GUNS ACROSS
THE BORDER

GUNS ACROSS THE BORDER

HOW AND WHY THE US GOVERNMENT

SMUGGLED GUNS INTO MEXICO:

THE INSIDE STORY

MIKE DETTY

FOREWORD BY
SHARYL ATTKISSON

INTRODUCTION BY
DAVID CODREA

SKYHORSE PUBLISHING

Disclaimer

The factual information presented herein is based on the experiences and recollections of the author.

However, the conversations reported within the text are written from memory and only represent the author's best recollection. These recollections are not intended to be statements of material facts, but rather the author's opinion of what was said and his interpretation of what those words meant.

Neither the author nor publisher claims that the words spoken during those conversations are accurately recorded herein. We apologize in advance for any omissions or errors in content or meaning.

All the people and events depicted are real. Some of the names have been changed for the protection of the individual.

Contents

Foreword

Mike Detty: Where "Fast and Furious" Meets "Wide Receiver"

AFTER BREAKING THE story of the Justice Department's Operation Fast and Furious scandal nationally on CBS News, I had only scratched the surface. There were scores of leads to follow. Many were unverifiable or dead-ends, but one source who had an interesting story and, more importantly, provable evidence was Mike Detty. Through Detty, we were able to report early on that the secret "gunwalking" by federal agents dated at least as far back as the Bush Administration. That's when the Bureau of Alcohol, Tobacco, and Firearms (ATF) began using Detty as a paid confidential informant. At the ATF's request, Detty sold a frightening arsenal of weapons from a makeshift showroom in his living room to traffickers for Mexican drug cartels. When I met Detty, the Justice Department was reviving the old Bush-era cases for prosecution, even as the Obama-era Fast and Furious scandal exploded. A foolhardy strategy that was tinkered with and apparently abandoned under Bush appeared to be resumed and expanded under Obama. But nobody was ready to own up to it yet. Besides "Fast and Furious" and "Wide Receiver," there was "Too Hot to Handle," "Castaway," and an array of other cases spanning states including Arizona, Florida, Nevada, Texas, and New Mexico. Like other gun dealers who assisted the ATF in this confidential effort, Detty felt betrayed and cast aside when he learned his efforts weren't helping the ATF arrest bad guys after all. Instead, he had inadvertently assisted them, thanks to the ATF. From his photographs to the paper trail and even audio recordings, Detty's story describes a piece of the gunwalking saga from a personal perspective that only he can tell.

Sharyl Attkisson
Emmy Award-winning investigative reporter

In 2012, Sharyl Attkisson was awarded the Emmy Award for Outstanding Investigative Journalism as well as the Murrow Award for Excellence in Investigative Reporting for her work on "Fast and Furious."

Introduction

"**A**RE YOU WORRIED about revenge?" I once asked Mike Detty. "What should readers know about not just the risks you took, but what coming forward like you have can mean?"

Mike is a firearms dealer and a gun writer, and he was the confidential informant at the heart of Operation Wide Receiver, an abortive attempt to track straw purchasers buying firearms on behalf of Mexican drug cartels with the ostensible purpose of identifying and bringing down trafficking organizations. As in the later notorious Operation Fast and Furious, some of the guns escaped ATF surveillance and were smuggled across the border.

In recounting the role he played, Detty explains key similarities and differences between the two operations, debunks some "common knowledge," and provides a first-hand account of his dealings with key players—both in the criminal underworld and in law enforcement—and in doing so reveals the flaws and foul-ups on both sides that make a real-life narrative so much more interesting than the way we're used to seeing such characters portrayed in fiction. In other words, don't expect *Scarface* meets *CSI*.

Detty first came onto my radar in March 2011. He'd noticed the work I'd been doing with colleague Mike Vanderboegh and our whistleblower contacts to get the Fast and Furious story noticed by the media and those tasked with government oversight in Congress. He informed me about Wide Receiver and told me that he'd sold guns as a CI to cartel straw purchasers for years.

"Most of the buys were late-night meetings at my house where I used my living room as a showroom," Detty told me. "These meetings often involved the bad guys, their bodyguards, and me alone in the house while agents listened to what was going on via the transmitter I wore.

"During these three years I took over eight hundred pages of notes," he continued. "I also have a digital copy of every phone call that I made or received from the bad guys. . . . When ATF discovered that I was keeping a journal and making copies of everything that I turned over to them, I went from Hero to Zero overnight."

This book is the result of those notes. And it checks out with much that has been subsequently proven.

People come to me all the time with stories they want my help gaining wider attention for, and they're invariably one-sided, where they've done everything right and been screwed over by people who did everything wrong, and corroboration to establish their credibility is often problematic, if not nearly impossible. That's why, in August 2011, knowing Detty had already been approached by the Office of Inspector General for the Department of Justice, I brought him together with an investigator working for the House Committee on Oversight and Government Reform with whom I'd previously communicated on Fast and Furious–related information.

In Mike's case, the information he provided, which became the source for numerous *Gun Rights Examiner* reports, checked out, with much of it substantially corroborated by the September 2012 OIG report.

Reading the manuscript for this book has been fascinating for me—I recognize a more fleshed-out version of a story Mike had allowed me to share that brought the picture into clearer focus. I also recognize instances, where, frankly, I wanted to shout at him, ask him how he could possibly believe those he was setting up wouldn't want to get even and that his handlers wouldn't screw him over, and demand to know what the hell it was he thought he was doing.

You don't do that unless you care about someone, and while we've never met in person, he's shared enough of his thoughts with me via correspondence—and with all of us in this book—that while reading it, I felt like I was watching a close friend wholly immersing himself into a crazy dangerous mess, and I was powerless to do a damn thing about it.

Some will no doubt be unsympathetic. Some will no doubt dismiss Detty as naïve or as a self-serving snitch and not care that those he worked for ended up betraying him or that those he worked against may yet do worse. Some may not care that his motivation for getting involved was because criminals approached him, and he saw an opportunity to make a difference and to do what he perceived was a duty.

"Of course I'm worried about revenge," Detty replied to my question. "Since most of these characters were sentenced to less than three years for straw purchases they'll all be getting out of prison sometime soon."

For his security, I won't go into measures he has taken to protect himself, except to note that if it were up to those who promote citizen disarmament edicts, the people who abandoned him and the people who hate him would be the only ones with guns.

David Codrea
Gun Rights Examiner (www.davidcodrea.com)
The War on Guns: Notes from the Resistance (www.waronguns.com)

1

The Proposition

GUNS ARE AS much a part of Arizona as the Saguaro cacti that dot the desert's floor. Used for protection, hunting, and competition, it's not uncommon to spot one in a pickup's rack or in the holster of a soccer mom putting gas in her minivan. The sight of people openly carrying guns causes no more concern than an errant Gila monster crossing the grocery store parking lot. Arizona is filled with rugged people who celebrate their pioneer spirit and take responsibility for their own safety. For the most part it is these honest, hard-working, God-fearing people who attend gun shows there. For the most part . . .

It was at the big February gun show in 2006 at the state fairgrounds in Phoenix that I first met Diego Rodriguez. I was helping one of my customers make a selection from the rifles I had on display when one of my helpers, Chenzo, came over and asked me if I had more AR-15 lowers than the six that were on display.

"That's all I brought," I told him. "Why?"

"The guy standing over there wants to buy all six and he wants to know if you have more." He pointed to a smiling young chubby Hispanic man with his hat on sideways, baggy shorts, and knee-high socks. Given his "gangster-like" appearance, I seriously doubted his background check would even go through.

The only real difference between an AR-15 rifle and the US military's M-16 rifle is that the AR-15 is semiautomatic while the M-16 is fully automatic. The AR-15 can be broken into two major assemblies: the upper and lower. The upper consists of the barrel, receiver, and bolt carrier group while the lower consists of the buttstock, pistol grip, and fire control components. The lower also possesses the serial number, and in the eyes of the federal government is considered a complete firearm—even if the upper assembly is not installed. For that reason, licensed dealers like me must do a background check on anybody purchasing a lower. Run by the FBI, the instant background check was mandated by the Brady Handgun Violence Prevention Act of 1993. The computerized system checked all state criminal records to see if the purchaser had any criminal background.

Several minutes later, Chenzo handed me a wad of cash totaling $1,600. "That's for the six lowers," he said. "His background check went through without any problems."

I went over to where we kept the #4473 forms and made sure the paperwork had been filled out correctly. It had. We had done everything by the book and had completed a legal transaction. But where did that young kid get so much cash, and why did he need so many lowers? Why was he asking if we had more? I dog-eared the form so that I could find it easily in the stack, just in case.

I didn't think much about it that night, but the following day the same young man returned to my display. He and a friend were holding bags of what I could tell were AR-15 lowers. I wondered if he wanted to return the ones he'd bought yesterday. He smiled at me and I walked over.

"Hey, you were busy yesterday when I was here, but I just wanted to introduce myself. I'm Diego Rodriguez," he said.

I shook his hand. "Mike Detty," I said. "Was there something wrong with the lowers I sold you?" I pointed to the bags he and his friend carried.

"No, we just bought these today from another guy. But I was wondering if you had any more lowers available?"

"Nope, you got them all yesterday. I've got twenty more on order from my supplier but they won't get here until next week."

"I'll take them all," said Rodriguez.

This erased any doubts that this kid might be doing something legitimate. In addition to the six he bought from me the day before, he and his friend were now holding at least eight AR-15 lowers and trying to broker a deal for twenty more. Fortunately we had the #4473 form on file and I had his full name, address, and social security number to pass on to the authorities.

I handed Diego a business card and told him to call me later in the week for the status of those twenty lowers.

The two-hour drive back to my home in Tucson gave me the opportunity to go over the weekend's events and I tried to imagine a scenario where someone would need so many AR-15 lowers. I couldn't come up with anything that made sense. No, there was no doubt in my mind that this kid was up to something illegal and was just not bright enough to be less obvious about it.

The Bureau of Alcohol, Tobacco, Firearms, and Explosives, more commonly referred to as the ATF, is a Department of Justice agency that oversees and regulates the firearms industry. Tucson has a small branch office in the federal building downtown and I had a contact there.

In the previous two years I had contacted Special Agent Spencer Edgar twice to report suspicions that my customers were doing something illegal—based solely on the volume of product they were buying. One case involved a Nogales, Arizona, cop who was buying AR-15 lowers and then transporting them across the border where they were being assembled into complete weapons. My involvement in this case was nothing more than reporting each transaction, along with the serial numbers, and faxing the form #4473 to Special Agent Edgar. The cop was confronted, and he resigned. I'm not sure what happened from there. It would not have been out of the ordinary for him to flip and turn over information in return for not being prosecuted or for a reduction in prison time.

A few weeks after the incident with the cop, an older Caucasian gentleman started buying lower receivers from me. The odd thing about this fellow was that he did not seem to know the first thing about shooting or AR-15 rifles. At first he bought five lower receivers at a time and then increased that amount to ten at a time. I contacted SA Edgar after his second purchase and Edgar asked me to inform him of any subsequent transactions. When the man approached me again at another gun show and asked if he could buy seventy-five lowers, I dutifully passed this information on to Edgar who gave me the go-ahead to complete the sale. I told the customer it would take me two weeks to get that many lowers and that we could do the transaction at the next gun show.

The day of the gun show I noticed the man walking slower than usual to my tables. All the color was gone from his face and he showed me the port his doctor had put in his arm for dialysis. Given his hunched posture and weathered looks, he seemed much older than the fifty-nine years his driver's license divulged. He was so frail that I closed my tables down to help carry the box of lowers out to his car for him. Of course, ATF agents were all around us and followed him back to his trailer in an impoverished part of town. According to Edgar, he confessed quickly saying that he saw nothing wrong with helping Mexican police officers get the parts they needed for good weapons. Apparently his source assuaged his fears by telling him that these parts were being used by Mexican law enforcement. He was indicted and then arrested as he was leaving his dialysis clinic one day. Not long afterwards, I read his obituary in the local paper.

Neither of these cases necessitated me devoting a great deal of time to the investigation or exposed me to any great danger. I wasn't paid in either case, and I imagined that the case with Diego Rodriguez would not be much different.

Monday morning I called SA Edgar and explained my conversation with Diego Rodriguez and my reason for concern. Edgar asked me to fax him the #4473 and said he was going to talk to his boss about the case. Later that afternoon Edgar called me back and asked if I could come down to the federal building the next day to meet with him.

After making my way through the metal detector and security on the ground floor of the federal building, I took the elevator to the eighth floor and nervously made my way to the office. I knocked several times but received no response, so I opened the door and walked into a sort of vestibule or antechamber, maybe six feet by six feet, with another door straight ahead and what looked like bulletproof glass overlooking an office on the left. After ringing the doorbell on the second door, I saw Edgar look around the corner through the glass and open the door from the inside.

Edgar ushered me into his cramped office where he introduced me to another field agent, Travis Lopez, who had just finished his training at the Federal Law Enforcement Training Center in Glynco, Georgia. I guessed Lopez to be in his late twenties and learned that he had played football on scholarship at a small Utah college before taking a job as a cop in Albuquerque, New Mexico. Tucson was his first posting with the ATF.

Edgar, who had been a Navy pilot, explained that he was now an Apache Longbow pilot with the National Guard and his unit was to deploy soon— first to Ft. Bliss for training and then on to Afghanistan. He'd be gone over a year. For that reason, Special Agent Lopez would be handling this case and I would be reporting to him from now on.

We went over my conversation with Rodriguez the previous weekend and I told them of my suspicions. Both listened intently. When I was finished speaking, Edgar agreed that this individual and his friend were up to something nefarious and they wanted to investigate this further. He told me he spoke with his boss, Jack Hinkley, the assistant special agent in charge of the Tucson office, and they wanted me to go ahead and sell those twenty lowers to Rodriguez. "Providing that you're cool with this and still want to help," he said.

"I don't mind helping you guys at all," I said immediately, without really considering what implications this decision might have.

"Good," said Edgar. "We'll put one of our agents behind the table with you at the gun show, just to be safe. And in the meantime I'd like you to let Travis know every time Rodriguez contacts you."

I made sure that my supplier did indeed ship the twenty lowers I needed. Rodriguez called a couple times in the next two weeks and we made plans to transfer the lowers first thing Saturday morning at the Mesa, Arizona, gun show.

Early Saturday morning, I met with Edgar and Lopez in the parking lot of the convention center where the gun show was being held. They introduced me to another agent who was tall, athletic, and physically imposing.

"This is Petey Palmer. We're going to put him behind the table with you today."

"Shit," I joked, "don't you have anyone bigger?"

I had brought along a shirt with the name and logo of the company whose rifles I sold and gave it to Palmer to wear behind the tables.

The show opened at nine o'clock as scheduled. Diego Rodriguez, on the other hand, was anything but on time. After 10 a.m. Palmer asked me to call Rodriguez and see where he was.

"We're on a job right now," Rodriguez said, "but we should be over there around noon."

"Alright Diego, but don't stand me up—I have other people who want to buy those lowers," I said, purposely sounding annoyed. I wanted him to know that it wasn't cool to set up a time and not keep an appointment.

Most of the Tucson ATF office had come down to observe the transaction and then follow Rodriguez to see where he went with the lowers. After hanging up with Rodriguez I passed on the news to Palmer who then relayed it to the rest of the team—some in the parking lot and some inside the show.

"Don't let it get to you Mike," Palmer told me. "He's on 'criminal time.' We're all used to it so don't let it bother you."

But it did bother me. The six agents who made the two-hour drive from Tucson to Mesa would have normally had Saturdays off. They must have been eager to get back home and spend time with their families or do whatever it was they would be doing on a non-working weekend.

It wasn't until about two-thirty in the afternoon that Rodriguez finally showed up, reeking of sweat in a very dirty work shirt. He stuck out a chubby paw to shake hands.

"Man, I'm glad you finally showed up. I was just about to sell your lowers to another dealer. Dude, you need to let me know when you're not going to be on time."

Rodriguez looked down sheepishly and apologized. I handed him a clipboard with a #4473 form to fill out for his background check while Special Agent Palmer started stacking the boxes with the lowers in them on top of the table and reading me the serial number to write down on the receipt. We chatted back and forth as we wrote and I noticed that SA Edgar was now standing next to Rodriguez pretending to look at the merchandise. He was wearing an Apache Longbow baseball cap pulled down low over his face.

Larry, one of my helpers for the show, saw Edgar's cap and started a conversation with him. Larry had worked for McDonnell Douglas in the early '90s and had been involved in the development of Longbow's upgraded weapons systems. Though Larry knew there was going to be an ATF presence for this purchase he had not yet been introduced to Edgar.

Once Rodriguez had finished completing his form, I used my cell phone to call in the background check to the National Instant Background Check System. Normally I knew within a minute or two if the sale could go through or not. One thing we had not gone over at my briefing was what to do if Rodriguez's background check came back "delayed" or "denied," so I held my breath until I got the "proceed" from NICS to transfer the lowers.

"Everything's a go," I said to Rodriguez as I hung up my cell phone. "I just need to collect $5,300 from you."

Rodriguez removed a fat white envelope from his front pocket and threw it on the table. It contained mostly $100 bills and I counted it quickly and placed the money in my fanny pack.

Rodriguez smiled at me and said, "I want to order fifty more receivers just like these."

"Fifty more!" I spoke loudly so Edgar and Palmer would hear me. "I can get them for you, Diego, but you're going to need to give me a $5,000 deposit. That's a year's worth of receivers for me and I don't want to get stuck with that inventory if you back out."

"No problem, bro. I'll give you a call when your deposit is ready but please go ahead and order the lowers. We'll need them as soon as possible."

I volunteered Petey Palmer to help Rodriguez to carry the lowers out to his car. Rodriguez took a couple of boxes and put them under one arm and left the remainder for Palmer to carry out. I had to laugh to myself. The kid was a piece of work!

After they left, I introduced Larry to SA Edgar. Larry had no idea that he was talking to an ATF agent the entire time and apparently Edgar enjoyed talking about the Longbow as much as Larry did. Edgar excused himself to take part in the surveillance, and not much later Palmer stopped back in to return the shirt I'd given him to wear.

I learned later that Rodriguez had started driving so erratically that the surveillance was cut short and the agents returned to Tucson.

I lost track of the number of times Rodriguez called me in the next ten days and while he was always respectful, calling me sir, bro, or Mike, he was something of a pain in the ass. He told me he wanted me to order the lowers and I stood firm that I would need a deposit to place the order. He kept telling me he was having trouble with his bank—a euphemism for what I understood to be the people or organization bankrolling his purchases. In the meantime, I had already ordered the fifty lowers from my supplier and had them sitting in my home warehouse. I wanted this transaction to go through as much as anyone else so I didn't get stuck with the merchandise.

Each time I spoke with Rodriguez I'd phone SA Lopez with a synopsis of the conversation. I was calling him so frequently I was afraid that I'd become the same pain in his ass that Rodriguez was to me. But Lopez was always quick to put me at ease. He was a good kid and I liked him immediately. Polite, courteous to a fault, he always seemed positive and upbeat.

I could tell by the way his colleagues spoke to him that they thought Lopez had the potential to become something more than just a standout agent. He was the kind of person people wanted to hang around, much like the star quarterback in high school. Of course, it didn't hurt matters that he was also good-looking, athletic, and always quick with a smile. Beyond all of that, he seemed to have intelligence and insight that most people his age do not possess. The more I got to know Lopez, the more I liked and even envied him. In a strange way, it almost made up for having to deal with Rodriguez.

After calling me for a week and a half to tell me he was working on getting the deposit, Rodriguez finally got some money. "But it's only half," he said, sounding almost ashamed. "I know you said you needed five thousand but I was only able to get twenty-five hundred. Is that enough for you to place the order with the factory? Our guys really want these lowers quick."

Something didn't make sense. They needed the lowers quickly but they only came up with half the deposit? But I didn't want to jeopardize the sale and risk getting stuck with the lowers, so I didn't question it.

"Yeah, I can do that," I said. "Once I have the cash, I'll place the order. But you have to understand that I won't transfer the lowers to you until the balance is paid."

"Sure, sure, Mike, I understand. That's great. Can we meet tonight?" He sounded relieved; like someone had lifted a weight from his chest.

"I've already got something going on tonight," I lied. "Let me see if I can move things around. I'll call you back." It was now mid-afternoon and I called SA Lopez with the news as soon as I hung up with Rodriguez.

"I'll bet that shithead stole the other half of the deposit," Lopez said with a chuckle.

I laughed too because it was something I hadn't even considered. "Yeah, you're probably right."

"See if you can get him to meet with you at the McDonald's on the corner of I-10 and Cortaro around seven tonight. We have something else going on nearby and that would make it easy for us."

When I called Rodriguez back he said that would be perfect as he was passing through Tucson on his way to the border town of Nogales that evening.

Tucson is a very spread-out city and it took me almost forty-five minutes to travel from my Northeast side home to the McDonald's on the far west side of town. About a half hour before I was supposed to meet Rodriguez, I met SA Travis Lopez at the Starbucks just down the street from the McDonald's. As I was pulling into the lot, a maroon Dodge Intrepid with blacked-out windows sped around the corner and pulled up next to my Yukon. SA Lopez and SA Palmer got out of the car and walked over to my driver's side door. Palmer said hello and then left Lopez and me alone to talk.

"Do you think tonight's meeting might be a possible reprisal for Rodriguez's car being followed after the last purchase?" Lopez asked me.

"Shit, I didn't think about that," I said. "I don't think so. Why would he tell me he only had half of the deposit if he was planning to shoot me tonight?"

Lopez agreed. He gave me a recording device called a "Hawk" to put in my pocket. It was about two and a half inches square and maybe three-eighths of an inch thick, with a brushed-aluminum housing and a single port to attach it to a computer. Small and innocuous, it would be very hard for anyone who didn't already know what it was to figure out exactly what it did. Even if it fell into bad guy hands it would be impossible for them to learn what was in it. The Hawk was designed expressly for law enforcement and intelligence work and the software to download, view, or listen to recorded data was tightly controlled.

Lopez showed me where the on/off switch was. "Don't let him pat you down, Mike. If he tries that, push him away and tell him that you'll kick his ass back to Mesa and he'll never get his guns."

As we talked, several other cars pulled into the lot and I saw some of the same faces I'd seen down at the federal building, but there were some others too that I didn't recognize.

Lopez pointed to one husky Hispanic guy who looked to be in his early forties. "He's one of our Tucson Police Department undercover guys," he said. "We just don't have the manpower for surveillances. Our side of the office only has seven agents, so we use TPD guys when we have something like this going on. If something goes wrong, he'll be inside to help you." I had to laugh because the TPD cop was wearing a shirt that said "I Love Hot Moms."

I drove back to the McDonald's and circled it once to see if Diego's gold Neon was already there. Not seeing it, I went inside, ordered a milkshake, and took a seat at a window that would allow me to see cars exiting I-10. I noticed that the TPD cop had ordered himself a Big Mac and was seated on the other side of the restaurant. After about ten minutes, Diego called and said he was very close. Not much later I saw the gold Neon drive by the window and my cell phone rang. It was Lopez telling me to activate the Hawk recorder.

Seconds later, Rodriguez entered the restaurant, took a quick look around, and spotted me. Before he sat down, he took an envelope from his waistband and handed it to me.

"Mind if I count it?" I asked. Holding the envelope below the table top, I thumbed my way through twenty-five $100 bills. I put them back in the envelope and stuffed the contents into my shirt pocket. We chatted for a little while and made small talk. When he was feeling more relaxed, Diego volunteered some interesting information. "You know how the AR-15s shoot kind of fast but not real fast?" He was referring to the AR-15's semi-automatic function compared to an M-16's ability to fire fully automatic. I nodded.

He smiled. "Well, we have a guy that machines them so they go real fast."

Now, I smiled. What a dumbass this kid is to volunteer information like that, I thought. "You know, Diego, when I was in the Marines I never thought that I would miss shooting a machine gun. But I have to admit I do. You think your guy would do one for me?"

"No problem bro—I'll be glad to hook you up." As he stood to leave he again mentioned that he had to drive down to Nogales that night.

"Do you have a girlfriend down there?"

"Nope, it's strictly business tonight."

I drove back to the Starbucks to return the Hawk and gave Lopez the information regarding the full auto conversions.

"He told you they were converting these lowers to full auto?" asked an incredulous Lopez.

"This kid isn't very bright, Travis."

The next morning I went down to the federal building to formalize the confidential informant agreement. Lopez gave me $200 cash and had me sign a voucher acknowledging that I had received the money. This would be my first payment as a confidential informant. He took me to a small booking room where I was fingerprinted and photographed and then gave me a copy of an informant agreement to read and sign. It was a standard ATF form with my name already typed in the blanks.

Among other things, it identified Special Agent Travis Lopez as the "controlling agent" of this investigation. It went on to say that I should not take part in any unlawful activities except insofar as the ATF determined it necessary for the investigation. Nor should I initiate plans to commit criminal acts or engage in acts of violence, and it noted that while I was working closely with the ATF, I should not hold myself out to be a law enforcement officer or agent of the government. I understood that I might be called upon to testify before a grand jury and at a subsequent trial, and in that case, I had an obligation to tell the truth and that any untrue statements made by me may make me liable for prosecution. If, as a result of being a cooperating witness, the ATF determined that my life may be in danger, I could apply to the Department of Justice for admittance into the Witness Security Program—a decision that would be made solely by and at the discretion of the Department of Justice. Any monies paid to me during the course of the investigation had to be reported as income to the IRS.

It was a document designed to give all the protection to the ATF and Department of Justice and virtually nothing to me, the informant. I laughed to myself as I signed it. I mean, what was I going to do? Send it to my lawyer for his OK? It was a ridiculously lopsided agreement and I was putting blind faith in these guys to take care of me. After all, I brought this case to them. I was a good guy and I trusted them implicitly. They'd never screw me over, right?

Lopez took me down the hallway to an office situated at the southwest corner of the building. It had a spectacular view of the city of Tucson, its beautiful desert mountains, and beyond. Inside, the office was nothing special—a Spartan mix of government office furniture, cheap carpet without padding, and walls that had been patched and painted for each new occupant. The walls were now bare—no family pictures, no group law enforcement class photos, no diplomas or certificates. Not a thing had been done to personalize this space.

Lopez offered me a chair and we made small talk until Jack Hinkley arrived and took his place behind his desk. He was a fit man who I guessed to be in his late forties. He was dressed in sharply ironed clothes and exuded professionalism. He reminded me of many of the career officers I'd known when I was in the Marine Corps.

Hinkley folded his hands, smiled, and leaned forward. "Mike, I'd like to thank you for bringing this information to our attention. It isn't often that a dealer will come to us with great intelligence that we can act on. Agent Lopez has informed me that you have been extremely cooperative with our requests and that your relaxed composure has garnered some very valuable information. I want you to know that your personal safety and the welfare of your business are our main concerns. We will not knowingly put our investigation ahead of your safety."

Even though I was smart enough to realize that Hinkley was giving me a slow, gentle hand job, I appreciated that he was addressing some of my concerns.

"Your initial suspicions regarding Diego Rodriguez proved correct," Hinkley continued. "We think he's a cartel associate and that he's moving these lowers to someone who is completing the rifles and taking them across the border."

Hinkley wasn't telling me anything I hadn't already suspected. "One of my concerns," I said, "is how many of these lowers will cross the border. I mean it's great for business, but there's also the moral aspect of this. Sooner or later one of these guns will kill someone. I'm worried about that as well as my liability."

Hinkley put up his hand as if it were a stop sign. "I understand, Mike. Frankly, I'd be worried about those things too. But I want you to know that our level of cooperation with the Mexican authorities is unprecedented. They'll be following your guns on the other side of the border and at some point in time they'll round them all up. As far as liability—you're working with us now, and you'll have the full weight of the United States government behind you."

This was exactly what I needed to hear. As crazy as it sounds, I was more concerned about the liability to my business than I was about the obvious health hazards of informing on a cartel. I had no desire to see my hard-earned profits depleted by legal fees and lawsuits because I chose to help the ATF.

More than that, I had no wish to see my guns being used in the savagery across the border. Mexico was a country I enjoyed and whose people I'd come to love. I'd honeymooned in Cancun, vacationed in Cabo San Lucas, and scuba dived in Guaymas. As bad as I felt about some of these weapons being used to harm innocent people, I also knew that if they didn't get them from me, they would find someone else. And those people might not be as likely to call the ATF and report the transactions.

"Mike," said Hinkley, "I think we really have a shot at taking out a powerful cartel. I couldn't care less about putting Diego Rodriguez or any of his punk friends in prison. They're small fry and we have no interest in them other than to use them to climb the ladder. What we want to do is follow the guns and the money, build a case against the kingpins, and hit them where it hurts. We want to seize bank accounts, businesses, mansions. We originally envisioned the investigation lasting a few weeks but it now looks like it will take a few months."

This was something I hadn't contemplated. I had imagined my involvement to be just a few weeks.

"What do you think Mike? Can you hang with us?"

2

NOTHING TO LOSE

COULD I HANG with them? I thought about those words for what seemed to be hours as I let my gaze hang on the view from Jack's eighth-floor corner office. My eyes followed I-10 west all the way to Picacho Peak, some thirty-five miles away, while I contemplated what path this decision would lead me down.

Up to that point I didn't feel there was any choice about reporting those kids. Based solely on the number of rifles and components they were acquiring, it was obvious they were up to something pretty serious. I just couldn't have let it go without telling the authorities, but I had never given any thought to the possibility that somehow I would end up being part of the investigation. Now reality was hitting me square in the face.

The timing couldn't have been more fortunate for the feds. I was a single man without any family, and possessed a sense of patriotic duty and a willingness to do whatever they asked me to do. But what made me especially useful for their cause was the reckless attitude I'd acquired through a series of unfortunate events.

Several years earlier, I had lost a job I'd held for seventeen years. I left that job with no retirement, pension, or even severance pay, but what really hurt was that it was my own brother who fired me from our family business.

My dad had been the head athletic trainer for the Philadelphia Eagles football team, and in the late 1960s he invented the neoprene sports medicine brace. Using neoprene scraps and my grandmother's sewing machine, he made braces for his injured players. They worked so well that he contracted with a wetsuit manufacturer to make the supports. As the popularity of these devices grew, new models were developed and my pop patented a number of his designs. Other NFL teams started buying his products, then the colleges and sports medicine clinics. By 1975, he had left the Eagles to devote all of his energy to his new company, Pro Orthopedic Devices.

About that same time, my brother was finishing graduate school and my dad offered him a job to help grow the business. Run out of the basement and garage of our home, the new company had seemingly meteoric growth. My sister was enlisted next to help with accounts payable and receivable. Despite the promising influx of money, my mom decided to finish out her career as an elementary school teacher.

It was an exciting time for my family. Though my dad had earned accolades, recognition, and respect in the NFL for his inventions, injury treatment, and rehabilitation protocols, he was never paid well. This was during an era before there were million-dollar athletes, and I can remember when my parents had a tough time making ends meet. Now my brother and sister were shopping for new cars and homes. Dad bought himself a Mercedes 450SL and Mom got a new Mazda RX7. My father had always been a rainbow chaser but I don't think he ever imagined that his pot of gold would be at the end of a sewing machine.

I finished high school with absolutely no idea of what I wanted to do and Dad talked me into giving college a try. So for two years I studied police science at the local community college and liked it so well that I decided to go on and get a Bachelor of Science degree. In February, 1979, Dad took me on a business trip to the University of Arizona. We left a frozen Philadelphia airport and it was in the seventies when we landed in Tucson. I immediately fell in love with the desert and its mountains. I filled out an application for the university before we left.

On that trip, Dad bought a house that he would call his vacation home. He'd never used his GI loan and his accountant was advising him to spend the money so it wouldn't be taxed. I spent my first two semesters in the dorm but lived in the new house once it was finished being built. Being away from home and responsible for myself for the first time in my life challenged me and helped me grow as a person, but as graduation approached my anxiety grew.

Dad had already told me that he wanted me to work for his business and I did feel indebted—the business had not only been good for the rest of the family but had also funded my college tuition and living costs. But I felt the need for adventure, to strike out on my own, to burn off some of my youthful exuberance and ambition. I wanted to be an FBI agent but I knew that would be next to impossible without some sort of law enforcement or military experience.

I always had bad ankles and had to use braces and crutches to get around when I was a kid. The chronic bleeds I had in my ankles disintegrated the joints' cartilage and eroded joint space. As I became a teenager, I got tired of listening to the taunts of classmates and decided that somehow I would transform my broken body into something that resembled that of an athlete. In that regard, I was successful. I'd often do thousands of calisthenics per workout. My junior year of high school I hung a heavy bag in the basement and Dad, who also used to train professional fighters, spent many evenings teaching me the basics of boxing. Sometimes I'd spend forty-five minutes or more just punching the heavy bag. I taught myself to skip rope and learned all of the intricate moves fighters practice. Using a leather rope with ball-bearing handles, I'd often skip for between a half hour and an hour as a warm-up to my workout.

By the time I finished college, I was working out for two or more hours a day and would run a minimum of three miles. All of this physical exertion had built my muscles but none of it improved the arthritis that already existed in my ankles—quite the opposite, in fact. But I was in spectacular shape and I thought that I was good enough to become a Marine officer.

I enrolled in Marine Corps Officer Candidates School and reported to Quantico, Virginia for twelve weeks of immersion into military life. It was the hardest challenge I had ever faced but I was well prepared physically. The marching and running didn't bother me too much. But jumping off the obstacles was pure torture. By now I had no joint space left in either ankle so it was bone-on-bone contact. I graduated and was commissioned a Second Lieutenant in August, 1982. After I was commissioned, I attended The Basic School—a kind of finishing school that all Marine officers must go through prior to going to their career specialty school. One day my platoon commander caught me limping after a run and ordered me to report to the base clinic for evaluation. The X-rays that were ordered led to my eventual medical discharge. Not only was I prevented from any future military career, even in the reserves, the medical discharge also negated any possibility of becoming a federal agent. Not being able to fulfill my commitment to the Marine Corps will always be a disappointment from which I have never fully recovered.

My goal was to serve my country and it is a decision that I've never regretted. The fact that I was at greater risk of injuring myself permanently never entered into my thought process. Like the other young and idealistic lieutenants, patriotism was my sole motivation.

I left Quantico Friday morning and made the short trip to the Philadelphia suburb of King of Prussia just after noon. Monday morning, I started work at Pro Orthopedic Devices. By now the business had outgrown the basement and Dad had moved it to another house that was commercially zoned. As I walked through the door to start work, I carried every ounce of frustration and angst for adventures unfulfilled, battles never fought, and victories never relished. I must have been a bear to deal with, yet Dad, ever patient, made sure he had room for me and that I was taken care of.

In terms of business it seemed like Dad's luck never ebbed. The house he had bought for the business was right in the middle of where a new big box office supply store wanted to put its driveway. Dad was very shrewd in his business deals and showed an extreme amount of savvy for someone who had never really been a businessman.

He used the windfall from his negotiations with the office supply store to move the company to Tucson which had had a much lower cost of living than Philadelphia and had a ready pool of skilled sewing machine operators to work in the factory.

My job was to sell sports medicine braces to sporting goods and drugstore chains. We had a moderate amount of success. At various times we sold accounts like Oshman's Sporting Goods, Academy Sports and Outdoors, Walmart, Big 5 Sporting Goods, Fred Meyer, JC Penney, etc. We weren't getting rich but we were all drawing salaries and making the payroll.

Dad's good luck started to wane when the NFL and NBA told us that our easily visible sports braces couldn't have our distinctive double diamond logo on them unless we paid a licensing fee. For years we'd enjoyed the free exposure of televised games but now we didn't have the budget to pay the fees.

Our next challenge regarded a new trend in retail sales that required us to pay for shelf space. I remember one sales call I made to a national drugstore chain when the buyer announced that the bidding was up to one million dollars, which meant that in return for eight feet of shelf space, we would need to give them one million dollars up front for a three-year contract. He speculated that we would lose money the first year and then break even the following year. But by the third year, he emphasized, we would make a lot of money. Then, of course, the contract would need to be renegotiated.

Even if our company were ten times its size we couldn't have afforded to take a million dollars out of our operating capital to get this account. Unfortunately, this was the trend on the retail side of the business that I'd be running into more and more.

My advice to my father was to either sell the company or become a strategic partner with a larger company. We talked with several companies and at one point Dad even hired a business broker to look for a buyer. The problem was that he thought his company was worth much more than it was. Pro had a great reputation and our distinctive diamond logo had some value but not enough to demand a price three times higher than what any business formula would dictate.

Dad's reasoning was that he wanted to get enough money for the business to settle his debts and still have a million dollars to bank. And, typically Dad, he wanted to make sure that my brother and I were taken care of.

We received no offers.

One afternoon Dad called me at work and told me we needed to talk. His sober tone alerted me that this would probably not be a good meeting.

I sat down at his kitchen table with him. It was his favorite spot. From there he could see his backyard and pool, watch his dogs play, and enjoy the view of the Rincon Mountains. Out the side window he could watch the quail, coyotes, and javelinas forage for food on the side of his house.

"Your brother wants to buy the company," he said.

I knew that my brother had always wanted the company for himself but I also knew he couldn't afford to buy it.

"He doesn't need you," Dad said flatly.

I was stunned. I'd never dreamed that my father would allow something like this to happen.

"Look," he said, leaning closer to me, "you and I both know that you're miserable working with him. I can't be there to referee you two anymore. You've always been so talented and there's so much you can do, Mike. You can be a full-time writer or open your own gun shop. This is all he has—it's all he can do."

"What kind of buyout will there be?" I asked.

"Nothing," he said. "There's no money there for you. He's not paying me anything either. I'm giving him the company for taking over the line of credit." He looked around the room. "Everything I own—my bank accounts, my investments, this house, guarantee the million dollar line of credit. I'll be gone before long and I don't want the bank coming after your mother and all that she owns. This is the only way I have of protecting her. If he bankrupts the company, that's something he'll have to deal with. At least Mom will be OK. Don't fight this, Mike. Let him have it."

He turned away from me in his seat and let his unfocused eyes settle on nothing in particular in the mountains. His huge shoulders rose and fell heavily as he sighed. I knew the conversation was over and his decision had been made. There was nothing more to talk about. I kissed him on the cheek and left.

After that, I worked briefly as a consultant for a company that manufactured CO_2 bike tire inflators. They were located literally within a stone's throw of Dad's factory. They were a major player in the bike specialty shops but had little experience or knowledge with dealing with chain stores. They hired me for this endeavor.

Their engineers had developed a CO_2 unit that could be used to clean computer keyboards with compressed gas. Before long, I had one of my old sales representatives present this item to a Walmart buyer.

Within the next five months we received the order, developed the packaging, and delivered the product. A phenomenal feat by anyone's standards! I was feeling pretty good about things. Maybe I'd have a future here?

After the product was delivered to Walmart, I had the accounting department issue the commission check to my sales rep, and a few days later the owner of the company came to speak to me. "That was quite a check we just gave your sales rep," he said.

"Yep, 8 percent—that's what we all agreed to."

"That's a one-time payment, right? I mean, we don't have to pay this guy again, do we?"

A feeling of dread came over me. "Sales reps get a commission on every order they place. He'll get the same percent commission on the next order we get from Walmart. That's industry standard."

"I can see paying him for getting the first order but then Walmart will reorder automatically. There's no need for us to pay him again."

"But that's how it works. If you don't pay your reps, the orders stop and you'll likely get sued."

My boss was now shaking his head from side to side. "I don't want to send this guy another check. He's not doing anything for it." He stood up and walked back to his office.

I phoned my sales rep and told him about the conversation.

"Don't worry about it, Mike. I have all the money I need. I only got involved to help you. Don't give it another thought, I'll call the buyer and let him know."

It took just a few moments to pack my desk and I was gone. On the drive home I made the decision that I would never again work for someone else. I'd never be at the mercy of another employer. I'd have to figure something out for myself.

I'd been writing for gun magazines for a number of years. The money wasn't great but I enjoyed writing the articles, and with the income from the articles, at least I'd be able to pay the bills until I figured out what to do next.

Within a month, I was contacted by the owner of ArmaLite—a high-end manufacturer of AR-15 and AR-10 (.308) rifles based in Geneseo, Illinois. I'd met him several times and had written about his guns. Earlier that month I'd helped them at a gun show in Phoenix.

At the time they were at war over some patent issues with a company based in Scottsdale, Arizona, that also manufactured AR rifles. ArmaLite decided they wanted a presence at every Arizona gun show—just to be a thorn in the side of their competitor. They offered to make me a distributor with special pricing and extended terms. Was I interested?

It seemed to be the perfect opportunity for me. I wasn't sure that I wanted to do this for a prolonged period or make a career out of it, but for the moment it looked as though it would keep me going. At least until I ran into another opportunity. I'd work a couple weekends a month and be able to write during the week. I'd be my own boss, set my own schedule, and do what I enjoyed most. I took $20,000 from my savings and placed my initial order with ArmaLite in the summer of 2001.

By August the order was delivered. I had only done one show before the tragic events of 9/11 occurred. I sold out of inventory within two weeks after that and ordered twice as much inventory, which also sold quickly. I was in the gun business, like it or not.

But my wife didn't like it. She would have much preferred that I get another corporate job with a fancy title. And if it weren't enough that she was unhappy with my career decision, she was even more unhappy that she had to get a job for the first time in our ten-year marriage.

She found a job doing collections which seemed to suit her disposition precisely. As the year stretched on, our relationship became more and more strained until she announced to me at her son's high school graduation that she was leaving. I really wasn't surprised—I saw all the signs, yet felt power-less to stop the deterioration of our relationship. She resented me and didn't even bother to hide her contempt.

Looking back, I can hardly blame her. I'd lost confidence in myself and she'd lost faith in me. I was only able to focus on myself and my problems and little else.

Toward the end of that summer, she moved out. I was alone, heart-broken, and miserable. I felt betrayed by those closest to me and even everyday activities seemed to be difficult. To make matters worse, I started a year-long course of Interferon to eradicate the Hepatitis C I'd contracted from a transfusion after surgery in 1986.

I have hemophilia and even though the surgery was on my elbow, I had to be transfused. We had waited to schedule the surgery until they had a good screen for HIV and we all knew I wouldn't be infected with AIDS. I never imagined there might be something else in the blood supply.

As far as I can tell, I was never sick a day from the Hep C but my doctors wanted me to start treatment as soon as the medicine became available. I felt like I had the flu every day and my energy level was zapped. To complicate things further, the Interferon that was saving my liver was also a heavy duty depressant and even though I was given antidepressants to counteract this side effect, my mood was usually dark and somber with too few happy or lighthearted moments.

The year came and went and I finished treatment. My doctor said my virus levels were undetectable and called it a cure. Even though I wasn't injecting myself any longer, the depression hung on me like a wet towel.

Everything seemed to hurt more than it used to.

As the years progressed, my ankles hurt more and more. Arthritis, by its very definition, is a degenerative disease and there wasn't anything I could do to slow its progress. But the change in careers actually accelerated the deterioration of my compromised joints.

Standing on cement for the duration of each gun show was agony for me. When I first started doing gun shows I'd take painkillers the night of the show to help ease the pain. Five years later, I was taking them almost every day just to function. This constant, chronic pain ate at me like a cancer and every doctor I saw held out no hope for me. The only surgical option was to fuse the entire joint which would mean that my ankle wouldn't be able to flex anymore.

There just didn't seem to be any hope in my future. I hated life and was sick of the misery in which I was mired. Too stupid and too stubborn to do anything else, I kept my head down and put one foot in front of the other. I was existing and that's about it.

There's an old adage that says the most dangerous man is the one with nothing to lose. That's exactly how I felt. I didn't place an ounce of value on my life, yet I didn't have the courage to take it either. Maybe one of these punks I'm working with will end my misery? It was a thought that didn't scare me in the least.

So that's how the ATF found me in 2006: divorced, depressed, and completely reckless. For their purposes I was perfect!

"Yeah, I can hang with you guys for a while," I said almost immediately.

3

TIJUANA CONNECTION

IF THERE IS one thing that Diego Rodriguez was it was unreliable. There was a gun show the weekend following his half-payment deposit and we were supposed to complete the transaction there. Rodriguez strung me along all weekend saying that he was calling from San Diego but he was still having problems with his bank. I had all fifty AR-15 lowers at the show and was ready to make the deal but, unfortunately, it never happened. Each phone call put a series of actions into motion and I wasn't the only one unhappy with him.

Of course, the ATF had to be at the gun show to observe this "buy" and each phone call Rodriguez made to me required me making a call to Lopez. This was his case and it was his decision to devote resources to it. I could sense his level of frustration was as high as mine. He had a handful of guys working this weekend and it was all for nothing.

On Sunday, Diego called me and said that he was having continued problems with his bank and would be unable to complete the deal that weekend, but that he hoped to have the money Monday or Tuesday. Monday came, then Tuesday, and on Wednesday Lopez had me call him and see what was going on. Diego said that he was still having problems getting the money. This nonsense dragged on for three weeks and I lost track of how many times I called Rodriguez at Lopez's behest. There were a couple times when it looked like he was going to come down with the money and I had to beg off because the ATF's guy was not available to install the tracking device on his car. But mostly it was Diego just shining me on and I was starting to get very frustrated.

Eventually Lopez had me call Diego and tell him that he had two days to get the money or I was going to sell them to another dealer. I left a voicemail message asking what address he wanted me to send the deposit money to. He called back in a panic saying that he was going to have the money that day. We called each other back and forth and by about six in the evening it became apparent that he was not going to be able to get the money. He said he was parked outside the money guy's house and that he was not answering the door or his cell phone. I was disgusted and hung up on him.

Later that evening I was in bed watching TV when the phone rang.

I heard an unfamiliar voice on the other end of the line. "My friend placed an order with you and I need to talk to you about it," he said. His uncongenial tone caused the hair to stand up on the back of my neck.

He identified himself as Ira Goldblatt. "I have your money, $10,700 in cash, and I will make good on his order. I'm looking at your cash right now."

Now I wondered if I was being set up for something. "I'm comfortable dealing with Diego. If you could just have him bring the cash and pick up the lowers, that's fine with me."

"I don't think Diego realizes how much trouble he's in. He missed his deadline and he's been relieved of duties. I'm making this right for him in order to help him and if I turn over $10,000, it's going from my hand to your hand."

Not only was this voice on the other end of the phone unfriendly, the subject of Diego made him sound downright hostile. I was afraid that he wanted to come over immediately to complete the deal so I asked him what his schedule looked like.

He said he had one plumbing job to do in the morning and then he'd come down to Tucson. "I'll be there sometime between one and three."

After I hung up I called Agent Lopez.

Lopez didn't seem to mind me calling so late and he sounded ecstatic that finally the logjam had been broken. He said he could arrange to have the chase team, tracking device installer, and security for me all at my house at the same time.

The next day two agents, Scott Languien and Armando "Mando" Arroyo came out to do a threat analysis of my home. They made a map of the entrances and layout, noted my security system, the security wrought iron that covered all the doors and windows, and also took pictures of my dogs.

The following afternoon around twelve thirty, I got a call from Goldblatt saying that he had my money and was seventy-four miles outside of Tucson and traveling at ninety mph. I gave him quick directions to my house and called Lopez as soon as I hung up. Lopez and his team made a beeline to my house to get there and set up before the bad guys arrived.

About a half hour later, Lopez and another agent showed up. Tall, slender, and young-looking, Special Agent Jim Shelty told me he was from Montana and had already put in six years with the ATF after spending time in the navy and then border patrol. He was going to sit in my living room under the pretense that he was waiting to go whitewater rafting with my stepson while I dealt with Goldblatt in the dining room.

Lopez put a wire transmitter on his fellow agent and worked diligently for about fifteen minutes to try to get it to work. Unable to do so, Lopez finally told him he'd be waiting in my gym at the back of the house and to yell really loud if there was a problem. Once Goldblatt came inside the house, Lopez and another agent would install the tracking device on his car.

We had a heads-up call from agents watching the intersection of Houghton and Ft. Lowell—about two miles from my home—to let us know the buyers were on the way. A couple minutes later Goldblatt called from my driveway to let me know he had arrived.

I walked outside to meet him and asked that he back his car up to my garage door. "I've got a nosey neighbor," I told him. "Don't want to give him anything to speculate about."

Goldblatt never questioned it but the real reason was that his car would now be out of sight from the living room, and the agents could install the tracking device without being discovered.

Goldblatt was tall at about six foot three, and very lean, with closely cropped hair. He looked athletic and seemed to be wound as tight as a clock. Another man, much smaller than Goldblatt, also exited the car. Goldblatt introduced him to me as Izmael and I recognized him as the man who had accompanied Diego Rodriguez when I first met him at the Phoenix gun show a couple months earlier. We all shook hands and walked up the flagstone walk to my front door.

They both seemed to balk when they saw the agent watching TV in the other room but I explained that he was waiting for my stepson and neither of them questioned it further. I had them both sit at the dining room table.

Once they were seated, I turned on the air conditioner. This was a prearranged signal to Lopez that we were all inside and that he could exit through a side door to install the tracker. I was hopeful that the noise from the old air conditioner would cover whatever noise they made exiting the gym.

Inside, I had Goldblatt start the paperwork. He had to fill out the #4473 background form and while he did that, I asked for his driver's license and started filling out a receipt. Before they arrived, I had entered all fifty serial numbers on my receipt and on the #4473 to save some time and reduce the risk of making a rushed mistake.

Based on the way he dressed and his fluent accent-free Spanish when he spoke to Izmael, I had guessed that Goldblatt was Hispanic so I was surprised to see that he had checked the box "White/Caucasian" for race on the form. He also listed his place of birth as New Hampshire and was only nineteen years old.

There were several times while doing his paperwork that I would glance up and catch him staring at me. It made me wonder—did he smell a trap? Did he catch a glimpse of the gun that my unbuttoned shirt barely covered, or did the man in the next room look too much like a federal agent?

I tried to keep Ira and Izmael engaged in conversation while we did the paperwork so that neither one would feel tempted to step outside for a smoke or to make a phone call. Every once in a while, we'd hear the person in my living room chuckle about something on TV enough so that they'd never guess he was eavesdropping on our conversation.

It only took a couple minutes for Goldblatt's background check to clear and I was given a "proceed" for the transaction.

"Will that be cash or credit?" I asked as I closed my cell phone. The two men laughed. Ira leaned over in his chair and pulled a wad of bills from his right hand pants pocket. It consisted mostly of $100 bills but also had a smattering of $20s and $50s. Ira counted it out in increments of $1,000 until we got to $10,000 and then he counted out another $700.

As I was afraid to leave the pile of cash sitting on the table with the two men, I stood up and unwittingly put the handful of cash into my pants cargo pocket that was already occupied by the Hawk recording device. Then I leaned over into the living room and said, "Jim, has my kid called you back yet?"

"Yeah, he said that he'd be here in about fifteen minutes." Unseen by the two in the other room, Shelty gave me the thumbs up sign to indicate that he had received a text saying the tracking device had been successfully installed and that the other two agents were clear of the car.

I explained to the two men that I would go through the house and meet them at the garage door after I turned off the alarm for that zone. They walked back out the front door and I ran down the hallway into the gym and then into the garage where I had the lowers already boxed up and ready to go.

We loaded as many boxes as we could into his trunk and when that was full we started stacking them on the backseat. I offered a blanket to cover the boxes and Goldblatt declined.

"Don't get pulled over for speeding," I advised.

"Don't worry," said Goldblatt, "we've got an escort."

We said goodbye and Ira and Izmael departed. I hurried inside to tell Special Agent Husky that they had an escort.

"They're probably referring to a radar detector," he said. "But it's not a problem anyway since we have the tracker on their car and can follow from a significant distance."

Lopez came back in through the door to my gym and collected the problematic transmitter, radios, and the Hawk. He handed me a shoe box that contained an old cassette recorder, an ear bud, and a box of blank tapes. After briefly showing me how to use the ear bud to record phone conversations, Lopez took an envelope from his pocket along with a voucher for me to sign. Inside the envelope was $200 cash. I was stunned. I'd spent three days getting ready for the sale and had little other time to devote to my writing or business. "That's it?" I asked.

He looked surprised. "How much do you think it should be, Mike?"

"I could have written an article with all the time I spent preparing for this buy."

"Well, don't forget you're also making a profit on this transaction," Lopez said tactfully.

That kind of pissed me off. There I was trying to help the government by selling guns from my home to known cartel associates. No one in the ATF office ever asked me what kind of profit margin I was making selling these lowers. It certainly wasn't significant enough to accept the risks involved. I didn't mind helping them but at least I expected to not lose money by doing so.

"Does our government really need Mike Detty to fund their investigations?" Hell, it hurt to think that these guys who I trusted would try to low-ball me like that.

Lopez could see that he was at a disadvantage. Unlike most confidential informants, I did not have charges pending or a looming prison sentence being held over my head. Nope, I was just a patriot trying to help his government take down a cartel and I expected my time to be covered.

"Let me talk to Jack about this," said Lopez. "We do appreciate what you're doing for us. I didn't realize how important your time is to your writing endeavors."

"Thanks Travis, I appreciate that. I'd hate for us to get off on the wrong foot."

Lopez would later bring me another $300 along with an apology from Jack Hinkley saying that my involvement, honesty, and hard work were critical to their success.

When he left my house, I felt a huge relief. I arranged to have dinner with an old friend who had retired from law enforcement. Frank had done work at the local and federal level and often helped me at gun shows. He was aware of what was going on. At dinner I clued him in on the day's events.

"Glad everything went well for you, buddy," he said. "I have to admit that I didn't get a wink of sleep last night worrying about you."

It was my understanding that the Tucson office would follow the gold Neon up to Casa Grande where the Phoenix office would take over the tail. But early Friday morning I received a call from SA Lopez.

"I just wanted to thank you for doing a great job yesterday. We're still up in Phoenix and it looks like things will be very successful—you're the man!" He sounded almost jubilant and I could hear the other agents in the car were also in a raucous, good-natured mood. I found out later that their excitement came from listening to the Hawk on a laptop computer and hearing my conversation. Apparently they were pleased with my questions and the answers I got.

A little later in the month, Ira Goldblatt found my tables at a gun show at the state fairgrounds in Phoenix and ordered another fifty lowers from me. He handed me a fat white envelope. "Don't count it here but there's $5,000 in there as a down payment for another fifty lowers."

"Rodriguez called me," I told him. "He said he thought you and Izmael were trying to cut him out of the profits."

"That pisses me off," said Goldblatt. "He's lucky he's not six feet under. I used my own money to get him out of trouble and then he says I'm screwing him?"

"Do you think Rodriguez took half of the down payment that was originally earmarked for me?" I asked casually.

"Yeah, and he couldn't replace the money in time to complete the deal. He even got a week off with pay and he still comes back with a bad attitude. We barely even talk anymore—maybe 'Good morning' and that's it."

"Diego told me they were replacing the semi-auto fire control parts with full auto parts and asked if I would take the semi-auto parts on trade towards the new lowers."

"That's bullshit," said Goldblatt indignantly, "they aren't replacing any parts. Rodriguez is full of shit."

I called Lopez after the show and he asked if I could come down to the federal building on Monday.

I'd prepared a two-page synopsis of my conversation with Goldblatt and gave it to Lopez when I arrived at the eighth-floor offices. Petey Palmer, the agent who worked behind my tables at the first observed buy in Mesa, came out of his office to say hello. Scott Languien and Armando "Mando" Arroyo also came out to say hello and hear about the latest development in the case. It felt good to have them all come out and say hello and slap me on the back. Languien wanted to hear the latest events with Goldblatt as he would be handling the case for Lopez while he went back to Albuquerque to get married and take a honeymoon.

Jack Hinkley put two fingers in my back as he walked by and said "Give me all of your money." He was on his way to the break room to wash out the plastic box that had held his lunch. When he returned Languien, Lopez, and I went into Jack's corner office.

"Mike, I want to thank you again for your help," said Hinkley. "You did a great job that day at your house. Travis expressed your concerns about your time being covered and I want to apologize for having overlooked that."

I smiled and nodded without saying anything.

Hinkley went on to say that the surveillance was stymied by some vision barriers and that they had discussed these problems and developed solutions to overcome them. "We get a little smarter each time," he said chuckling. "Did I hear you say that you ran into Goldblatt at the gun show last weekend?"

"Yeah, he brought me a $5,000 cash down payment for another fifty lowers."

"Perfect," said Hinkley with a big smile.

"He also wanted some grenade launchers. I specifically asked him if he wanted the legal-to-own 37 mm flare launchers, those are really nothing more than toys, or if he wants the authentic 40 mm military weapon. He wants the real thing!"

The agents discussed among themselves the possibility of borrowing an M-16 with a grenade launcher from Davis Monthan, a Tucson Air Force base, as they had done in other cases but this would require a buy-bust, meaning they would have to arrest them as soon as they took possession of the gun and that's not what they wanted to do at that point in the game.

"If we wanted them," said Jack, "we could have busted them already. Quite frankly, Mike, I don't care about Ira or Diego. If they want to cooperate, that's fine, and if they don't, we can work around it. What I want is to seize businesses, homes, vehicles. I want to take a huge slice out of this cartel."

I told them I had placed the order for the next fifty lowers that Ira had ordered on Saturday with the factory earlier in the morning and would probably have them by the following Wednesday. "We could do it on Thursday," said Jack. "That way the surveillance wouldn't run into the weekend." The agents appeared happy at the thought of not having to work on the weekend. Jack said they would set up video surveillance for the buy, possibly using the Hawk with a button camera that would be worn by the agent in my house.

I told them Ira had said more than once that he needed as much time as possible to arrange the delivery. When I asked if he'd had any problems on the trip home with his lowers he said that he had a lot of eyes on him and was well protected.

Jack shook his head slowly. "Mike, this guy is a gangster wannabe—they had no one with them, I can tell you that for a fact. They have been trained though. They made the return like they had a load of dope in their car. They were turning down side streets, making U-turns, and doubling back to make sure that no one was following them. There were a number of places where he pulled into areas we couldn't observe and that's why we aren't sure where the lowers were unloaded."

When I told them what Goldblatt had said about Rodriguez, Hinkley sounded pleased. "Good, we might be able to use this broken friendship for leverage at some point in the future—assuming they don't kill Diego first."

"He also denied replacing any parts."

"Well that just confirms what we already knew about Rodriguez," said Hinkley. "He's a lying piece of trash. I wouldn't be surprised if his own guys are going to kill him."

Goldblatt called me the following day and sounded pissed. "I thought you were going to call me yesterday."

"Ah geez, Ira, I'm sorry. I completely spaced getting back to you. I spoke with the factory and they thought it would be a week to ten days before I get the lowers that you ordered."

"I want to give you my new cell phone number. The one that you have now is my work number."

I copied down the number and promised to stay in touch if I heard anything. I was overly apologetic; I wanted him to know that he was very much in charge and that I was going to follow his direction. This was a person who wanted to embrace the thug culture of the cartels and had once told me that he was the "muscle" for the Phoenix group. He wanted to portray himself as hard and ruthless and I wanted him to think that I perceived him exactly that way. Jack had asked me to try to get his email address so that they could use it as some sort of Trojan Horse to collect information. Specifically, they wanted to know where they were getting the upper assemblies to turn the lowers into complete weapons. But when I asked Goldblatt for his email address he rebuffed me and said that the new cell number would be the best way to get hold of him.

As was often the case, my suppliers let me down. The lowers I thought I would have by the following week took several weeks to get to me. Once I had a firm delivery date, I called Goldblatt.

"I'm in Tijuana right now on vacation," he said, sounding thoroughly relaxed.

"Well, I hope that you have a beautiful señorita on each arm."

"That's the plan."

I explained that we'd have the lowers the following week and should be able to transfer them at the gun show at the state fairgrounds. Again,

Goldblatt said his guy wanted the grenade launchers and I told him that I would check a source and see if we could get them.

After I got off the phone I called SA Languien and reported the conversation.

"Tijuana, huh? Well, it's all starting to make sense now. Those guns are most likely going to the Arellano Felix cartel."

When I called Goldblatt back to say we had the lowers, he said that he had to work all day Saturday and I told him that a Sunday pickup would be fine. Lopez seemed to be relieved to hear that he'd be able to spend Saturday with his new bride. I'm sure the long hours and demanding nature of his job would play havoc with any marriage.

It was a miserable hot day at the gun show. The building was not air conditioned and the swamp coolers were not working. By noon I had already drank three Gatorades and had sweated through my shirt and shorts. To make matters worse, sales were terrible, and all I wanted to do was drive home and jump into my swimming pool. Around noon, Lopez called me and asked me to meet him outside. He took the Hawk recording device from its protective container and started attaching an external microphone to it with the idea that he would tape the mic to my chest. But my shirt was already so wet that it would have clung to the mic and its cable. We decided to use the Hawk like we did the last time, and I dropped it into my cargo pocket.

Lopez told me that there would be eyes on me inside—meaning that there would be an agent in the vicinity in case there was any trouble. About an hour later, Petey Palmer phoned me and told me that they just saw a gold Neon pull into the parking lot and confirmed the plate—Ira and Izmael were on their way in.

I held the Hawk in my right hand inside the cargo pocket of my shorts, with my thumb on the record switch so that I could activate it when I saw Goldblatt. As I scanned the crowd, I saw Mando making his way down the aisle. He was a tall Mexican American, who before going to work for the ATF had been enlisted in the air force, worked for the Federal Bureau of Prisons, and had also been a border patrol agent. He was a good guy and I always enjoyed talking to him. Mando shared my love of guns and was always excited to see the latest gun I was evaluating for the gun magazines.

Finally I saw Goldblatt through the crowd about sixty feet away. I activated the record switch and let the Hawk fall to the bottom of my pocket.

As they got closer, I could see the much shorter Izmael walking next to Ira. We shook hands and exchanged pleasantries. Ira asked to sit down as he filled out the form #4473.

Izmael came behind the table with Ira. He shook my hand and pulled me closer. "It is important to our boss that we apologize for the problems that Diego created and let you know this is not how we normally do business," he told me. "We value our relationship with you and we want it to be an ongoing one. Our boss is embarrassed about what happened and promises that nothing like this will happen again."

He said all of this while maintaining a firm hold on my hand and looking me directly in the eye. I told them I didn't hold Diego's screwup against them and that I felt they'd always treated me with respect and it was my privilege to do business with men of honor. They both smiled widely when they heard this. But it made me wonder. It seemed very important for Izmael to send this message to me before we did anything else. I wondered if it was a direct order from the big boss—whoever that was. What I had thought was a dead issue had suddenly become a very important issue to them. Perhaps the boss understood that it was important for me to be happy, as I could rapidly bring much unwanted attention to them and their cohorts by alerting the ATF. It also made me feel good to know that at least at that moment neither of them suspected anything.

"How is Diego doing?" I asked.

"He's been sent home," said Ira. "He's been fired."

"Is he back in Yuma?"

Both men shrugged as if to say—sure, if that's what you want to believe.

Izmael told me he was the "money man" that Diego kept mentioning when he was trying to get the lowers. Supposedly at one point Diego told the other two men that he was going to call me to cancel the order.

"Who the hell is he to cancel an order for our boss?" said Izmael. "We made a decision that he would no longer be involved in this project."

"Shit, even the Boy Scouts will kick you out for stealing, what was he thinking?"

Both men laughed again and Ira said that Diego was too stupid for his own good. I was inclined to agree with him.

Compared to the last time I saw him, Izmael was unusually chatty. While Ira completed his paperwork, he rehashed his apology and told me that his boss was aware of me and that he appreciated my help. At one point Izmael mentioned that his boss was using the lowers (and I assumed an upper to make a complete weapon) as gifts.

Just then a uniformed Maricopa County Sheriff's Deputy leaned over and slammed both fists into the top of my table. In a loud voice he said, "What's up, gentleman?"

Izmael and Ira looked shocked and said nothing but I couldn't help laughing. I'd known Jason for quite a while. He was a sergeant on the SWAT team and was working security at the show. I'd already spoken to him and let him know that I had something going on with the feds but I guess he had forgotten. "Don't worry," I told Ira and Izmael. "He's an old friend."

I called in the background check while one of my helpers loaded the boxes filled with lowers onto a hand truck. Izmael excused himself to move the car closer to the building. Ira walked with me while I pushed the cart with his lowers.

While we walked, I asked him if he had lived in Phoenix for a long time.

"No not really. I've probably moved fifty times since I was thirteen years old—that's when I left home."

"You left when you were just thirteen? Do you ever talk to your mom?"

"Oh yeah, me and my mom are fine. In fact, I just bought her a twenty-acre spread in Georgia so she can have her horses."

"I thought maybe since you left so early you didn't get along with one of her boyfriends or something."

Goldblatt chuckled. "No, I never let her have any boyfriends. I was just ready to leave when I was thirteen."

"How was your vacation in Tijuana? When I was a little kid I grew up in San Diego. My memory of TJ is that it was a dirty place where sailors went to get drunk. Is it still like that or are there some nice places?"

"Well, the place where I stayed charges $240 a night. It's a beautiful resort. It's called Las Angelitas."

"Think an old white guy like me would have any problems if I went down there?"

"Actually, if you want to go there, you call me first and I'll arrange everything. You won't pay $240 for a room."

"So, you're connected there? There any trim down there?"

"I'll make sure you're well taken care of. You might even get to meet the big boss."

"That's a little scary—maybe he'll want to use me for a piñata."

"No, he'll probably kiss you on the cheek to show his appreciation."

Wow, I thought, imagining my unlikely meeting with a drug kingpin. Somehow, at that moment, it all seemed so possible and probable. My life had been transformed into a B movie full of all the typical gangster clichés. How in the world did I get myself into this?

I took the opportunity to ask Goldblatt who was assembling the lowers to uppers. He didn't tell me but he gave me the impression that it was someone in California. He also told me they were ordering ten-inch top ends from a source on the Internet and paying $450 for each upper.

AR-15 rifles have two basic groups—uppers and lowers. In the eyes of the US government, the lowers, like the ones I had been selling Goldblatt and friends, were viewed as a complete firearm which is why a background check and paperwork had to be done as if it were a complete gun.

Uppers were unregulated so individuals could order those parts over the Internet and have them shipped directly to their homes. However, unless very specific paperwork was filed with the ATF and approved and a special tax was paid, it was illegal to possess a rifle with a barrel shorter than sixteen inches. The six inches in length saved made these AR-15 carbines incredibly short, fast-handling, and easy to conceal. I knew Lopez and the agents at the ATF would be very interested in this information because besides the obvious trafficking aspect to the case, assembling a rifle with a barrel length of less than sixteen inches was also a felony.

When Izmael arrived and we loaded fifty AR-15 lowers into the back of their Neon, I decided to take a paternal tone with them.

"Look," I said, trying to sound tentative, "I don't have to worry about these things popping up at drive-bys or Circle K robberies in Phoenix, do I?"

"Absolutely not," said Ira. His answer, accompanied by a knowing smile, assured me that these lowers were going south.

Izmael removed a sealed white envelope from his pocket and handed it to me.

"Eighty-two hundred?" I asked.

"Yep."

I gave each one a fifty-dollar bill and told them to have dinner on me. They both seemed genuinely appreciative. For me the show was over. I saved the money envelope in a plastic sandwich bag to see if the ATF could get Izmael's fingerprints, and by 3 p.m. I had packed my goods into my Suburban and started the two-hour drive home.

Travis called the following morning and said he'd broken off the stakeout the previous night at about eight. He asked if I was able to come down to the federal building and drop off the Hawk.

Travis met me at the front door when I arrived so we wouldn't have to put the Hawk through the X-ray machine for security. As I walked through the metal detector it screeched loudly but the security guy waved me through without making me take anything off. I guessed I was sacred as long as I was with Lopez. We went upstairs and sat down with Scott Languien.

I relayed as much of the conversation with Izmael and Ira as I could remember. Especially how Diego had been fired and sent home.

"Well, there hasn't been any activity on his cell phone," Languien said. "Maybe they buried it with him." We all laughed, but I more nervously than the others.

"I hate to think that asshole got himself killed for $2,500," I said.

"Fuck him," said Languien. "He knew exactly who he was dealing with and what would happen to him if he took their money."

I agreed, but Languien's callous response and the news that a player I had dealt with had met his demise, or what we assumed was his end, hit home with me. If those guys had no problem taking out one of their own, they'd certainly have no problem killing me.

I shrugged off the risk and told Languien and Lopez what Goldblatt had told me about the short top ends. Languien said that according to a recent ruling just finding them with the ten-inch uppers and complete lowers wouldn't be enough to charge them with illegal possession of a short-barreled rifle. We had to get conclusive proof on tape that they were assembling the short top ends onto the complete M4 lowers.

At one point the Tucson office had me checking sources to see if I could supply Goldblatt's people with the short top ends so that they could better track these weapons. In the end, the special agent in charge of the Phoenix ATF office, Bill Newell, vetoed this idea as he had reservations about the CI providing both parts to manufacture an illegal arm. I ended up telling Goldblatt I couldn't beat the $450 price they were already paying.

I was eager to hear about what happened after Ira and Izmael left the fairgrounds. Travis mentioned that during the stakeout they watched the two pull their Neon into a garage and close the door. Several minutes later, the garage door opened and they backed the car out and parked it. He said that after a few minutes he did a walk-by and saw that the back seat was empty.

"You walked by," I said incredulously. He nodded. "Man, you got big balls!"

"Yep, that's me—cajones grandes!"

Less than a month later I was getting ready for another gun show in Mesa and had sent Lopez an email asking if he wanted me to pick up the Hawk in case I ran into Ira and Izmael. I received a phone call from Lopez a few minutes later.

"Our investigation took a turn last week," he said. "Turns out that Izmael shipped some lowers from a UPS Store. After he left, the suspicious owner, a retired Secret Service Agent—who thought the box might contain dope—opened it and discovered the lowers. He called the Phoenix ATF office and the lowers were seized. We got involved and tried to get approval for the shipment to go through, but the special agent in charge of the San Diego district refused to let that happen. He said something to the effect that he didn't need our guns over there causing problems for him."

Izmael was tracking the shipment on the computer and when it became apparent there was a problem he went into the UPS Store where the owner told him that the lowers were seized. Lopez said there were two other phone calls to the UPS Store, he thought from Izmael's boss, to check on the lowers. The ATF had yet to contact Izmael.

"We may just end up arresting both Goldblatt and Izmael," said Lopez. "We've got plenty on both of them."

My heart sank . . . after all that work to end up busting them for a relatively minor offense that would no doubt be plead down to an even lesser charge with very little prison time. It was far from seizing businesses, vehicles, and homes, and toppling a cartel as Jack Hinkley had envisioned.

The next day I parked just outside the building by the fountains and called Lopez on my cell to let him know I was there to pick up the Hawk just in case Goldblatt or Izmael approached me that weekend.

Lopez seemed disappointed yet resigned. "We're still not sure what we're going to do," he said. "Obviously we'd like to keep the investigation going."

He told me to act angry if they showed and told me what had happened. He also said to ask Goldblatt if he'd used his real address on his #4473 and tell him that if he hadn't been contacted yet they probably couldn't find him.

"Is it a bogus address?"

He nodded. "That's another charge we can hit him with."

4

DYSLEXIC DIVERSION

FOR A WHILE I received sporadic calls from Lopez to let me know that they were still investigating the case. He told me that they were using forensic accountants to see if the HVAC company that Goldblatt and Rodriguez worked for had any involvement in the gun trafficking.

Occasionally Lopez would ask me to call Goldblatt and check in. Ira was straight up with me when I spoke with him after the UPS Store debacle and put the blame on Izmael for the seized lowers. A couple months later, Lopez told me that Izmael's bank accounts had been emptied and were inactive and asked me to call Goldblatt to see if Izmael was still around.

"I really don't know where he is right now," said Goldblatt when I called. "Basically, it was the same thing as Diego. He got too greedy and got knocked off the payroll. He's doing OK but he's not with us anymore."

"Did this have anything to do with the lowers getting seized?"

"No, not really," he said, but then he paused for a moment before adding, "Maybe it did have something to do with him leaving—he's such a little bitch."

That was about all Goldblatt would say about Izmael and it made the guys at the Tucson ATF office wonder if he'd been killed for losing the lowers or stealing from the cartel.

The case did seem to be dead in the water, though every once in a while I would hear from Goldblatt. He'd ask if I'd be able to get together twenty lowers. It sounded to me like he was trying to broker his own deal by doing an end around on the middleman in San Diego with whom he'd previously dealt. Money seemed to be his problem as he never did put together a big buy. He did, however, send one of his workers to a Phoenix area gun show in November 2006 to buy five lowers with the idea of using the profits to buy increasingly bigger amounts. But it never happened.

At the same November gun show I was approached by another individual whose reckless abandon and disregard immediately raised my suspicions. Santini "Rey" Ayala cared nothing about being clever or subtle and had his son buy seven rifles the first day I met them. A couple weeks later he had another son do the paperwork for four rifles on a Friday and then had his girlfriend fill out the form for eight more rifles on Sunday.

This case was handled by the Phoenix ATF office and I couldn't have been more disappointed. I was assigned to SA Jodi Pederman—and from what I had heard, she was not known for her efficiency or intellect amongst her peers. In fact, based solely on my interaction with her, I am amazed that this person was allowed to be a federal agent.

I'd asked Lopez if he could handle the case after Rey bought his first guns. After discussing it with Hinkley, and then Hinkley with the Phoenix special agent in charge, it was decided that the Phoenix office should have the case and I was given SA Pederman's contact information.

Based on my first conversation with Ayala it was apparent that he was looking for a dealer for a continued supply of these guns. I told him that if he didn't mind driving to Tucson to pick up the guns we could take care of his needs between shows. Tucson is just about an hour's drive from Mexico and is situated between Phoenix and the border.

"Shit, Tucson is right on my way," said Ayala.

While the Tucson office had tried to have a presence at every transaction I did with Rodriguez or Goldblatt, SA Pederman did not apparently see the need when I sold guns to Ayala from my home.

"Just fax us the #4473 when you're done so that we have the serial numbers," she said. Her apathetic attitude was not a morale booster!

If something went wrong I could have been dead for days before someone found me. That was the problem, amongst other things, with this case being run out of the Phoenix office.

Ayala called me the day after the first gun show where his girlfriend and son had bought twelve rifles and said that he needed four more. He was supposed to be at my house by nine that evening and at about ten thirty

I got undressed and went to bed. About a half hour later he called and said that he was at the far end of town—at least forty-five minutes away.

I was nervous about dealing with Rey. He had told me during our first meeting how some gang kids had given his girlfriend and kids a hard time at a convenience store and how he confronted them with a pistol and told them he would kill them if it ever happened again—pistol-whipping one of them to make his point.

Rey was not a physically imposing man but with a gun in his hand there was no need for brawn. He was as unkempt as he was unintelligent and usually desperately needed a shave and shower. But what was most scary about him was his apathy towards getting caught. Perhaps we were more alike than I cared to imagine. He too seemed to have nothing to lose.

Because of this, I carried two .45s that night—one behind my right hip and the other, a Kimber Ultra lightweight subcompact, in an ankle holster on my left leg. I also secreted a couple pistols around the area where he'd be doing the paperwork.

Jodi had asked me to run a tape and I set up the recorder on the wet bar in my dining room behind a box that held the cremated remains of my old Labrador, Sarge. When Rey called from my driveway to let me know he'd arrived, I started the recorder and met him at the door.

This night he had another son with him to do the paperwork. My guess is that he thought he'd fly under the radar by using a different buyer each time to do the paperwork. We sat down and chatted at my dining room table while his son completed the background form.

"I've been trying to work with a dealer in Phoenix, but every time I called him I'd hear a 'click.' I was asking how much it would be for eight different rifles and he said that he'd have to check. When I called back, I heard the click again. Can you believe that asshole was taping me?"

"Fuck him. Rey," I said. "You don't need to deal with that shit. Look, you're filling out the required forms and doing everything legal. If you need more guns just get them from me. I'll take care of whatever . . ."

I was interrupted by a loud clunk from the wet bar. Adrenaline shot through my veins as I looked to see Rey's reaction. Apparently, I had put the tape in upside down and the recorder shut itself off loudly when it slammed to the end of the tape.

"That's the plumbing for the wet bar," I said. "Happens so often that I don't even pay attention to it anymore."

He bought my response. How ironic, I thought, he's telling me a story about some gun dealer recording him when my own cassette machine interrupts us. Things could have been much worse. If he'd stood up and looked behind Sarge's urn, our evening might have finished very differently.

After I called in his son's background check, Rey started pulling cash out of his pocket. The first time he did this I thought it was some sort of test—maybe he knew exactly how much cash he had and just wanted to check my honesty by counting it. But this was the fourth time he'd done it and now I realized that this guy was either severely dyslexic or just couldn't count. There were $20s, $100s, and $50s and I counted out the $2,700 he owed me and pushed the rest of the cash back to him. "I hope this is the beginning of a long business relationship," I said. He shook my hand and said that he hoped so too. I didn't push too hard to ask where the guns were going or what he was doing with them.

I walked out with them carrying a gun in each hand. They had a white Ford F150 truck that was just two years old, according to Rey. I made a mental note of the license plate and placed the guns in the back seat of the extended cab. By midnight, they were on their way to wherever they were going.

The following weekend I saw Rey and another son at the gun show at the Pima County fairgrounds in Tucson. He wanted to buy ten of my cheapest AR-15 rifles—a DPMS Panther-Lite. I only had nine left and he bought them all. This time he took a wad of bills from his pocket and pulled a couple hundreds off the stack and put them back in his pocket before handing me the cash. I counted out $7,000 and handed the remainder back to him. They left the guns at my tables while they went shopping for handguns. In particular, Rey was looking for Sig pistols and some hot defense ammunition for them. When he returned to my tables he held several different pistol boxes. He must have spent thousands more on these expensive handguns. I offered to help carry the rifles out but he declined my help when another son showed up.

Just three days later, Rey called again and wanted to know how much it would be for another ten rifles.

"Let's see," I said, "$675 times ten is $6,750."

""Would you take $6,600?"

"Absolutely not, these are my most economical guns and I don't have any room to discount them."

"OK then, I'll stop and get more money. I should be at your house by four."

I called SA Pederman. She had told me the day before that she would like to bring a team down from Phoenix the next time he made a purchase. It wasn't quite noon when I called, so she'd have time to get her people together and come to Tucson.

Before anyone arrived, I pulled the rifles from inventory and started filling out a receipt with the serial number. I also filled out as much of the #4473 as I could so that things would go as smoothly and as quickly as possible.

I saw two agents position their cars on the street in front of my house and on the side street. Rey ended up being late, as usual, but I kept myself busy in the meantime. I was under the gun to meet a deadline for one of the gun magazines I wrote for. My photographer, Allen, a young man just out of college, came over to pick up a rifle I was doing an article on. He'd be doing studio shots of the gun for my piece. Inside the house I gave him some quick directions on which of the rifle's features to concentrate on. He put the gun back in its case, slung it over his shoulder, and left in his white Ford F150. As soon as he turned the corner, I saw the car parked on the side of my house follow quickly behind him. I called Jodi as fast as I could on my cell phone and explained that the person in the Ford was not one of the players. "Break off—that's not our vehicle—and return to position," I heard her shouting into her radio. It almost made me laugh! Of course, poor Allen had no idea what was going on.

As I looked out my large front picture window, I saw my neighbor Sharon back out of her driveway and then sit for a second in the street while looking at the silver Dodge Intrepid with blacked-out windows parked on the side of the road near her property line.

Oh Christ, I thought, she's going to call the Sheriff's department and report a suspicious vehicle. A few moments later, she backed out of the driveway again and up to the driver's side door of the Intrepid. I saw the window on the Intrepid go down and a brief conversation between the two drivers and then Sharon left.

SA Pederman later told me that she "badged" the neighbor (flashed her badge) and told her that she was doing police work and not to worry. Great, I thought, it was obvious that she was positioned to watch my house—who knew what type of trouble my busybody neighbor might cause?

Rey got there a few seconds after this encounter and said he'd brought along enough money to buy all ten rifles. He had his son fill out the #4473 for me and Rey started pulling cash from his pockets and throwing the bills on the table. His equally challenged son attempted to help his dad count the cash while I called in his background check. Rather than arrange the bills by denominations, they started trying to make mixed stacks of bills that totaled $1,000 each. It was a mess and required recounting the money several times.

"Business is pretty good right now, huh?" I asked Rey.

He smiled broadly, his front lower teeth missing. "What can we do to make it better?" I asked.

"That's a good question," he said. "Let me talk to someone about this. You know, Mike, I like you. You're exactly the kind of person I want to do business with. We take care of those that take care of us. If anyone ever bothers you, just let me know. We'll take care of 'em."

How awesome is that, I thought, I now had a presumed cartel associate telling me that he'd take out anyone causing problems for me. If I said a couple people's names didn't come immediately to mind I'd be lying.

I helped them carry the guns out and pile them into the back of the Grand Cherokee. It took us two trips. I looked at the silver Intrepid sitting at the corner on the other side of Sharon's house and wondered if Rey had noticed the car or suspected anything. If he did, it wasn't obvious to me.

I had gained his confidence and he liked me. That should make things easier if the investigation continues, I thought. Then he showed me a S&W Sigma .40 pistol he had bought. It was tucked between the two front seats in a cheap black nylon holster. As I turned it over in my hand, I told him I thought he got a good buy at $400, and then I stepped back away from Rey so that Jodi could see me give the gun back to him and see him put it back between the front seats.

We said goodbye and he took off. The silver Dodge Intrepid was about thirty seconds behind him.

I went to dinner at Austin's, a hamburger place on Broadway. About seven o'clock Jodi called me. She had lost the subjects—they had pulled off the main highway and into pitch black after turning off their lights.

"But I don't see how they could have made us, Mike. There was only one car with them when they did this and he was a quarter mile behind them."

"I don't think it would be possible to underestimate these guys' stupidity. I don't think they have the ability to be cagey."

"We think they ended up in a trailer park somewhere near the Cortaro exit. Do you think they use a Phoenix address and really bring the guns down here?"

"It's possible but they talk an awful lot about the Phoenix area. I don't think they're smart enough to develop a cover story complete with fake addresses."

She asked if the boy had any tattoos. I couldn't remember but I did notice that he had some piercings on his face. She said she thought he was a member of a gang. "Maybe that's where the guns are going," she said. We both agreed if that was the case these rifles would start popping up really soon at crime scenes and traffic stops. I mentioned this theory to Lopez and he laughed.

"You know, I like Jodi but she's not the brightest person," he said. "This close to the border we can almost guarantee that they are going south. These aren't typical gang guns—too expensive. Now if they were buying twenty Ruger P89s"—a budget-priced semiautomatic 9 mm handgun—"at a time I might be inclined to believe that they were going to gangs. But I'll guarantee you that these rifles are going to Mexico."

I faxed the receipt and #4473 to Jodi. Travis asked me if she'd mentioned paying me and I told him that it was never discussed and he said he would take care of it. So, at least she knows now that I expect something other than a good citizen award when this is all over, I thought.

A couple days before Christmas 2006, Rey called again and said he needed four more rifles. He said he'd be out at my place between seven or eight that evening. About eleven he called and woke me up and said that he'd be at my house shortly. I got up and got dressed and tried to shake off my drowsiness.

I'd be doing the buy alone again. Jodi and her team couldn't make it down and she didn't seem too concerned. In addition to the Kimber pistols I normally wore for these events, I had a new item to add to that night's dress list—a digital recorder.

Larry, one of my regular gun show helpers, was a full-time IT guy for a Fortune 500 company and after I relayed my near-catastrophic experience with the cassette recorder to him, he suggested I buy a digital recorder. Much smaller and lighter, my new digital recorder had better recording qualities than the cassette recorder, files could easily be downloaded to my computer and saved, I could easily burn a conversation to a CD or email some of the shorter conversations, and it had twelve hours of recording time versus the one hour on a cassette tape. There appeared to be no downside to my $70 investment.

On this night, Rey brought along one of his overweight sons and his girlfriend's son to do the paperwork. They were gone before midnight with their four rifles and I went back to bed. I wouldn't see or hear from Rey for three weeks.

I was at a Phoenix gun show the third weekend of January 2007 when Rey stopped by to say hello. He mentioned that he had bought five AK-47s from another dealer who gave him a good price, and he asked me to look at some guns another dealer had for sale.

They were Saiga brand rifles made in Russia using an AK-47 action but fitted with clumsy sporterized buttstocks to make them eligible for import to the United States.

"Do your customers want guns with stocks like this, Rey?"

"All they told me was that they wanted AK-47s and the guy here says that these are AK-47s."

"Most people don't want these style stocks on their rifles. I'd call your guys before you buy them."

"I'm going to go ahead and get them," said Rey.

The reason was obvious—they were much cheaper than the guns with military-style stocks and Rey wanted to broaden his profit margin. I later watched as Rey and his sons walked out with ten rifles. The dealer who sold them to him packed his tables and went home since he had nothing left to sell the following day. Before he left, Rey gave me the vendor's business card.

"Maybe you two guys can work something out?"

"Yeah, I'll give him a call."

I knew Jodi would appreciate getting that dealer's information.

We took our time closing my tables down. Larry and I were going to have dinner at a local Mexican restaurant close to the hotel where I was staying in Phoenix. The gun show parking lot was empty save for a few cars. I spotted Rey talking with his son and some other people and waved. I sat in my car pretending to make a phone call and copied down the license plate numbers for the two cars I had not seen before. We already had plate numbers for Rey's Ford F150 and Jeep Grand Cherokee, but now there was also a maroon Nissan Altima and a silver Lincoln Town Car. I emailed that information along with the dealer's info to SA Pederman that night.

Five days later Rey called me in the morning and asked for a price for a variety of AR-15 and AK-47 semi auto rifles. The total for the eighteen rifles he wanted came to $11,740. Rey told me that he'd be there by one in the afternoon.

I called and relayed the information to SA Pederman. She asked me to call him back with some sort of excuse to see if we could push the time to three so that she'd have a chance to get down there with her people. I called Rey and told him that I'd forgotten a doctor's appointment and wouldn't be available until later and this didn't seem to be a problem for him.

About an hour later Lopez called me. I could tell by his tone that he was pissed off.

"Mike, has Jodi said anything to you about taking down your buyer tonight?"

"Absolutely not."

"Has she paid you anything for your work or told you that she was going to pay you?"

"Nope."

"That fucking bitch! I don't need her coming down from Phoenix and burning my CI."

"The last time she was down here she never even knocked on my door to introduce herself," I said. "She sat right outside my house but couldn't be bothered to knock on my door. I still don't know what she looks like."

"Let me clue you in—she is as ugly as she is stupid. She had plans to take you down with the bad guys in your driveway and handcuff you in front of your neighbors."

"What? Are you fucking kidding me?"

"I wish I was. I'm trying to put together a team of Tucson agents so that we can help Jodi take these guys down away from your house."

I felt betrayed and used. Why would any agent think it was OK to arrest and handcuff a confidential informant at his house? This was the thanks I got for helping them take down a gun trafficker? I could understand her wanting to throw suspicion off me but at the cost of destroying my reputation? There were other ways to handle this and thankfully Lopez had put together a hasty plan. "A friend of mine from FLETC will call you after the bust to let you know what's going on," he said. "His name is Doug. I'll be involved with the interrogations and may not have the time to call you, OK?"

I sat at the dining room table working on my laptop when Rey arrived. He had walked up to my front door without me realizing it and I didn't even have time to activate my digital recorder. With him was one of his ugly sons and a tall young black man who was holding hands with a short and dumpy Hispanic woman. As I let them through the front door my fourteen-year-old Ridgeback-mix woke up and started barking. I used this excuse to put her outside and activated my recorder.

Rey seemed agitated and quickly told me a story about his friend stealing his truck, which had nine of our rifles in it, and driving it to Mexico where cops arrested him and seized the rifles.

As Rey was telling me the story, his son showed me a picture he had taken with his cell phone of the Mexican newspaper and the front page story of the seizure.

"Why did he steal your truck?" I asked.

Rey shrugged. "I don't know," he mumbled.

It was an incredible story that Rey must have concocted because his delivery guy got caught. He even told me that he'd driven down to try to get his truck back with no luck.

Rey asked if I minded if he went through the boxes of rifles. I told him to go ahead. Even though I had already taken the detachable iron sights off the AR-15s, had removed some of the cleaning kits, and taken all of the extra mags and bayonets out of the AK boxes, he never noticed.

Rey explained that the young black man was his son's friend and that they'd be doing the paperwork. I had him start filling out the #4473 for the background check. I looked at the form as he filled it out so that I could put the same name on the receipt. I was surprised to see that the person's name was Sally Dougs—she was a nineteen-year-old woman.

While I filled out the paperwork Rey paced nervously in my living room stopping to look out the front window and also peering through the blinds on my side windows.

"Hey, the last time I was out here there was a silver Dodge Intrepid that followed me all of the way to Casa Grande. Every time I took an exit she would follow and then they would be right behind me again on I-10. I took my pistol and was going to shoot that bitch in the head."

His story matched what Jodi had told me though she said it was someone else who was a quarter mile behind them. Apparently she was close enough he could tell she was a woman.

I watched him carefully. Was he accusing me of setting him up? Was he confronting me? "Do you think it was a cop or someone trying to rip you off?" I asked.

Rey shrugged again. "I dunno."

"How many people knew you were coming down here with all that cash and who knew you were bringing guns back with you?"

"There's a couple people and right now I'm trying to figure out who would double-cross me."

"That's some scary shit, Rey. Let me know what you figure out. But I don't need those kinds of problems here, OK?"

Rey nodded and I felt as though I had dodged a bullet.

Rey had brought all $20 bills and I had put a bunch of rubber bands on the table prior to them coming so I could band together $1,000 at a time. I got to $11,700. "OK, we're only $40 short now." He looked a little shocked that I actually asked for the missing cash. He opened his wallet and took out another $40.

I offered to help Rey carry the guns out to his car. I took a pistol out of the wet bar drawer and put it in my waistband. I winked at him. "Just in case . . ."

Rey was driving a nice new white Nissan Armada. It still had the new car smell. "Wow," I said, "this is as big as my Chevy Suburban—looks like a really nice SUV."

"I can get you one for 15Gs," he said.

I chuckled. "Yeah, but will it come with a title?"

Rey let out a short laugh but didn't answer. He and his son had begun fighting over how to stack the gun boxes in the back. He nodded when I asked if I could look at his car.

I opened each door pretending to look inside until I saw him and his son head back inside to pick up another load of guns. Then I hurried to the driver's side door and opened the center console. Inside, I could see two auto pistols. One was a Smith & Wesson and the other a Sig. I dropped the mag partway on both of them and ejected the round in the chamber before pushing the mag back into place and pocketing the two rounds. Unless they checked them, they would get a click instead of a bang if they tried to use them tonight.

I said goodbye to Rey and told him to be careful. We shook hands. He trusted me implicitly and I truly did feel bad for what was about to happen to him.

By 4 p.m. all four were in the car and back on the road. Shortly after they left, Travis's friend Doug called and said they were on Rey's tail. I told him about the pistols in the console and he said he would pass on that information.

I got the money ready for deposit, did the necessary paperwork, and logged the guns out of my bound book. It was still relatively early so I decided to go out for Mexican food.

After I was finished eating, my cell phone rang and it was Doug Molson. He said that he didn't know how much in the loop Jodi kept me and I told him it was zero. I was still fuming over her original plan to take me down in my driveway without telling me.

"Well, we took down your guys at an apartment complex at Golf Links and Aviation Highway. We have like eight in custody including Rey's boss. He was reluctant to talk at first but ended up spilling the beans." He told me they started asking Rey questions about the dirty gun dealer that had sold him the guns. Rey reportedly said, "Oh no, don't drag Mike into this. He's a nice guy and did everything legal. This is all on me."

An hour or so later Travis called me. He said they had done some preliminary interviews and Rey had confessed. It was fortunate the way things happened because had they taken him down at my house they would have never gotten his boss and money guy. When they surrounded them at an apartment complex, a guy came out of his unit and asked what they were doing to his friends. This turned out to be the money guy and he confessed as well.

Travis said Rey was almost relieved because his boss was pushing him to buy more and more guns everyday—until that was all he did. As we spoke the crew was being transported to Phoenix. I asked if all of his kids were going to be rounded up. My concern was that one of them would target me while I walked to my car after a gun show.

"That's a good question and only Jodi can answer it for you."

But she never did. In fact, I still have no idea what happened to Rey or any of his family members. I don't know if they were prosecuted or flipped and turned informants to get out of trouble. I sent numerous emails to Jodi with no response in regards to this matter. That was the big "thank you" I got for bringing them the case. At no point in time did Jodi say, "Hey thanks, Mike, this is a really nice bust. You took some big chances on our behalf and we are truly grateful for what you've done for us." Nope, nothing like that; in fact, I never even received a good citizen's award.

Many months later, I did finally get some confidential informant money. Jodi sent another agent to a Phoenix gun show to give me the cash. He handed me a voucher to sign that listed the amount as $700.

"Are you serious? Seven hundred dollars for all the work I did?"

The agent shrugged unapologetically, "Look, I'm just making the delivery. I didn't work this case. If there's a problem, you'll have to discuss that with Jodi."

I called SA Pederman when the gun show ended and she didn't seem surprised to hear from me.

"We just don't have huge amounts of cash to give our CIs. That was the best I could do for you. Don't forget, I'll put you in for a sizeable reward once this case is adjudicated." Somehow I knew that would never happen. Being screwed over like that after the risks I took by dealing with Rey and his family from my home sapped every bit of motivation from me. While this bust would be a feather in her cap, she cared absolutely nothing for the person who brought her the case and took all the risks.

Well, I thought, it's done. Goldblatt is on hold and my days of helping the ATF are over. Maybe now I could get back to a semblance of normal life.

5

NOT DEAD AFTER ALL

IT WAS SATURDAY February 3, 2007, and I'd returned home after working all day at a gun show at the Pima County fairgrounds. After feeding my dog Morgan, I checked my answering machine.

There was a garbled message from someone—it was hard to understand as he was not speaking clearly. I had to play it several times before I realized that it was Diego Rodriguez. So he was still alive! I grabbed my digital recorder, attached the ear bud mic, and called him back.

"Hey buddy," he said, "I have some friends that need guns and I told them about you. We wanted to see if we could come over and take a look."

I told him that all of my guns were on display at the fairgrounds and that I'd be happy to show them to his guys if they wanted to come by on Sunday and take a look.

The Super Bowl was the following day and Diego called around two to say that he and his friends were out by Three Points, very close to the Sasabe border crossing, and that they couldn't make it to the show before it closed. We chatted for a while and I tried to elicit as much information from him as I could without making him suspicious.

The following day I sent this email to SA Lopez.

Hey Travis,

Diego Rodriguez is still alive! He called and left a message for me Saturday and I called him when I got home from the gun show. I have subsequently had another conversation with him via phone and here is what I found out.

    He has a friend that is looking for guns and interested primarily in AK47s.

    He said that he is struggling to get on his feet and is working at Florolite, a lighted sign company, as an electrician for $10/hour. He's living with a friend in a trailer at the Malibu Trailer Park near the airport. He owns a '93 Camaro but is having lots of problems with it and it is not currently drivable.

    Rodriguez said that he's tried to call Izmael a couple times but his phone was disconnected. "That's unusual for him—he always has a phone on."

    He wanted to know if I could meet him somewhere tonight and I told him that because of my license I could only work from this address or a gun show. I asked him if this guy was "cool" and he replied that he wouldn't bring him to my house if he wasn't.

    Let me know what you'd like me to do with him.

Lopez's email response:

YOU ARE THE MANNNNNNN!!!!!!! Nice work Mike . . . I was just going to head out to that trailer park this morning . . . I think I know which trailer he is staying in . . . we will be there tonight . . . I will give you a call when I get situated . . . thanks Mike

Prior to my meeting with Diego, I arranged some guns just inside the front door of my living room. As a bachelor I'd had little need to fill the room with furniture after my divorce so it made a perfect sales room and eliminated the need to take these guys farther into my home where they could study its layout.

I made stacks of multiple guns that I knew they would be interested in seeing. I had AKs with regular stocks, side-folding stocks, and under-folding stocks. I also had AK pistols—very much like the rifles except there was no buttstock and the barrel was shorter by two inches. I also put out some of my more popular AR-15 rifles that were set up to look like the military's M4 carbine. I made several stacks of these rifles in order to fill up the room and send the message that I had plenty of inventory.

I really had no idea what to expect. Diego's friend could have been interested in shooting and just needed one gun. But that's not the impression I got.

When they arrived, I noticed Diego was slimmer than I remembered. He introduced me to three friends as they came through the door. One of them he identified as *Gordo*, a Spanish nickname meaning Fatso, and said he was the buyer.

The four milled around my living room speaking in Spanish to each other while they picked up the guns and played with them. Gordo selected two of the AK-47 folders and one rifle. After counting his money he also chose one of the AK-47 pistols.

"Who is going to do the paperwork?" I asked Diego.

"I will," he said.

While he was doing the paperwork I leaned closer to him and quietly asked if these guns were going south to Mexico.

He smiled, "Yeah, dude, they are all going South," and gave me a look like he couldn't believe I even needed to ask.

As I filled out the receipt I saw a flash of light near the rear end of the car in the driveway and then my motion-sensor security lights went off. No one else noticed or seemed to care. An agent had used his flashlight to get a license plate number and had unwittingly activated the floodlights in front of my garage. It blew my mind that someone, especially a trained agent, could be so careless.

Gordo asked Diego in Spanish to ask what the cost of a real M-16 would be. I told him that if they bought them legally, jumping through all the government's hoops, it would cost tens of thousands of dollars, but it would be much cheaper if you had someone modify an AR-15 to fire full auto.

"Diego," I said, "didn't you have a guy who was converting your lowers for you?"

"Yeah, but he's in Tijuana." He said it was the same guy who gave him the money for lowers. He also said he bought the uppers, he called them "tops," off the Internet. Diego thought the guy might have been be Izmael's cousin or "they grew up together, or something."

As I walked the group outside, I asked Diego if he had to deliver the rifles or if someone came and got them from him. He said someone usually came and picked them up. "They take an old car and make special places to hide the guns before they cross the border."

He had arrived in a white '86 Ford T-Bird with a large New York Yankees logo smack in the middle of the rear window. It belonged to Santos—Diego's roommate and homeboy. The distinctive window decal will make following this particular vehicle very easy, I thought. They loaded the guns into both the trunk and back seat. As the careless agent had already taken it down, I didn't need to worry about getting a license plate number this time.

"We'll buy more next time," Diego promised. "These are samples to see what the guys want."

I shook hands with Gordo and said, "Buenas noches," to which he replied the same.

I felt more comfortable outside. I knew that there were more than a few friendly eyes on me and many of them within M4 range. But I hadn't felt particularly threatened that evening. My job was now over and it would be up to the agents to follow the car and find out where the guns went.

Two days later Lopez asked me to come down to the federal building to ID the people who were at my house that night. He had six pictures out of which I picked the three people I'd met. They all looked like driver's license photos that he most likely got from DMV so I think he had already identified all involved.

I asked Lopez who had lit up the license plate and triggered my floodlights and he laughed and asked if it caused me any problems. It made me wonder if it was him. We could both laugh about it now the danger had passed and I was safe, but it was a stupid mistake that could have caused some very serious problems for me.

Lopez said they tailed the guys almost all the way back to the trailer park but then they had turned down a cul-de-sac. They broke off the tail fearing that they might have been made.

"No sense in making them paranoid at this point," said Lopez.

He talked about scooping up Diego one day when he wouldn't be missed by anyone. His goal was to turn him. He had enough evidence to charge him and his carrot would be to keep his ass out of prison by setting up the rest of his buyers and providing info about the Tijuana cartel. I thought he would be successful in flipping him. Diego was soft and would not fare well in prison. But it would also give him a chance to be a big shot and put the screws to Ira Goldblatt and associates who Diego already felt had betrayed him.

I asked Travis to give me an idea of when it would go down so I didn't overload myself with too much inventory.

"It'll be sometime soon but I'll let you know," he said.

Rodriguez came out with Gordo a couple days later. The AK-47 pistol they had purchased was not working properly—its trigger was not resetting after it fired—and they wanted to return it. I took a look at it and offered to trade it for another.

Gordo spoke to Diego in Spanish and then Diego asked if they could see the AR-15 pistol I had shown them the other night. It was a Rock River Arms gun that for all intents and purposes was an AR-15 rifle but without a buttstock and with a short ten-inch barrel.

Gordo asked if Rock River was a good brand of guns. I took a catalog from the table and showed it to them. "Look, it is the choice of the DEA."

Both men smiled. Diego slowly repeated the letters D-E-A.

Seemed like that was all Gordo needed to hear—he wanted the gun. I told Diego I'd made a mistake the last time they were there. The AK-47 pistol he bought had the same regulations as any other handgun and the purchaser had to be older than twenty-one. Diego was only nineteen.

I had spoken about this mistake with Lopez when I was in his office. "Listen Mike," Lopez had said, "as long as you're working with us you're golden. But obviously we'd rather not have this issue to deal with."

I explained the problem to Diego, and Gordo offered to do the paperwork. It didn't seem to be a big deal to him.

After he finished his #4473 form, I called it in and it went through without a hitch. As I made out his receipt, I saw that Gordo's name was Pedro Armando Trujillo and he was much younger than I guessed—just twenty-two years old.

They had brought a different car so I made a point of walking them outside. It was a gray Nissan Sentra and I memorized the plate number as I stood talking to them. After a couple minutes they were on their way and we had some very new and significant information on this new buyer.

Diego would call every couple days saying he needed one or two rifles at a time. I finally told him to hold onto his money until he could come up with a good size order of ten or more guns. He whined a little about this and asked if he could come to the gun show the following weekend and get two AK-47s they needed.

The Tucson convention center was one of the nicer gun show venues. It had a clean tile floor and was air conditioned in the summer and heated in the winter. There was a snack bar and clean restrooms and, for the most part, vendors and customers stayed comfortable. Along one wall above the show floor were a couple offices with windows looking out onto the exhibition floor. The ATF and the Tucson police department's gang unit often taped black plastic over the windows and cut small ports for observation and photography during the gun shows. My tables were directly underneath these windows.

The show was painfully slow on Saturday and even worse on Sunday. Most of the agents I knew stopped by and said hello. Morty Bedouin stopped by on Sunday with his son and said he wasn't working that day so he thought he'd bring his boy to look around. Morty was among the minority of agents who seemed to actually enjoy guns and shooting. We were still talking when Pedro and Diego walked up to my tables.

I cut Morty off mid-sentence. "I'll have to talk with you later. These guys are some of my best customers."

Morty smiled and nodded and walked away. I took out the two AK-47s for inspection and Diego started filling out the form #4473 while Pedro looked around at the other tables.

"Hey," said Diego, "there's a guy over that has a TEC-9 for $400. Is that a good deal?"

"That's about the going rate for them these days."

"Do you know him? Will he cut you a special deal?"

"Nah, that guy's a dick. We don't like each other."

And that was pretty much the truth. I had seen that dealer for the past year or so at every gun show I'd attended. This pudgy myopic gent often dressed in camouflage and would tell anyone who would listen that he'd been involved with Israeli Special Forces. He called himself "Captain" and someone told me his nickname came from having a maritime license. He'd usually have three tables full of handguns. I made a point of counting his inventory at every show and he'd have between 90 and 130 guns. He was one of the people who took advantage of what politicians called the "gun show loophole."

The Captain's inventory seemed ever-changing and he'd often buy a gun from someone walking the show and then set that gun on his tables for sale. In short, he was in the business of dealing firearms, but unlike me and many of the other dealers, he had no federal license to do so and did all of his transactions without background checks or any of the federal paperwork dealers are required to do by law.

When Diego finished his #4473, I called in his background check and made out his receipt for the two rifles. Pedro handed him thirteen $100 bills which he then handed to me. They picked up the rifle cases and walked back over to the Captain's tables.

While Diego looked at a bulletproof vest on the Captain's table, I watched the Captain remove the TEC-9 from the table and place it underneath. A couple seconds later, he set a plastic bag on top of the table and collected money from Pedro.

I was disgusted—that was the kind of crap that gave gun shows and honest dealers like me a bad rap. I hoped that transaction would bring enough heat to the Captain that he would quit or be forced to quit doing gun shows.

The following day I received an email from SA Lopez saying that he had posted a picture taken surreptitiously from the windows above the gun show of me talking to our two buyers. Lopez had labeled both of the bad guys with their names but drew a circle around his fellow agent, Morty, asking for information leading to the arrest of the third party.

"What was he thinking saying he couldn't work and then coming to the same gun show where we were working? I guess every office has one," said Lopez.

Diego called during the week to tell me that he wanted another two rifles. "But you need to raise the price $50 each and give that money to me."

"I can't do that, Diego, Pedro already knows what my price is. Why don't you just cut him out of the picture like Ira and Izmael did to you?"

"I can't cut him out of the picture, Mike. His cousin is the money guy."

Later that night, Diego and Pedro came out with another handful of friends. There was no ATF presence at the meeting, and that always made me nervous, and I had absolutely no idea who the other people were that they had brought into my house. Diego was in a pissy mood because I didn't raise my prices, and I wasn't too happy about him trying to extort extra money for himself. The fact that he was there with Pedro told me that he'd been paid a finder's fee and was probably getting money for every rifle he did paperwork for.

But everything went OK and they were on their way in about a half hour.

The next day Travis and Mando Arroyo came out to give me some CI cash and pick up the CD containing the recording of the previous night's activities. Travis and Mando had shared the same office since SA Edgar left for his National Guard deployment.

"I don't like that you can see me but I can't see you through the screen," said Lopez, as they stood outside my front security door.

"Unfortunately, it works just the opposite at night," I said.

Lopez told me they had to do a bust in Phoenix on a home with security iron much like mine and had used a hydraulic jack thinking they could make a quick and easy entry—it had turned out to be neither. That story made me feel a little bit better about my home security. Besides an alarm and watchdogs, I had security wrought iron over every door and window in the house and garage and while someone might have been able to breach them, it wouldn't be quick and they'd make a lot of noise doing it and that, most likely, would make me cranky!

We sat down around my dining room table where I always did the paperwork with the bad guys. Lopez handed me eight $100 bills and had me sign a voucher which Arroyo witnessed with his signature. I pushed a CD over the table to Lopez as he started to outline his plan for our friend, Diego Rodriguez.

"Our plan is to grab him Friday morning on his way to work. I've planned to have him call you and record the conversation. You just talk to him like you would normally and this will help throw any suspicion off you."

"Can you really get someone to flip that quickly?" I asked.

"It all depends on how bad they want to stay out of jail," said Mando.

"I've always thought that Diego is on the soft side. I don't think you'll have much trouble convincing him that it's in his best interest to start talking," I said.

The following evening around nine I was sitting in my living room reading when I heard the doorbell ring. Shit! The outside light was off and my interior lights were all on. I'd have to walk to the front door illuminated without knowing who was there. I took the pistol sitting on my end table and tucked it in my waistband and pulled my shirt over it. My dog Morgan was already at the door barking ferociously when I turned the outside light on. It was Pedro and he appeared to be by himself.

"Let me put my dog outside before I let you in," I yelled through the closed door.

I grabbed her collar and walked her to the back door. I was able to pick up my digital recorder, which was also sitting on the end table, and activate it before dropping it in my pocket and returning to the front door.

"Buenas noches, Pedro," I said.

"Hi Mike, I'm sorry to bother you. I hope it's not too late," said Pedro in perfect English.

I was astonished! "I didn't know you could speak English," I said, laughing.

Pedro smiled sheepishly. "Yeah, I grew up in Tucson. But my first language is Spanish. Everybody in my family and at work speaks Spanish."

"Where do you work?" I asked innocently.

"I work for a company that paints houses here in Tucson."

That explained his dark tan. I invited him in from the foyer and offered him a seat at the dining room table.

"What brings you out tonight?"

"I was talking with my cousin. He's the one that we're getting guns for in Caborca. I told him that Diego is demanding more and more money from me. He suggested I come talk with you and see if I could buy the guns without Diego."

I had to laugh. Were there no limits to Diego's stupidity? He had a perfectly good deal but screwed it up, once again, by getting too greedy.

"Sure," I said, "I don't mind dealing directly with you. Diego was also asking me for money for every gun I sold to you."

"Really?" Pedro asked in astonishment. Then he too had to laugh at Diego's stupidity.

Pedro wanted an AK-47 pistol and I happened to have one available, but he also asked about a .25 Beretta for his uncle and wanted to know how many Colt .38 Supers I could get.

"I can get you as many as you want. But if you want more than five, you'll need to give me a 50 percent deposit because that's not normally a gun I carry in inventory and it would take me a while to get rid of them if you backed out on the deal."

Pedro said that would be alright. We did the paperwork for his AK-47 pistol and I walked him out to his car. Through the tinted windows I could see that someone was sitting inside and I pulled up short.

Pedro noticed and chuckled, "That's my wife Angelina—did she scare you?"

"Why didn't you bring her inside with you, Pedro? She's welcome here."

"Our baby had barely just fallen asleep and we didn't want to wake her up."

A very young and rotund lady got out of the Nissan Sentra. She shook hands with me. "*Mucho gusto.*"

"She doesn't speak any English, Mike."

"*El gusto es mio*," I said, trying my best to remember eighth grade conversational Spanish.

The next morning I met Travis in a parking lot behind a realtor's office at the southeast corner of Broadway and Country Club to give him the CD of my unexpected meeting with Pedro.

We talked about Pedro coming out without an appointment. It was my opinion that the meeting wasn't so much about buying an AK-47 pistol as it was to see if I'd agree to cut Diego out of the picture.

"You're armed when these guys come out to your house, aren't you?" Travis asked.

"I'm always armed when we're doing a buy. Fortunately I had a pistol sitting next to me on my end table when he rang the doorbell."

"Good, I'm glad that you're taking care of yourself," he said.

We didn't speak about this further, but I always felt that this topic was intentionally not addressed. That way if something happened there'd be some deniability on their part.

On February 27, 2007, Travis called to let me know that they had Diego in custody. He said they would have Diego call me in about fifteen minutes and he would be asking questions about how to obliterate serial numbers. Travis said he would be taping the conversation on his end.

When Diego called he sounded like he was about to throw up. "Hey buddy, I have a question for you. You know, we're a little worried about having these guns and we want to know how to get rid of the serial numbers."

I told him where to look to find the numbers and that he needed a powerful tool like a Dremel or an electric drill with a carbide tip to deface them.

"I also wanted to ask you about that thing we talked about at the gun show," he said.

"We talked about a lot of things, remind me what in particular?"

"You know, the grenade launchers. Do you have that guy's number?"

I told him to hold on a minute while I searched for his card. I shuffled some papers around for about twenty seconds and then got back on the phone with "Dave's" number.

"OK, buddy, I'll talk to you later," he said.

"Diego, you sound funny. Do you feel OK today?" I was sure this comment caused Mando and Travis to give each other a quick smile.

There was a pause. "No man, I'm straight up."

Travis called a couple hours later. "Hey, thanks for playing along. Diego flipped as easy as we thought. We don't think he knows too much, which is what we suspected. We also had him call Pedro while he was here. They may be out sometime this week to pick up some more guns. It turns out that Pedro was paying Diego $100 for every gun that he purchased."

"That son of a bitch," I said. "I knew he was shaking them down. Just imagine how much those guns sell for in Mexico if he can afford to pay $100 each gun. No wonder Pedro was trying to cut Diego out of the picture."

"We don't think Pedro has shared too much information with Diego. We're not entirely sure that they trust him. I gave Diego a small cassette recorder like the one we initially gave you to record the purchase at your house. He was pretty nervous. He said, 'Mike even asked if I was OK.'"

I laughed and asked if Goldblatt's name came up.

"Oh yeah, we went over all of that. We told him that his trailer, phone, and car had been bugged and that's how we got all the information."

We both laughed hysterically at the legal implications of this scenario and how the nineteen-year-old Diego must have swallowed hard when he heard this lie.

A couple days later Travis and Petey came over and Travis told me that Jodi had sent a nasty email to his boss, Jack Hinkley, saying that he had failed to get her the tapes and #4473s from "his CI." What a load of crap! I asked Travis why she didn't pick up the tapes at the gun show in Phoenix like she was supposed to and he said she never got a call from me. Of course she never told me to call her and she knew I would be there all weekend. I gave Travis the tapes and the CD of my meetings with Rey Ayala. I was thoughtful enough to put a copy of an infamous lingerie shot of me wearing a black bra and panties on the CD for Jodi. That should get her motor running, I thought.

Petey and Travis both complained about her. "She obviously lacks people skills but I think the real problem is that she's a complete idiot," said Travis.

"I can't stand her," said Petey. "I'm glad that she doesn't work in our office. She's worthless. She's not only incompetent, but I would feel that I was actually in more danger if I was working with her. I would do everything possible to make sure that I didn't have to count on her to watch my back."

I relayed the story about her parking next to the neighborhood's busy-body and badging her when the neighbor asked why she was parked there.

"A couple weeks later I was walking down my driveway just as another neighbor from across the street walked down to get the mail. I said "hi" to her but she just looked down at her feet and mumbled back. I wondered to myself why she would be pissed off at me. Then I remembered Jodi badging Sharon. It must be all over the neighborhood."

"Yeah," said Travis, "there's really only one house that you can survey from that spot—it's very obvious."

"What an idiot," said Petey. "She really doesn't have a clue."

I asked if she was coming to pick up the tapes and Travis said that he would just FedEx the stuff to her. I told him that I could have done it but apparently it would have broken the chain of evidence. Travis said he would put a post-it note on the file that said, "Mike says you haven't paid him yet."

"I can't believe that she didn't pay you," said Petey incredulously, "or even say thank you."

I asked Travis how he would get useable information from Diego if Pedro Trujillo's group had already excluded him from future transactions. Travis said that the only way might be to get them to buy a grenade launcher. "That way, we have a lot more charges and heavier prison time. Then we'll get him to roll like we did Diego."

Travis made Petey and me laugh when he reenacted how nervous Rodriguez had been before he made the phone calls. "He's sitting there trying to psych himself up, hitting himself in the head and hyperventilating and after twenty, thirty seconds of this nonsense, he announces, 'Let's do this.'"

A couple days later, Pedro called me and said that Diego told him he couldn't do the paperwork for his guns anymore because he had gotten a DUI. I relayed the info to Lopez who was skeptical of the veracity of Diego's claim but said that he'd check on it. More likely was that Rodriguez figured this story would extricate him from his predicament. At least for now, we didn't have to worry about how we were going to get the wayward Diego back involved with a group that had already determined he was no longer useful for their needs.

6

LITTLE MAN—HUGE ATTITUDE

PEDRO HAD NOT yet made a significant purchase but he called me frequently to ask about the availability and price of a variety of weapons. He arranged to come out with some friends the third week of March 2007.

When he arrived I saw he had a stack of cash in a toy Barbie purse. "Does Angelina know that you have her money?" I joked.

Pedro laughed. "She doesn't know that I broke into her piggy bank."

He stood by my front door and introduced his friends as they came into the house. First through the door was a young clean-cut Hispanic man in his twenties. Pedro introduced him as Fernando. Next in was a tall Hispanic man wearing ostrich skin cowboy books. He was about thirty-five years old, with a beer belly and black hair with a streak of white that gave his head a skunk-like appearance. Pedro introduced him as Omar. With Omar was a small-framed man, maybe forty-five or so, who had the weathered appearance of a laborer and was missing two fingers on his right hand.

While they were looking at an AK pistol, Pedro told me that he had given Diego $100 earlier in the week to come out and buy some guns but Diego cancelled and never gave him his money back. I shook my head in disgust and related some of the problems that Diego caused for the other "group" out of Phoenix.

Fernando said he wanted to buy a Colt .38 Super pistol and I had him sit down to fill out the form #4473. As I wrote the receipt, Pedro took money out of his stack of cash and pushed it over to me to pay for the pistol. With the background check completed and approved, Fernando picked up his gun and gave it to skunk-head, who was now sitting on the couch by my front window. For the rest of the visit Omar sat and played with the pistol, racking the slide and snapping the hammer like a kid playing with his toy Christmas morning.

Pedro didn't know how much money he'd brought that evening. He'd picked up the cash at his uncle's house before heading out to my house. He originally thought that he'd have enough for ten AK rifles and a couple pistols but once we counted his cash he ended up buying eighteen AKM rifles with wire folding stocks and vertical foregrips, an AK-47 rifle and pistol, and two .38 Supers.

While I worked on the receipt my cell phone rang. The caller ID showed as "Restricted." I knew it was SA Lopez calling to check on me as there was no ATF presence at my home that evening.

"Hi Susie," I said, referring to an imaginary girlfriend.

"Hey Mike, just checking on you to see if everything is OK."

"Yeah, I'm doing fine. Just working with some really good customers right now." I looked at Pedro and smiled.

"Do me a favor and call me when they leave. Don't forget OK?"

"No problem, Susie, I'll call you soon."

"Thanks sweetie. I love you," said Lopez.

"I love you too."

Pedro was doing the paperwork for the guns that he'd selected and I could tell that he was ambivalent about it. I tried to assuage his fears and explained that the completed form did not get faxed or mailed anywhere. "It stays with me until I retire my license. In fact, the only time a cop might see the paperwork is if the guns are found at a crime scene. Then they'll trace the serial number back to me to see who bought it." I told him he could cut Diego out of the picture without any problems and have a lot more money to spend on guns.

This seemed to ease Pedro's fears, whatever they may have been. He pointed to the .38 Super and told me that it was for his cousin José in Caborca and the other guns were for people in José's organization.

I helped Pedro and his friends carry his rifle boxes out to his Sentra. We'd opened his trunk and had started stacking the boxes inside when my neighbor turned the corner and did a double take when he saw us. In fact, he took such a hard look over his shoulder that he nearly missed his driveway.

It must have been quite a sight for him—four Hispanic men and me standing at the rear of a car trying to load a stack of nineteen rifle boxes into the subcompact's trunk. My neighbor pulled into his garage and closed the garage door before he even got out of the car. I wondered if this would eventually cause a problem with him calling a tip into one of the anonymous crime hotlines or making an anonymous complaint. I also wondered if he'd ever get together to compare notes with my other neighbor Sharon—the one that Jodi Pederman had badged.

We loaded as many boxes as we could into the trunk and then had the passengers get into the back seat and stacked the rest of the boxes on their knees to make them all fit.

After they left, I called Lopez to let him know that I was alright and he asked if I could bring a copy of the conversation down to the federal building the following morning. I finished up the paperwork, faxed the #4473s, and downloaded the digital recorder onto my laptop and burned a CD.

The next day I got a call from Pedro after I had already dropped off the CD downtown. He wanted to know if I'd be able to get twenty AK-47 pistols and eight .38 Supers. He also asked how many ARs I had, which styles, and their approximate pricing. I asked him if he really needed twenty AK pistols. "Yes," he said, "because one guy wants like five and another guy wants ten."

"Oh, so do you have more customers besides your cousin José?"

"Well, they are all my cousins."

My hunch was correct. The earlier small purchases were just to feel me out and see if I was trustworthy. It appeared that they were now taking orders in Caborca for guns they intended to get from me.

I spoke with Lopez and he told me to go ahead and order the guns. Hinkley was out of the office but he said if he had any heartache with this transaction they would do a low-key traffic stop with a marked TPD unit close to Pedro Trujillo's house so they could round up the guns before they found their way to Mexico. He warned me that this might be his last buy so I shouldn't order more inventory than what Pedro had ordered.

But before the inventory for that big order arrived, Pedro called me and said he needed some guns really quick. Lopez told me to go ahead with the sale but that he couldn't make it out to watch it. I'd be alone again that night and Pedro was bringing someone new to do the paperwork. It was Friday and I'd been setting up my tables for a gun show at the Pima County fairgrounds in Tucson.

Pedro arrived around six in the evening and brought along a clean-cut associate by the name of Joaquin Serrano to replace Diego to do the paperwork.

Pedro looked among the guns I had laid out in my dining room. I had ordered a Beretta .25 pistol for his uncle. Pedro asked the price and when I said $300 he opened his phone and called his uncle.

"My uncle says that's too much," he said after he hung up. "So, I'll take the gun—I don't want to make you mad, Mike."

I had laid out the two AR pistols I had, also the high-dollar DPMS "Agency," an AR with all the bells and whistles, and the eight AK pistols I had left. I also had an S&W M22 target pistol that I had ordered because Pedro said that one of his uncles wanted a cheap semi-auto target gun.

Pedro had brought his money in a plastic grocery bag this time and I asked if Angelina wouldn't let him have her Barbie purse any more.

He laughed. "No, she wouldn't let me have it—she hid it from me."

Pedro had told me he had to close escrow the previous Friday so I asked him about his new house purchase. He said it was in the Drexel area and that he paid $169K for it. He said that the name of the street was *Los Mananitas*.

I remembered that it was the title to a popular Mexican folk song often sung by Mariachis. "That means little mornings or tomorrows, right?"

He nodded. "That's why I'm doing this." He pointed to the guns and money on the table. He told me that his house had a garage, which would be good so that he could drive into it and unload the guns without anyone seeing him.

Joaquin Serrano completed the #4473 while Pedro counted out the money and I called in the background check. Serrano's background check came back as a "Delay" meaning that I couldn't transfer the guns until I heard back from NICS or five business days—whichever came first. I told Pedro that maybe they would call back on Monday with a "proceed" and then I could transfer them. Or if they didn't call back before Thursday, I could transfer the guns then. Either way, they wouldn't be leaving with the guns. (On Monday NICS called and said that Joaquin was a DENY and asked for the address given on the #4473.)

Pedro stood and pondered for a moment looking around at the guns that littered the floor of my living room. "OK, I'll do the papers," he said.

Pedro ended up buying eight AK pistols, two AR-15 pistols, one AMD wire folding stock AK-47, the Beretta .25 that his uncle said was too much money, and three .38 Colt Supers. The total came to $12,900. Rather than arrange the money by denominations, Pedro made little piles; $600 here for this gun, $800 there for that other gun, etc. This really slowed the process down and as he found that he had more money than he thought, he would add another gun or two to the pile.

"Don't you know how much money you came with?"

"I know about how much. My uncle gave me the bag." Whatever business was laundering their money must have done a lot of small transactions as there was over $1,500 in $5 bills. It must have taken forty-five minutes just to count the money.

I offered to help carry the guns outside with the specific intent of getting the license number. Pedro had driven his 2000 Chevy K1500 metallic blue truck with a custom lid on the bed and twenty-inch chrome wheels. He showed me his CD player that also stored digital pictures.

"Here's my truck when it was black," he said. "I was on my honeymoon in Rocky Point in this picture." He also had pictures of his daughter that played like a slideshow. I had not ever seen a unit like that before. Pedro and Joaquin were on their way by 8 p.m.

Pedro came by during the gun show the next day with his skunk-head friend and mentioned that he had a buyer that he wanted to bring over the next week. "He's going to buy a lot of guns, I think."

I assumed that this was the customer that generated all of the calls from Pedro inquiring about the prices and availability of a multitude of assault style guns.

On Tuesday April 3, 2007, I had an appointment at the University Medical Center and arranged to meet SA Lopez in the parking lot of a Boston Market just down the street from the hospital. I brought along a CD containing the conversation of my meeting with Pedro the previous Friday.

At the arranged time I pulled into the parking lot and saw Travis and Mando sitting in a green Cougar. It was a non-descript car that wouldn't raise anyone's suspicions and I'm sure that they acquired it in some sort of seizure with the windows already tinted.

I pulled into the space next to them as they got out of the car. Travis had questions about who Pedro wanted to bring to the house tonight and what they wanted to buy. I told him that based on Pedro's calls it was someone other than his cousins or uncles because he called him a friend.

"We're getting a lot of heat about these guns going South so this will probably be his last purchase. We just can't keep letting these guns go to Mexico with impunity."

"I understand, no problem," I said.

That evening Lopez came out early and set up the Hawk. He brought a box of Kleenex that had a pinhole in it and taped the Hawk inside it. "I'm going to turn it on right now so be careful—anything you say is going to be recorded." This setup would allow the Hawk to digitally record audio and video. He placed the box on the counter of the living room wet sink and aimed it at the dining room table where we normally did paperwork. I moved the chairs around so that they were mostly on the opposite side of the table—kind of like they do on TV sitcoms. I took another extra chair and put it in the kitchen so that it wouldn't look so lopsided.

I was wearing shorts with a T-shirt and had a button-down over that to conceal the Kimber Ultra .45 that I had behind my back in a Fobus paddle holster. I had tucked the T-shirt in back so that I wouldn't get a handful of shirt if I grabbed for my gun.

Lopez asked me to run my digital recorder as he thought the sound would be of better quality. I would also be wearing a transmitter that would let Lopez hear the conversation from his car.

During the three years that I worked with the Tucson ATF office they used the same old transmitter that, according to agents, was of dubious quality, got uncomfortably hot when it was in use, and would sometimes shut itself off without warning. Lopez had duct taped an old athletic sock around the unit in an attempt to keep it from burning me while it was in the cargo pocket of my shorts.

"See if you can engage them in dialogue and see if they say where these guns are going and where the new players are from," said Lopez. "Stuff like what port they're taking the guns through and who's doing it for them. Anything you can think of that would be helpful."

I asked Lopez how many guys he had out here tonight. "All of us," he said.

Lopez was only gone about ten minutes when two cars pulled into the driveway. I was surprised that they didn't all come in one car. I started my recorder. "This is April the third and it is approximately 1900 hours," I said, and I slid it into my pocket with the front towards my body so they couldn't see the red recording light through my clothes.

When I answered the door there were three new faces—two males and one female, and they were all Hispanic. Pedro was first through the door and the shorter Hispanic man shook my hand briefly and nodded when I introduced myself. He did not respond when I told him my name and he didn't look me in the eye. He just pushed his way past me into the living room. Behind him was a taller man, about six feet four, and reeking of Old Spice aftershave whom I presumed to be the first man's bodyguard. He was in his mid-thirties and was well muscled. Behind him was a pudgy gal who I guessed was about thirty years old.

Before they arrived, I had set cases of rifles around the floor of my formal dining room. I had several different variations of AR-15 rifles from both DPMS and Rock River, several variations of AK-47 guns and Colt .38 Supers. The stacks of guns made my living room look like a Middle Eastern arms bazaar.

The shorter man made a small lap around the living room, seemingly to size things up. He walked from the living room into my kitchen, took a quick look, turned around and came back into the area where I had the guns displayed. Maybe he was looking for other people or trying to see if this were some sort of trap? Satisfied, he turned his attention to the guns.

He was immediately drawn to the AK pistols and felt the need to insert and lock a magazine into place. Then he held it at his side. He also held it under his arm as if he had an imaginary harness under his jacket to suspend it. He picked up several of the ARs and examined them, asking Pedro for a price for each gun. I would tell Pedro the price and then Pedro would add a couple hundred dollars to the price before interpreting. Finally, the guy started repeating the price that I gave him in English and Pedro knew he was busted.

He went back to the AK pistol and held it at his hip pretending to fire it full auto. I laughed to myself wondering if he knew that these were semi-auto guns. I wasn't going to volunteer anything. He asked me in Spanish if the gun would get hot if he fired it.

"*Claro que si*," —of course—I answered. They all laughed.

He played with the threaded muzzle cap on the end of one of the AK pistols and asked me, through Pedro, if I had silencers for them.

"No," I said, "I don't have the right type of license for that stuff." Then, as an afterthought, I turned to Pedro. "You know who has those? Dave—the guy with the grenade launchers also has silencers."

Pedro's face brightened and he translated the information to his friend, whose eyebrows went up. It seemed like we had managed to impress him. I hoped that move would get Pedro to call the fictional Dave and allow the ATF to tack on a host of new charges.

I offered a seat on the couch to the young lady in the group. "That's OK, I've been sitting a long time—you live a far ways away," she said in English.

The taller of the two Mexicans followed the shorter guy around and would look at a gun only after his presumed boss was done looking at it. The shorter guy lifted the digitally camouflaged M4 and smiled. I could tell he loved the way it looked and I could imagine him carrying the gun with his ostrich skin cowboy boots and matching belt. I think he was imagining this picture too.

I showed him one of my high-end rifles after turning on its Eotech electronic sight. "Wow," he said and insisted that his associate look through the holographic sight too. He handed it back to me and I bent to put the rifle back into its case.

Just then I heard, "This is April the third at approximately 1900 hours . . ." Shit! My recorder had started playing back! Apparently the "play" button somehow got depressed when I bent over. I lifted my T-shirt and took the cell phone from its carrier pretending to talk into it as I went out the front door. I continued the imaginary conversation as I turned off the digital recorder with my other hand. I casually glanced over my shoulder and could see the group continuing to look at different guns. No one seemed to notice. I took a moment to gather myself and restarted the recorder using a different file.

The group was looking at a Rock River AR-15 when I returned. "This is the same rifle that the DEA uses," I said. Pedro started to interpret but he didn't have to, this guy understood exactly what I'd said.

After a while the little guy said something in Spanish to Pedro and looked at me while Pedro was talking. "He likes your guns," said Pedro, "but thinks your prices are too high."

I laughed. "Pedro, why did you bring this shithead here? You should take him to Walmart." The little man's eyebrows rose. Apparently he did understand me.

He nodded, seemingly acknowledging what I had told him, and then smiled. His bluff had been called. He slapped his hands together and then rubbed them and sighed. He walked through the piles of guns and selected them by pointing to them. His bodyguard would then gather up that gun and lean it against the wall. It wasn't the order I had hoped for. He had a DPMS Panther-Lite, a Rock River 16"AR-15 Carbine, a Colt .38 Super, and an AK pistol. He asked me for a price and I used the calculator on the dining room table to figure it, making sure I didn't block the video from the Kleenex box. The total came to $3,850.

His cell phone rang and he answered it. I could hear him say Fort Lowell and Houghton—the major crossroads near my house—before he hung up. Pedro said he was giving directions to his wife. "She is bringing him the money." Seconds later the phone rang again and he seemed annoyed and headed out the door with his bodyguard.

Pedro said that he had to go find his wife because she was lost but that he'd be back. "He's buying these guns for samples. He said that maybe next week he'd be back for twenty or more rifles."

Then my phone rang—it was Special Agent Lopez. "Hi sweetie," he said.

I took his cue. "Hi Susie, how are you?" I walked out the back door leaving Pedro and his female friend to chat by themselves.

He asked how many guns this guy was buying and when I told him that it was only four he said that there wouldn't be any arrests that night.

"According to Pedro, this guy is just buying samples but will come back next week and pick up at least twenty more."

With the two strangers gone, Pedro and the woman and I sat at the table and Pedro explained that the woman, Maria Valenzuela, was his cousin's wife and that she was the one that knew the shorter Mexican—she called him Eduardo. She said Eduardo was also her cousin. She told me that she lived near Park and Silver Lake by the UPS hub.

I learned later that Maria Valenzuela's husband was in a federal prison on drug trafficking charges. She would host BBQs at her home and tell the nefarious types that attended that she had a hookup for guns—as long as she got a commission for every gun they bought. In the months that followed, Pedro would bring several of these BBQ hookups to buy guns from me.

"I'm surprised that he said my prices were too high."

"He knows that your prices are good," said Maria. "He's just feeling you out. He can get $3,000 for that AK pistol in Mexico."

"He's really clean cut, is he a cop in Mexico?"

"He's exactly the opposite," she said, snickering. Pedro laughed too.

I asked why Eduardo's wife didn't just come with him and Maria grinned again. "Because he doesn't know you. His wife is a bitch; I'm glad that she didn't come. I can't stand her."

Remembering Lopez's instructions, I asked if Eduardo was from Caborca too. Pedro said that he was but he wasn't associated with his cousin, José. "I don't even know if they know each other. But José is friends with his boss."

"Things are crazy there," said Maria. "Everyone has guns. It's like the Wild West there."

"I guess I won't go to Caborca on vacation then," I said.

She giggled. "No, you shouldn't." She then asked if I had a charger that would fit her cell phone and I showed her my cell phone. "Perfect that will fit—do you mind charging it for me?"

I went to get the charger from the bedroom and when I got back Eduardo and his bodyguard had returned. Apparently he didn't want his wife here. He now held a plastic baggy with a stack of money in it.

He asked in Spanish if I had any other guns. Pedro said that I had a really neat .22 pistol and he asked to see it. I went out to the garage to get it. As I came back into the living room, the taller Mexican had picked up the urn that held the remains of my dog Sarge from the wet bar. He was looking behind it, obviously searching for some sort of recording device. He didn't move anything else on the shelf or counter and I watched him nervously as he moved past the box of Kleenex.

I sat back down at the table and began writing the receipt for Eduardo's purchase. Suddenly the hair stood up on the back of my neck and I realized the bodyguard was standing directly behind me. I scooted forward in my seat in case I needed to make a quick grab for my gun. There was nothing behind me and no reason for him to be standing there other than to make me nervous or intimidate me.

"Pedro," I said in a stern voice, "tell this guy to go over and sit down on the couch."

Pedro could see I was pissed and told the bodyguard in apologetic Spanish that I did not want him standing behind me. I spun my chair to look him in the eye. He didn't like being told what to do. We stared at each other for what seemed like minutes but he finally walked over and sat down on the couch. His boss looked at him and smiled, cocking his head to the side. The bodyguard returned his smile and shrugged.

Trying to lighten the mood, Pedro told me that while I was in the other room they were talking about how there are "probably fifteen or twenty people outside watching us."

My heart jumped into my throat and I felt my face blush. "I'll tell you what," I said slowly and as menacingly as I could, "if someone comes through that front door without knocking, they're going to get a big surprise." Pedro smiled and Eduardo nodded and smiled weakly. Then he told Pedro that he wanted the .22 pistol as well. He also wanted five AR-15 magazines and I went back out to the garage to get them.

I had completed my invoice and the total came to $4,230. He had put $4,000 of $100 bills on the table and said, "*Es todo, OK?*" and made a wiping motion with his hands.

I laughed. "Pedro, why did you bring this guy to my house?" I turned and looked at Eduardo. He looked at me for a moment expressionless, smiled, and then slapped me on the back. He took out another $240 and handed it to me. I counted it and gave him $20 back. "Here's your discount." It was $10 off the invoice price.

If he had been trying to feel me out, he now knew where he stood with me. I could not be intimidated and apparently I wasn't the weakling he'd hoped for. Pedro had discovered a few weeks before that my prices were not negotiable.

While we were still at the table, Eduardo reached over and handed Pedro $500 and a moment later handed him another $100 bill. Pedro gave the $100 bill to Maria who was still sitting next to him. We all shook hands, with the exception of the bodyguard who walked out ahead of his boss, and they departed.

Just moments later, Travis called me and asked how many guns they'd left with. "Hold on a sec," he said as he picked up his radio. I heard him instruct the other agents not to follow Pedro as the guns were in the red Ford Explorer that Eduardo had driven.

A minute or two later, Travis was in my house. He had asked me to turn off the Hawk. I held my watch in front of the Kleenex box and said the day and time out loud before opening the box and turning it off. Lopez placed the recording device into its protective padded case. I asked him if he wanted me to burn him a copy of the #4473 and he told me I could just fax it to him.

"Hey, do you think you'll be anywhere near downtown tomorrow?" he asked.

"Sure, I can drop off the CD of the meeting. Do you need me to do a summary or anything?"

"Nah, just bring the CD."

The next day before I left home for the federal building, I noticed the plastic bag that Eduardo had brought his cash in on the dining room table. I took it and put it inside another plastic sandwich bag just in case they wanted to fingerprint it.

At the federal building Lopez started to take me into his office just as Jack walked out of his. He stopped to chat. "Thanks for making me work last night," he said. "I hope that you understand that we're getting a lot of political pressure to keep the number of guns going to Mexico to a minimum. So we'll probably bust this guy on his next purchase. To be honest, Mike, we're not interested in these mules or even guys like Pedro. We want the money guys, the head honchos. Quite honestly, we might not even indict Pedro if he cooperates. But Diego is a whole different matter. I'm going to indict the shit out of that little asshole."

"Did you ever get your cassette recorder back from Diego?" I asked Lopez.

He shook his head with disgust. Diego had not kept his promise to call Lopez periodically. In fact, he had not heard from him since he dropped him off at work after kidnapping him.

I told Jack that Eduardo had the capability to make Pedro's cousin's business look like peanuts.

"Yeah, he's an experienced dope dealer," Jack said. "That's why he had his wife deliver the money. He didn't know what he was walking into at your house. We'll take him down and insulate you and Pedro. That way, he'll suspect Pedro if anybody. We're still trying to ID the big guy. We think there may be a chance that he's wanted in Mexico for a couple murders."

"Oh great," I said and recounted my real life Mexican standoff the previous night.

"You have to stay in control, Mike, especially when there are multiple people in your house. Never let someone get behind you. Use your best judgment but never hesitate when the time comes. You did a great job."

Hinkley's words were sobering.

"In the worst case scenario we'll pay to have the blood stains shampooed out of your carpets," he joked.

I showed him the plastic bag. "I dunno if you can print this, but I brought it just in case."

"Oh yeah, we can have TPD's ID section print it for us."

The Tucson Police Department's forensic and ID lab was housed in their headquarters building just a few blocks from the federal building and the Tucson ATF office relied heavily on them for this kind of work.

But Travis rolled his eyes, "They still have guns I gave them to print from last year."

"Call Jeff over there and he'll make sure that it gets expedited," said Jack.

I wasn't sure if he put on this display on for my benefit or if he was sincere about wanting to print the bag, but he always made a point of making me feel like I was a part of the team.

Scott Languien walked out of his office and walked over to shake hands. It had been a while since I'd seen him, maybe the last time was at the Tucson Convention Center gun show and we didn't get to talk. Then Petey walked by and hollered and waved to me too. These guys always treated me with respect and made me feel like they appreciated what I did for them. What a contrast to the way that Jodi Petersen from the Phoenix office had treated me.

"Jodi still hasn't given me any money," I said to Travis.

"You're never going to see any money from her, Mike."

"That's why when I find something in Phoenix I'm bringing it to you."

Later that day Pedro called and said that Eduardo wanted ten more of the DPMS rifles. I told him it would take a week or more for me to get the guns in and he said it wasn't a problem because he was leaving for Caborca in the morning. Pedro said that he'd be taking orders and that we'd get together the following week.

"I know that those AK pistols will sell. My other friends will want them too once they see them."

I told Pedro that the best way for us to make sure that these guys don't back out of orders is to take deposits so they don't change their minds. He agreed and said that he would ask for money up front before the order was placed.

"I bought a gun magazine the other day and I was reading it," he said. "Then I saw your picture, 'Hey I know that guy.'"

"Yeah, didn't you know that about me? I write for gun magazines."

"Wow, that's funny, huh? I saw your picture."

When I mentioned this to Travis later he said I was lucky the picture wasn't with a cop. At the time I was also writing for some law-enforcement magazines and had attended a number of law-enforcement-only seminars and training classes. The sad truth was that if Pedro had Googled my name he would have found many of these articles and pictures and would have seen that I had strong ties to the police community. I had to remind myself before every buy that Pedro or one of his associates might have researched me and figured out that they were being set up.

The following day Pedro called and told me that Eduardo wanted twenty-one more .38 Supers. Later, he called again and said that Eduardo wanted even more guns. It appeared as though we had stumbled onto a very serious player.

On Wednesday, April 11, 2007, SA Lopez showed up around six with a clock radio in hand. This neat little thing not only recorded audio and video, but could also transmit the picture and sound. Outside, a big Ford F250 with a matching white cap pulled up curbside. Lopez told me the back of the truck was filled with electronics and had enough room for two agents. Agents could move from the front seat to the enclosed back without exiting the truck, and the windows were very darkly tinted to protect the occupants. He had Special Agent Paul Harcum come to the door and introduced us.

"Paul will most likely retrieve the clock radio when we're done here tonight. I'll probably be following these guys."

Lopez had me move my phone stand that is normally next to my entertainment center to next to the couch in the formal living room. From that position, Harcum was able to capture almost all of the room. Lopez and Harcum spoke back and forth on their cell phones, adjusting the camera's angle and then doing a sound check to make sure the audio was good.

While he was setting up the radio, Lopez told me they had an ATF agent in Mexico who worked with a Mexican task force and it was their hope that they could track these weapons to see where they were going and where the money was coming from. He said he was doubtful about the Mexicans' cooperation because of their notorious corruption. If all went well, there could be many more of these buys.

Lopez also briefed me about what questions I should ask this guy Eduardo. "Play tough with him, Mike. Let him know that you're in charge, not him. We need to know what port they're taking these things through. Also ask him how many days he holds them until someone picks them up. I don't think he'd rip you for twenty .38 Supers but stranger things have happened." He was touching on something that had never really been said to me before, though it had been implied. He looked at my Kimber Custom Ultra .45 lying in a Fobus paddle holster on the dining room table. "If things go bad, you do whatever you need to do. It will take us a few seconds to get to you and I'm sure that the shooting will be over by then. Just keep in mind when we come into the room, we don't want to see your muzzle, OK?" He smiled slightly.

Lopez normally parked his car on the shoulder of the road down the street. From that position, he could see whoever entered my driveway and my front door. But that spot was over eighty yards away from my front door. I told him that I would leave the security door to the gym open and that would be his most likely avenue of entry. I also told him that I'd leave the back door to the patio open, just in case.

His reassurance made me feel better, though it still amazed me how I got to this point. Here we were having a conversation about shooting a cartel member inside my living room. Life had certainly gotten much more interesting in the last year!

"There'll be four of us coming through the door if something goes wrong. If they grab you or things start to go badly yell as loud as you can and we'll get to you as soon as possible. In the meantime you fight for your life."

"How many guys are out this evening?"

"All of us."

"Even Jack?"

"Yep, Jack's out here too."

"Wow, these guys must hate me."

Lopez stopped in his tracks, "Let me tell you something, Mike, there's not one guy here who doesn't love doing this shit. This is what we live for. All of the guys think the world of you."

With the clock radio set up, he went to meet the other agents at a nearby McDonald's I warned him about the reformed addicts that worked at that location and lived in a nearby halfway house. "Go inside to the counter if you can. Otherwise your order will be fucked up."

While Lopez was gone I noticed an unusual amount of traffic on my normally quiet street. When I looked outside there was a white compact car that I'd never seen before parked directly in front of my house. I was scrambling to find Travis's cell phone number when my houseline rang—it was Travis asking if I knew whose car it was. Apparently my neighbors across the street were having a party that night. We realized that the extra cars along the street would be good cover for the agents and no one would question the white electronics truck or Travis's Cougar. I warned Lopez that I had seen one of my neighbors out and about. "So be prepared for a chubby, red–headed lady with her daughter to ask you why you're sitting in your car not far from her property."

Pedro called at seven to say that he was just leaving. He showed up around seven forty-five in his truck and Eduardo was right behind him in a silver van.

Pedro and Eduardo met me at the front door and I welcomed them in with a handshake. Behind Eduardo was another man, approximately forty years old, five foot five, and 140 pounds. This man had the haggard look of a laborer that had spent way too much time in the sun. He was a *viejo*—an old man—before his time. Eduardo introduced him as his cousin. Noticeably absent was Eduardo's bodyguard and I couldn't have been more happy.

I noticed right away that Eduardo was acting differently; more polite and less obnoxious than his last visit. I wondered if maybe he finally realized how much money he could make with me as his supplier.

I had laid out fifteen different long guns, AK pistols, and had stacked his twenty-one .38 Supers in a pile in the middle of my formal living room. Eduardo walked through the guns picking each one up and looking at it and then handing it to his "cousin."

"I think he's going to take ten of the .38 Supers tonight," Pedro told me.

I felt my face flush with anger. "What? He's supposed to take them all. What happened?"

"He's having a problem getting the money tonight. He only has $13,000 with him. Maybe tomorrow we'll come back and get the rest."

I was pissed. I'd made it clear to Pedro that Eduardo was supposed to take all twenty-one pistols with him. The other stuff was placed out for him to look at, but the Supers were supposed to be a done deal. I could feel my frustration growing and I think Pedro also understood that I was upset. As we talked, Eduardo fielded call after call on his cell phone. Something was going on.

I invited Eduardo to sit at the table and poured him a 7-Up in a glass I'd wiped down, hoping they would be able to print it. The ATF still didn't have an ID on this guy. Pedro wanted a Pepsi and the "cousin" asked for a glass of water.

Eduardo asked through Pedro how many pistols he could take with him for $13,000. After some quick calculations I told him nine. He said he was going to take the nine Supers and the Beretta .380 that I had ordered especially for him and he would return in one hour with the rest of the money.

But before he left he told me he wanted all twenty-one .38 Supers, three WASR Romanian AK rifles, his Beretta .380, the DPMS Agency AR-15 rifle with EoTech holographic sight and Surefire light, and one of the AMD wire folding stock AK rifles. The total came out to a little more than $34,000.

While we were sitting at the table, I had the opportunity to ask some of the questions Travis had wanted me to ask Eduardo.

"I've been doing this a long time and so far I have not ended up in prison so I must be doing something right," I said. "The best way for all of us to stay out of trouble is for these guns to go to Mexico as quickly as possible. Once they're in Mexico, it's no longer a problem for me. But if they stay here a week or longer and somebody finds them, then it comes back to me because of the serial numbers on the gun."

Pedro translated and Eduardo nodded his head, "*Yo entiendo, si, si mon.*"

I asked how long the guns usually stay here. "*Llegan manana,*" he said—they're leaving tomorrow.

"Perfect, perfect," I said.

"You don't drive these to Mexico do you?"

He said that he had people to do that for him and that the trucks had secret compartments in them to hide the guns.

Eduardo went out to his van and came back in with a big box of baby wipes. Inside the box were bundles of money that had a piece of notebook paper wrapped around each stack with an amount written on it. He said that there was $13,350 there. Most of the stacks had lower denominations—$5s and $10s. Oh fuck me! This will take hours to count.

Before he left, he asked the price of several other guns and how many of each I had. He wrote these numbers down on a piece of paper that I gave him.

Eduardo and his "cousin" left to get the remainder of the money. "You guys will be back in one hour?" I said, as clearly as I could. I wanted to make sure the agents outside would hear and understand that they would be coming back.

Not long after they left Travis called and asked what was going on.

"Hi Susie, how are you?" I headed to the back door to talk to him, leaving Pedro by himself in the living room. I stepped out onto the patio and bent down to pet Morgan.

"Are they going to get more money?"

"Yeah, the shithead only brought $13,000 with him."

"That knucklehead! Did you tell him that it's your rules or the highway?"

"It's funny, I didn't have to. He is acting completely different tonight."

"Really? I wonder why?"

"I dunno but it's a nice change. Maybe Pedro told him that he pissed me off."

"We're tailing him right now to see if he goes back to that house to get the money. Do me a favor—when he gets back help him carry the other guns out to the car. We need to know if he dropped the guns off at the money house or if they're still in the van."

I hung up and walked back into the living room where Pedro was still sitting at the table. He offered to help me count the money.

"Sure, I'd really appreciate it."

The bricks of $5 bills stood about four inches tall for $1,000. Many were well-worn and torn and this slowed the process. With two hundred bills making up a $1,000 bundle it was easy to lose count. Pedro and I stacked the money by denominations in piles of $1,000 and I got some paper money bands from my office to bind the stacks.

As I was counting, Pedro said to me, "Remember when you asked if Eduardo knew my relatives in Caborca?"

I nodded.

"Well it turns out that my cousin, José, is friends with his boss. That's why he's being nicer. He knows that if I say something to my cousin then he will get in trouble."

Well, that explained his contrite behavior.

As Pedro spoke about Eduardo, it was obvious he didn't like him any more than I did.

"That's the problem with this business," I said, "you never know who you are dealing with." I looked him directly in the eye and he had a hard time maintaining eye contact with me and looked away quickly. I turned to the clock radio and mugged for the camera. I was hoping that Agent Harcum was having a good laugh in the truck.

After the money was counted and banded I placed it in the baby wipes box that Eduardo had used to bring the money inside and carried it into the office where I stored it in my large gun safe.

When I came back into the living room Eduardo and friend were just walking up the walkway. Eduardo was carrying a white plastic "Target" bag with him. Inside the bag was a smaller freezer bag box that he started pulling cash out of and laying on the table. When he was done, he reached back into the bag and pulled out a brick of cash that was vacuum-packed in plastic wrap and marked as $15,000. Each end of the brick had $10 bills facing outward. Most of the other cash was in $20 bills and it was quicker and easier to count out the $6,000 needed for the balance.

I looked at the ten-inch thick block of money and sighed. It was almost ten fifteen and I dreaded counting out the money.

"This is $15,000?" I asked Eduardo.

"*Si, quince mil.*"

"I can trust you? I don't need to count this?"

"Nah, nah, *es* OK."

I had completed the paperwork and the background check on Pedro shortly after Eduardo departed the first time. Everything was ready to be boxed up and put in the van.

I picked up four Colt Supers, two in each hand, and followed Eduardo out to the van. He opened the side door, folded the middle seat down, and climbed over it. Then he pulled a blanket back and I could see the first guns he'd taken when he left the first time. Good—he didn't drop anything off at the money house. Travis would be glad to get this news.

I came back inside and grabbed another couple guns and went back out to the van. Pedro carried an armful of guns and we stood and watched as Eduardo arranged them in the back of the van. He was laying them flat so that if someone shone a flashlight there wouldn't be any obvious bulges or bulky packages to warrant further examination. As he worked, Pedro asked him in Spanish when the guns would leave and Eduardo said they would go the next day. Seeing the opportunity, I asked Pedro what port they take the guns through. He said they all go to Caborca.

"Yeah, I know, but what port at the border do they use?"

Pedro asked in Spanish what port they used and Eduardo said Sasabe. "They only have one checkpoint and it's easy to bribe the police there," Pedro said. More good information that will help the good guys track these guns, I thought.

I said good night to everyone and went back into the house—when I turned off the recorder it was 10:20 p.m.

A few minutes later Agent Harcum knocked on the front door. He collected the clock radio and put it in a protective case. "You did really well. Either you're an old pro or Travis has trained you very well."

He said that the quality of the video and audio was excellent and that he was able to hear everything being said at the table.

I also gave him the empty baby wipe box and the plastic baggie box—both of which Eduardo had handled and should have his prints on it. I put my fingers inside the glass of 7-Up, took it over to the kitchen sink, and dumped its contents. Paul held a Ziploc bag while I placed it inside. He put the baby wipes box in a larger garbage bag that I supplied. He was gone a few minutes later.

I put a frozen pizza in the oven and started organizing the money. I still had a couple hours of paperwork to do and I really felt like just crawling in bed. I put all of the money back in the Target bag and put it in the safe. I took my gun off and found that the paddle holster had left a sweaty impression on the small of my back. I moved a loaded AR-15 from the closet to a spot next to me on the couch while I did some paperwork. I always felt a little paranoid when I dealt with those guys because who knew what they were thinking. There I was sitting with $34K of their money (or so I thought) and I could imagine one of the lower-level guys thinking they'd rip me and get the cash and more guns. I finally went to bed at about one although it was a restless sleep. Little sounds woke me and there were a number of times when I sat up in bed to listen for noises. Morgan slept next to me on her little bed. While she may have been senile and had a host of health problems, she wasn't shy about barking and always let me know when someone was approaching.

I got up when my alarm went off at 6:30 a.m. I had a lot to do that day. I was half expecting Travis to call in the morning and ask me to come down to the federal building and deliver the CD like we had talked about the night before. After reading the paper and getting a good workout, I took the bag of money out of the safe and got a deposit slip ready.

I recounted the bundles of money several times until I was comfortable with the amount for the deposit. I left the $15K in the vacuum-sealed bag as I just didn't have the energy to take it out and count and band it. I called the bank and asked for Jackie—the woman who processed my line of credit. She knew what I did for a living and it would make it a lot easier if I didn't have any questions to answer.

When I was on my way to the bank, Lopez called. "Hey Mike, we're just getting back to the office."

"Are you kidding me? You guys have been up all night?"

"Yeah, we lost the guys in a neighborhood and we've been sitting on it all this time waiting for the van to come out of one of the garages. But I think he just drove through the neighborhood without stopping. I'm beat; I'm going home in a little while. Give me a call if you hear anything from Pedro. Ask him if the guns left for Mexico and if they had any problems last night."

Jackie saw me enter the bank with my box of money. She grabbed Rebecca, one of the tellers, and took me back to the manager's office, cleared the desk, and emptied my cardboard box full of cash.

Rebecca was about twenty-five, thirty years old and I could tell that it was killing her to know where this cash came from and why $15K was in a sealed plastic bag.

"Did you save up for a long time?"

"No, not really," I said.

After a pregnant pause she said, "Did you sell something last night?"

"Uh huh, I sold a lot of things last night." I didn't say anything else. She seemed to purposely avoid eye contact after that.

She had unplugged the money counter from the pedestal behind the counter and had brought it into the manager's office. She started with the five-dollar bills and then the tens and finally the twenties. Once that was done, we finally cut open the plastic bag. Both ends had bundles of ten dollar bills but the centers were all fives.

When she was done she told me that the total was $29,000.

"There's a problem," I said.

"How much did you think the deposit would be?" Jackie asked.

"Thirty-four thousand. How much was in the plastic bag?"

Rebecca looked at her post-it note with amounts written on it. "$9,995," she said.

"Dammit, someone is getting shot," I growled.

7

CONTENTIOUS RELATIONS

EDUARDO'S ATTEMPT TO burn me for $5,000 presented a new threat to the investigation. Lopez did his best to calm me down. He said he could understand being pissed off at Eduardo, but it was important to keep doing business with him. Because they lost these guys Wednesday night it was as if this purchase had never happened. They needed to be able to follow the guns from my house to the border. Eduardo was already indictable but they wanted to know where he was getting his money and where the guns were going.

He told me Jack had mentioned buying me a money counter like banks use so that we wouldn't have this problem again. But the reality of this situation was that I screwed up—I trusted a criminal. That wouldn't happen again! Now, for the sake of the investigation, I needed to get over the feeling that I had to even the score with Eduardo. I decided to spend several hundred dollars to buy myself a bank-quality money counter.

I called Pedro to let him know that Eduardo shorted me and he seemed as incensed as I was. He spoke to Eduardo who denied it emphatically and said it was my responsibility to count the money.

"I'm sorry Mike," said Pedro. "I don't know what he's thinking. But I don't want no problems with you. I'll make this right."

And he did—over the next few days Pedro brought me some cash and returned some of the guns he'd bought that night with Eduardo until the $5,000 debt was satisfied.

Things got quiet for a week and I wondered if the problem with Eduardo had screwed everything up. Then too, since the day Lopez kidnapped him there was always a concern that Diego might tip off Pedro. Diego had never contacted Lopez as promised and that was a huge problem. There was just no way of knowing for sure.

But the last weekend of April, Pedro called me while I was working a gun show at the old indoor swap meet on the south side of town. He said that Eduardo had called him and needed thirty-three more .38 Supers. Pedro said he would drop by the gun show as it was not far from his new home.

I was ambivalent about contacting Travis because he'd told me it was his anniversary weekend and he intended to take his bride camping in the mountains. After thinking about this for a while, I decided it was too important to wait. When I called, Lopez told me they'd be working on another case for most of the following week and to do everything possible not to have them take any guns that day. He also said that towards the end of the next week they had tentative plans to go to Mexico to meet their Mexican counterparts and help them to better track the guns on their side of the border.

This was a surprise to me as I thought it had already been taken care of back when we were dealing with Goldblatt. All of this time I had been under the impression that Mexican authorities were tracking these guns on the other side of the border. Lopez told me at a later date that their trip had been canceled but did not elaborate.

With regards to Eduardo, Lopez had some special advice. "Look Mike, I know I don't need to tell you to act pissed off. This little prick thinks he just got over on you to the tune of five grand. Let him know that you're in charge and if he wants to play games he can take a hike. It's a tough spot to be in, I know, but I think you'll handle it fine."

As I was speaking to Lopez on the phone, I saw Pedro's wife walk up on the left side of the table. She smiled and waved and I looked frantically for Pedro and Eduardo whom I saw standing at the end cap of my tables looking at my rack of AK-47s. I told Travis I saw someone who owed me money and said a hurried goodbye.

I shook hands with Pedro first and he seemed to be enjoying the uneasy position Eduardo was in. I extended my hand to Eduardo but did not smile. I wanted him to feel very uncomfortable. Through Pedro, Eduardo told me he needed another thirty-three Colt .38 Supers.

I informed him, still without smiling, that he'd need to put down a 50 percent deposit before I would order anything for him. In this case, it would be $23,000. To my surprise, he said that would be fine and he already had the money together. He had yet to look me in the eye.

Around eight that evening Pedro showed up at my home. He said Eduardo was driving separately and would be there soon with the cash deposit. With Lopez camping in the mountains I'd be on my own again. I didn't have much to worry about that night, though. Most of my guns were at the gun show and it wouldn't make sense for Eduardo or any of his cohorts to try to rip me. I was in a good spot for the moment—his boss had sent him back to me to get more guns and he'd be in trouble if he couldn't make it happen.

Pedro told me that these guns were not for the guys in Caborca. Eduardo had told him they were going to another group and that was an important development. It made Pedro happy too because he was getting a slice of this new business just for doing the paperwork.

Eduardo showed up about ten minutes later carrying a weighty plastic grocery bag. The money was all $20 bills rubber-banded together into bricks of $5,000.

As I sat and counted each brick, Pedro told Eduardo a story in Spanish. I could tell by the astonished expression on Eduardo's face that Pedro had just related a very scary event. With my limited Spanish all I could understand was that the tale involved his cousin and a car. But Eduardo's eyes were open wide and his skinny porn-star mustache made a perfect half circle around his mouth when he said, "Wow!" I coughed loudly a couple times to page-mark the recording so a Spanish speaker at the ATF could interpret Pedro's impressive anecdote later.

Eduardo only brought me $20,000 in cash but lowered his order to thirty instead of thirty-three Colt .38 Supers.

Eduardo asked me to make a catalog of sorts that displayed each of the weapons I sold. He wanted to be able to print this out or email it to his associates and take orders. When I asked for his email address, Eduardo opened his cell phone and made a call and then wrote the address at the top of the receipt I had prepared for his deposit. He said it was his girlfriend's email. I asked Pedro if Eduardo also had a wife and he shrugged and said yes but she lives in Mexico. Eduardo lived with Charlene, a student at the university, in a rental house not very far from me. Charlene was the woman Maria had referred to as Eduardo's wife at our first meeting when she said that she was glad she didn't come because she couldn't stand her.

On May 7, 2007, Pedro called me mid-morning and told me Eduardo had a car that was getting ready to head to Mexico and he wanted to know if they could come get some guns. I told him I had a doctor's appointment in the afternoon but would call and see if I could change it.

I called Travis as soon as I hung up. "Stand by and I'll talk to Jack about it," he said. "We may have you call him back."

About fifteen minutes later he called back and told me to try to arrange for the buy to take place that evening. After I arranged for Pedro to come at six, I piled all the AK pistols in their boxes in stacks in the formal living room. I opened the top box and lay the gun on top of it so they could tell what was in the boxes below. I also brought out the four under-folding AKs from various manufacturers. I had twenty more .38 Super pistols stacked in three piles. It was an impressive load of guns and I was hoping that Eduardo would come through and buy most of the stuff.

Travis came at about four and dropped off the transmitter. He left for the briefing but returned about forty-five minutes later and called to tell me that he was in position, parked just down from nosey Sharon's house. A little while later, I watched another nondescript sedan with blacked-out windows drive down my street and park at the end of my cul-de-sac. All seven agents would be out on this tonight.

Pedro pulled into my driveway in his Nissan Sentra at about six fifteen. He was wearing a white T-shirt and jeans and it seemed like he had already showered. He must have finished work early. I invited him in and he looked around at the guns that I had laid out and told me that Eduardo should be there soon.

He sat down at the table and noticed my new AccuBank money counting machine. "Ah cool, you got your machine," he said. He struggled to pull a big stack of twenties out of his pocket so that he could see the machine working.

"How much did you bring?" I asked.

"I'm not sure. My cousin just handed me a bunch of money and said, 'Here, buy something.'"

I ran his money through the machine and both of us were amazed at just how fast it worked. It made my bank's machine look absolutely prehistoric.

In no time, we found that Pedro's cousin had given him $4,500 in cash. "I'm definitely going to buy something tonight," he said. "We'll see what Eduardo wants and I'll buy what he leaves."

Eduardo was late and Pedro tried calling him several times to see where he was but there was no answer. We made small talk and drank Gatorade as we sat at the table waiting for Eduardo to show. Pedro told me about his childhood and how he and his mother and siblings were once deported back to Mexico. He could recall his brother carrying him on his shoulders as they crossed back into the US through the desert.

He told me of another time when he was going to Puerto Penasco, Mexico, the closest beach destination for people in southeastern Arizona. He had forgotten his driver's license and the Mexican police stopped him at the border and would not allow him to enter. He sent his friend all the way home to get the license. When the Mexican border-guard looked at his ID and saw his last name was Trujillo he asked if he was related to José Trujillo in Caborca. "Yeah, that's my cousin," he'd said. "Why didn't you say something?" the guard had said apologetically. "Please go!"

My cell phone rang and it was Travis. I excused myself and walked out back onto the patio with my dog Morgan. "Hey," he said, "it looks like Eduardo is still at home. Maybe he's waiting for the money. Do me a favor . . . ask more questions about which port and what kind of vehicles they use to transport these guns."

I sat back down at the table and Pedro told me he still could not get hold of Eduardo. It was now seven thirty.

When I started the conversation about taking the guns south, Pedro acknowledged they had been using Sasabe port. I asked if they paid the guard ahead of time or waited until they had a problem. He said that it depended—sometimes they paid the guy ahead of time so there wouldn't be any problems, but other times they didn't pay anyone and took a chance on them not finding the secret compartments in the truck. If they were found out then they would have to pay more to make the problem go away.

Sometimes Pedro's cousin took the guns apart and hid them in the gas tanks. He said they also had trucks that were specially modified with compartments to hide cargo. I asked if they used the same trucks that bring dope up to take the guns back down and he said they used different vehicles.

"What about Eduardo?" I asked Pedro. "What does he do all day? I mean, remember you told me he can't travel because he doesn't have a passport, so he must be doing something to justify his organization paying him to stay up here."

"I dunno know, Mike. The only time I ever see him is when we come over here to buy guns."

I knew this was a lie because he had told me many times that he saw him over at Maria's house. I looked at him in the eye. "What is Eduardo's last name?"

He looked away. "I don't know."

I cocked my head and continued to look at him until he started squirming in his seat. After a second or two he said, "Maybe it is Valenzuela, like Maria."

"So, they really are cousins?"

"Yeah, they are cousins."

Lopez still did not have a solid ID on him and I was hoping this news might make it easier. It also told me that Pedro was not as forthcoming as he tried to appear to be.

We made small talk for a while longer. After eight, my phone rang again and I immediately got up and walked out to the patio. It was Lopez and he said that he was happy with my questions and the responses but he wanted me to take it to the next level. "Ask him who Eduardo's boss is."

When I came back, Pedro was just getting off his phone. He looked at me dejectedly. "Eduardo can't make it tonight. He has some important guys at his house from Mexico and now he can't come."

"Too important to miss this chance to get these guns to Mexico? It must be a really big dope deal?"

Pedro shrugged. "Yeah, I guess so."

He looked through the guns and set several aside. He ended up getting two Century AK-47 underfolders, a Wise Lite AK pistol and a Century AK pistol that had been outfitted with black plastic furniture. He also wanted to get three Beta Mags 100-round magazines for AR-15s. It was over $4,000 worth of stuff.

As I was counting his money I asked Pedro the name of Eduardo's boss.

Pedro looked up with a shocked expression. Almost as if he couldn't believe that I had asked such a question, but I looked him in the eye without blinking.

"His boss is Paez. In Spanish it means peace."

I handed him a pen. "How do you spell this name?"

"P-A-E-Z," he said and wrote the name on top of a cardboard box on my dining room table.

"And this cartel, is it one of the biggest?"

"Umm, maybe middle size."

"How about your cousin, José? Who does he work for?"

Pedro moved his hands in wide circles. "In Caborca there are many groups." I could tell that my questions made him feel uneasy but my directness also somehow disarmed him. But, even so, he didn't give me the name of any specific cartels.

I helped him carry the guns out to his car and loaded them into his empty trunk. It was almost eight thirty when he left.

A few minutes later, Travis pulled into my driveway. He was smiling as he came through my front door.

"I'm sorry man," I said. "Got all of you out here tonight and that fucking asshole didn't even show up."

"Don't feel bad at all, Mike. We got some great information. Tell me again who Eduardo's boss is?"

"Paez."

Lopez's smile widened. "Ignacio 'Nacho' Paez Soto! He's a major player, Mike. This is great news."

"It sounds to me like you already had a pretty good guess."

"Yeah, but this confirms things for us. You got us some really good information tonight. You did great, man!"

I handed Travis the transmitter which was now quite hot. "Just be happy we didn't tape this up under your nut sack," he joked.

I offered to make a CD of the conversation and bring it by the office.

"Let's try to reschedule this buy for Wednesday or Thursday," he said. "Tomorrow is bad for us as we'll be working a home invasion."

The way he spoke made me curious. "Has this invasion happened yet or is it going to happen?"

"Some assholes decided it would be a good idea to do a home invasion on our safe house," he said, laughing. I started laughing too, trying to imagine the surprised look on these idiots' faces when they broke through the front door of a house and ended up being confronted by a bunch of feds holding automatic weapons.

After he left, I cleaned up and took myself out to dinner. It seemed like every time I had to deal with the asshole Eduardo, I ended up eating late because of his bullshit. I was almost at the restaurant when Travis called again. It was nine o'clock. He had a question about Pedro's cousin and wanted to know if he told me the name of his cartel—which he hadn't. He still seemed exuberant about the information regarding Paez and thanked me again. We also spent some time talking about Jodi in Phoenix. I told him I was going to write a letter to the SAC in Phoenix to complain that I had still not been paid. His advice was not to do it. He said that if he was me he would wait until Jodi called me and needed something from me, and then to tell her I wouldn't work with her anymore because of the way that she treated me.

"I want you to know that we treat you differently than we treat any other CI because all the information you bring us is accurate and actionable. We appreciate everything you do for us and we enjoy working with you. Don't let this bitch's unethical behavior color the way you think of us."

He was right, of course, and I never considered not working with the Tucson office because of Jodi's bullshit. There was never a time when I visited the Tucson office that each of the guys didn't come out of their office to shake hands with me and say hi. They did seem genuinely appreciative and always made me feel like part of the team.

The following day was no different. Just as I got off of the elevator on the eighth floor of the federal building, I ran into Jack Hinkley. He was smiling broadly. "Hey, that was great last night, good job," he said, as he ducked into the men's room. "I'll be in to say hi in a couple minutes."

I rang the doorbell in the secure vestibule and Joey Pequeno spotted me through the Plexiglas window and came to let me in. Travis was on the phone but Mando came out to see me. Morty also stopped to say hello. There was a buzz in the office and it was obvious that something was going on, and then I remembered the home invasion Lopez had told me about.

Despite the obvious danger they would be facing that night, the agents all seemed relaxed and focused. There didn't seem to be any nervous Nellies sitting in a corner biting their nails.

Petey walked by on his way to lunch and made a point of waving and saying hi before he went out the door. Travis got off of the phone and handed me another $800 and had me sign a voucher. Joey Pequeno countersigned the voucher but then ripped the money out of my hand to count it. Jack told Travis to come back after lunch and Travis said that he wasn't going to take a lunch because he had to serve a subpoena at two. What a life these guys live, I thought. Maybe it was just perception on my part, but Travis seemed to really work his butt off while the older guys seemed to coast a little. Or perhaps it was because this case he was working with me was bigger than anything else their office was working on.

Lopez invited me into his office to look at the chain of command for the Paez Cartel. Most of the positions in the chart had silhouettes and question marks indicating that they had not yet identified those individuals. He pointed to several places on the chart that were only a person or two removed from Nacho Soto Paez and explained that he'd like to ID those guys.

Mando asked Lopez if he told me about the guy that got blown up.

"Oh yeah, Mike," said Lopez, "remember when you said they were talking about Pedro's cousin and you coughed to mark the conversation? Mando listened to it and they were talking about Pedro's cousin, José. He was supposed to go pick up a car that had just had a new stereo system put in it but he was too busy and he sent one of his guys instead. The car blew up when he started it. That happened in Hermosillo."

No wonder Eduardo had seemed so shocked.

"By the way, Pedro is not the innocent dolt he pretends to be. Judging by the questions he asked Eduardo about the drug trade, we think he's more involved than he wants anyone to believe. Be careful, Mike, these guys are dangerous. Don't ever let your guard down when you're around them."

Travis had a pretty good idea about finding IDs on the other henchmen. He suggested I talk to Pedro and make presents of some .38 Supers. "Tell him you'll have their names engraved in the slides."

"In Mexico, a gun like that is a status symbol," said Mando. "They don't use those pistols for fighting—that's what the AK-47s are for."

"That will give us the IDs of these top lieutenants," said Travis, "and will also provide an indictable offense when they're caught carrying a gun with their name engraved on it."

I could tell they had plenty to do before their big event that night, so I didn't linger. Travis thanked me for the CD. I shook his hand and told him to be careful. "You be careful too," he said emphatically.

The next day Travis called me early in the morning and asked me to reschedule the buy with Eduardo. "Sure, no problem. I'll send you the recording as soon as I get off the phone with him. How did it go last night?"

"Actually, nothing happened."

"You mean my criminals aren't the only unreliable criminals in the world?" I asked, chuckling.

Lopez laughed. "They did show up but they didn't go through with the rip off. They spotted the SWAT tank and it spooked them."

"Well, you have to give them credit. Most of these guys would have just said, wow, what a coincidence here's the SWAT tank parked on the same block where we're going to do a home invasion."

"They parked it over four blocks away but somehow they managed to spot it."

"So, you never even got to go 'off safe'?"(flicking the safety lever of his weapon from "safe" to "fire.")

"No, not even."

I know that he must have been disappointed and truthfully I was too as I would have loved to hear about the shootout that ensued when these assholes kicked in the front door to the feds' safe house.

I called Pedro a little later and we made plans for him and Eduardo to come out at four so that Eduardo could look at the AK pistols to figure out which ones he needed and how much they would cost.

Lopez had other things going on that evening and asked if I felt OK dealing with these guys by myself again. Quite honestly, I did feel safe. I had $20K of Eduardo's money so it wouldn't make sense for him to try to rip me, Pedro didn't have the tough guy mentality, and Eduardo certainly didn't have the muscle—as long as he didn't bring his bodyguard. Travis told me to get real specific about the names of the cartel people and where they fit in the overall organization.

I laid out all of my AK pistol and rifles, stacked the boxes, and left a representative sample on the top box. That way Eduardo would know how many I had of each model. They both showed up right on time, one right behind the other. Eduardo walked through the samples picking up guns and handling them and occasionally asking Pedro a question that was, in turn, translated for me.

After about fifteen minutes Eduardo asked for a price on eleven AK pistols and nine other AK-47 rifles. The total came to $13,900. Of course he'd already put a $20K deposit down on the thirty .38 Colt Supers. So, he would need to bring an additional $35,900 cash with him when he came to pick up the guns the next day.

I handed him a Kalashnikov knife I had in stock and tried to explain in my limited Spanish that it was a switchblade. He looked at it and I could see that he was holding it backwards. I think Pedro noticed too but neither of us said anything when he pressed the button. He nearly cut himself. I bent over laughing while Pedro snorted.

He told Pedro that he wanted to buy the Beretta M84 Cheetah in .380 and M92FS in 9 mm that night. Pedro did the paperwork and we arranged to meet the next day at two o'clock. Eduardo left with the pistols.

Travis had asked me to call him after the duo left. It was about six and he was at home. I told him we were still on for the next day at two. "But you know how unreliable these fuckers are, especially Eduardo," I said.

The next day Lopez called again and asked me to call Pedro to confirm our appointment at two. He also asked me to have Pedro show up early or stay a little later so that we could talk privately about the Mexican bosses and whose names we should have engraved on the .38 Supers.

After I emailed my digitally recorded phone conversation with Pedro, Lopez called back. "We'll come out between twelve thirty and one to set up. We have to get lunch because it will be a long night and then we have to have a briefing before these guys arrive."

When Mando and Travis arrived later that day, Mando listened to the section of the previous night's recording when Pedro and Eduardo were talking between themselves in Spanish while Travis prepared the transmitter for me. It was more involved than I realized. It looked like he had to put a memory card in it—not unlike the one that I used in my digital camera— and then reattach a cover plate of some sort. The unit had a nine-inch flexible external antenna.

He also set up the Kleenex box with the pinhole video camera. The Hawk would record but would not transmit the picture like the clock radio we had used previously.

"Push Pedro for some answers today," said Lopez. "Ask him who his cousin's boss is and try to get details about the people he works with. And ask Eduardo when his stuff is getting packed and when he thinks it will cross the border."

While Lopez took the opportunity to use my bathroom before his stake-out began, I showed Mando one of the AK-47 switchblades and told him about Eduardo opening it backwards. In fact, I played the recording of that meeting and he heard Pedro and me laughing hysterically at the jerk when he almost cut himself.

Pedro called at about one thirty and said that Eduardo told him he was too busy to come over. I felt my face blush with anger. That fucking prick! "Pedro, call him back and see what time he wants to come over. We have to get this done today."

Pedro called back after a couple minutes and said that they would be there between six and seven. I relayed this information to Travis with an apology.

"Don't sweat it," he said. "We'll use the opportunity to go set up at his house and watch him for a while. Mando is interested in finding out more about the drug dealing side of Eduardo's business."

I made myself a bowl of soup for lunch and then used the time to start filling out the back of #4473s and Multiple Disposition forms that listed all the serial numbers of handguns whenever more than one handgun was purchased at the same time for the .38 Super purchases, trying to get as much of the paperwork done as I could so I could get these guys in and out as quickly as possible.

At about six twenty Lopez called to tell me that Pedro had arrived. He asked me to activate the Hawk in the Kleenex box as well as the transmitter. I also turned on my digital recorder and put it in the knife pocket of my trousers.

I welcomed Pedro into the house. He showed me a plastic bag full of money. "I'm going to buy some guns today," he said. "I just picked up this money from my uncle myself." He pulled out some stacks of cash from the bag and I could see that it was all $20s, $50s, and $100s. Thankfully the bag was not full of $5s like he had brought previously. Not that it would matter now that I had my money counter, which I left on the counter of the wet bar in the living room.

I asked him if Eduardo was still coming and he replied that he was.

Pedro selected eight Colt .38 Supers. He also wanted four of the Wise-Lite Generation III AK-47 pistols and four Rock River Arms AR-15s. I still had two of the AR-15 Beta Mags left and he took both of those too. His tab for the purchases was just over $15,000.

While we did the paperwork, I asked him to call Eduardo and see where he was. The prick had his phone turned off.

"What could be more important to him than completing this deal?" Pedro shook his head with disgust.

"Do you think he has a big drug deal going on?"

"Maybe, but these guns are for his brother, and I think he is having a hard time getting the money." Apparently Eduardo's brother was not as well-funded as Paez.

"Maybe he's having a hard time getting the money," I repeated—this time for the benefit of the agents listening in. "Do you think he might not come tonight?"

"Yeah, I dunno. It's already after seven and he has his phone turned off." He tried dialing again for my benefit.

I could see that Pedro felt really bad about this. Once again he was in the position where he had to apologize for Eduardo. I was really starting to hate that bastard!

Pedro wanted another one of the Rock River rifles and I had to go out into my storage area to get it. While I was out there, I took out the transmitter and spoke into it. "I don't know if you heard it clearly, but it looks like Eduardo is not coming." I put the transmitter back in my cargo pocket and started back into the living room. Just then my cell phone rang. I walked into my bedroom and went into my walk-in closet where I could speak.

"Mike, I got your message about Eduardo. Let's use this time to ask more questions about Pedro's cousin. See who his boss is and tell him you're fascinated with that lifestyle."

While I finished the paperwork for Pedro's buy he asked if I had gotten the Colt Commander that he ordered for his cousin. This gave me the opening I was looking for to converse about his cousin without being too obvious.

I asked him how old his cousin was and he said that he was only about thirty-five but that he had a very nice house and BMW and lots of toys.

"Does he have a pretty wife?"

"Oh yeah, right now he already has three kids."

"Does he have some girlfriends?"

He looked at me incredulously. "Of course."

"His organization . . . is it big? I mean, does he have a lot of people working for him?"

"Oh yeah, probably over a hundred."

"And his boss, what's his name?"

"No, no, he doesn't have a boss."

"How about Paez . . . he's not his boss?"

"No, they are friends. He doesn't work for Paez. You know those fancy .38 Supers? He gave one of those to Nacho Paez as a present."

His phone rang and I could understand with my limited Spanish that he was telling someone that he was there now and buying the Colts. When he hung up he said that was his cousin José and that he said to say "hi" to me.

"I thought you said your cousin was in Mexico."

"Yeah, he is. He just called me right now."

He opened his cell phone and showed me the long string of numbers indicating a call from a foreign country.

"Wow, I'm impressed! How come you don't work for him full time?"

"He said that maybe next year I can work for him full time. But right now I am working more and more for him. He said he wants me to do my uncle's job but I didn't want him to fire my uncle. I don't want to cause no problems for him."

"It sounds like all of your family is in this business."

"My father is the only brother that didn't do this work. He was a landscaper and worked hard all of his life. Now he is disabled. Sometimes they give him some money. My mom, she is sick too with asthma and diabetes. She told me not to get involved with these guys because they were bad news." He chuckled. "But she'll take their money when it is offered."

To me it sounded like a sort of Mexican-style social security. At least they were taking care of their own. But now, for me at least, things were not as black and white as I had seen them previously.

I asked if any of his brothers worked for his cousin and he said no. "Nobody really knows what I do. But it is hard for me being a painter. I only make $10.85 an hour and don't have any insurance. I need this money."

I asked him if he would have a wife and a girlfriend like Eduardo when he got rich.

"No, I don't have a girlfriend but sometimes we go to Valentino's and I meet a girl. Not a girlfriend, but, you know . . ."

"You're not picking up hookers down on Miracle Mile, are you?"

"No, no," he said laughing.

"Because some of those hookers are men."

"Oh no, no . . ."

"Now that your wife is getting her Green Card, she'll divorce you and take your house."

He shook his head from side to side, laughing.

I asked if his wife had a driver's license and he said that she didn't even know how to drive. "I don't want to teach her."

Pedro tried calling Eduardo one more time and shook his head. "I'm sorry, Mike, I don't like this guy either. If you want, we won't do business with him anymore."

"No, I want his business and his money. I just don't want to put up with this cocksucker's bullshit anymore."

"I'm sorry. My cousin says right now that he is going to order fifteen or more guns at a time. We'll do some nice business without Eduardo."

"When will you get these guns loaded up?"

"Probably tomorrow. Today is Mother's Day in Mexico and I have to take my wife to dinner. But tomorrow I will load them and send them."

"Are you going to do this at your house?"

He nodded.

"Who is going to take them to Mexico?"

"Ah, we have some guys to do that."

"Hey, I want to make some nice custom .38 Supers for José and his top guys. You know, engraved with their names and pearl grips to thank him for his business."

"José will love that. I'll talk with him and see whose names he wants on the guns."

There was still some daylight outside when I helped Pedro carry out the guns. He carried a box of AK pistols and I had a Rock River Arms gun case in each hand. My neighbor sped around the corner as we both headed down the walkway. He stared at us hard and nearly missed his driveway again. He got out of his car still looking at me and my customer. Finally he muttered a hello.

"I hope he doesn't cause any problems," I told Pedro.

"Yeah, he doesn't look friendly. Does he know you sell guns?"

I nodded, wondering again if he was going to place a call with our anonymous tip line or call the Sheriff's department. While Jack could go talk to him, it would just be another headache we'd rather not have to deal with.

We loaded the guns into Pedro's trunk and he promised to call the next day and tell me if he got hold of Eduardo.

After he left, Lopez came to the front door and I waved him in. He was smiling again and said that we got some good information. He collected the Hawk in its Kleenex box and the transmitter.

He asked me to fax him a copy of the receipt I had written for Pedro that had all the serial numbers on it.

When I told him that Pedro got the money from his uncle's house he said he was pretty sure he knew where Pedro's uncle lived.

"That shithead Eduardo will probably call tomorrow morning to demand his guns," I said.

"Tell him, too bad, you'll do this on your schedule not his. He's out of luck."

"The problem with that, Travis, is that I have to pay for all of the guns that you see sitting here. Pedro dropped $15K tonight but I really need that other $35K that Eduardo was supposed to bring tonight. It's difficult to give you an accurate figure because I get the guns from five different suppliers and they all have different terms."

"On Tuesday we're flying down to Mexico to meet with our counterparts about this case. We get back on Thursday. That sort of shoots the shit out of next week. Can we do it the following week?"

I nodded but he could see that I wasn't happy. I was disgusted with Eduardo. I knew that Lopez had spent a lot of time and energy putting together the surveillance and once again Eduardo had not shown up. I told Travis that I hoped that the rest of the guys were not pissed off at me.

"We deal with criminals all the time. Believe me, we're used to this."

On May 11, 2007, I received an email from Lopez.

Thanks Mike . . . I know that you are a little frustrated but don't let it get to you . . . these types of things are expected when the customer is a bad guy . . . If Eduardo calls you tomorrow and wants to buy the guns, let me know and we will move forward with it . . . I talked to the guys about it and we don't want you to get stuck with some late payments . . . hopefully he will call in the morning . . . if not, we will get something figured out . . . take care and keep up the good work, it is much appreciated . . . Travis

Pedro would normally finish work early on Fridays and then drive down to Mexico. Even though he said he was not transporting the guns himself, I suspected that he was. It was important for Lopez to be able to follow the guns from my house to Pedro's and then from his house to the border. Travis called around ten in the morning on Friday and said he was sitting outside Pedro's house. Apparently his company work truck was gone before they arrived for the stakeout. "Hey, would you call him on the pretense of asking about Eduardo but then ask him if the guns were loaded yet?"

Pedro said he hadn't heard from Eduardo but would try him soon. He said that he got home late last night from dinner but would load the stuff today and get it on its way to Mexico. He promised to call later about Eduardo.

At two Travis called again and said they were still sitting outside Pedro's house waiting to see if there was someone coming to transport the guns.

I called Pedro and he said he'd just finished work and was on his way home. I told him to have a nice weekend and said that we would transfer the other guns the following week.

I called Travis back to let him know that he was done work and Travis said that he pulled up just after he called me. That day was the first of the year to hit 100 degrees and he said that he was sweltering and miserable.

"Doesn't your car have air conditioning?"

"Yeah, but I don't want it to catch fire."

I could only imagine how uncomfortable it must have been. They couldn't roll their windows down all the way for ventilation and they had to wear something that would help them conceal their sidearm.

About 5:45 p.m. Travis called again. I asked if he was still working. "Actually we just called the stakeout. This is a tough neighborhood to do surveillance. Someone called the police on us."

I started laughing.

"What's so funny?"

"I'm just trying to imagine that call . . . '911—What is your emergency?' 'There's a white man sitting outside of my house.'"

He started laughing too. "That's about the size of it. Some kids started riding their bikes around our cars and trying to look inside. I also wanted to let you know that I canceled our trip to Mexico next week. So we'll be around all week to do the buy. Maybe Tuesday or Wednesday will work."

"Well, I hope that you didn't do that on my account."

"No, this whole thing seemed to be poorly organized. It always seems that way when we deal with the Mexicans. We had no clear-cut mission or agenda for going so I canceled it."

There was no progress the following week. Pedro called a couple times to say that Eduardo had the money but Lopez couldn't get his troops lined up quickly enough for surveillance so I had to beg off. This made things tough on me. Gun shows always slowed down during the hot months in Arizona and I didn't have the money to pay for the guns I had purchased for Eduardo. I had to go deep into my line of credit with a stupidly high interest rate to pay my invoices as they came due.

Before I left for a gun show in Phoenix I received an email from Lopez

Good job Mike . . . I know that delaying this hurts you but we just don't have the personnel to cover it . . . we are already getting the people together for next week and are in the process of getting a DPS plane so they can be followed outside the city limits . . . let's plan on Tuesday at 5pm . . . maybe if we delay them a little bit it will make them move the guns to MX a little faster . . . thanks and have a good weekend . . . if you need anything call me at anytime . . . Travis

The weekend was a bust. Any hopes I had of making enough money to cover Eduardo's invoices were dashed. It was insanely hot and the building had no air-conditioning. The promoters put industrial swamp coolers at both ends of the facility but they did little to cool us. I think I only sold eight rifles all weekend long. Of course, I had to pay for gas, hotel, and meals, and for a helper both days. I also had to pay a dog sitter to stay with Morgan while I was gone.

The following Tuesday, we arranged to do the deal at two in the afternoon, but that morning I got a call from Pedro saying that Eduardo wanted to pick up the guns up at 10 a.m. instead. I told Pedro I could not accommodate them until at least two o'clock. He said he understood and would call Eduardo.

After we hung up, I called Travis to let him know. "There's just no way we can get everyone into position right now. Let me know what he has to say when he calls back."

Pedro called back a few minutes later. "Ah, this guy is a fucking asshole. Now he says he wants to do it tomorrow. He has to go to Phoenix."

I felt like my head was going to explode. "You know what, Pedro, call that fucking asshole back and tell him that I don't want his business. He's not getting his guns and he'll get his deposit back when I get around to it. I'm tired of this guy treating me like this. Tell him I'm not his bitch and don't want his business."

My frustration had gotten the better of me. I wasn't going to let this stretch on any further. There was no acting this time.

A few minutes later Pedro called me back. He had Eduardo on his other cell phone and I could hear him speaking to him in Spanish. He finished quickly and told me that Eduardo was going to deliver the money to Maria and that he would get the money and then deliver the .38 Supers to her. Pedro also wanted to do some shopping while he was in town. He asked if we could push our appointment back to 5 p.m. I told him that would be fine and called Travis to let him know.

Now I had several conversations that I had taped with my digital recorder that I needed to download into my computer and email to Travis. It was getting tiring. A two-minute conversation ended up taking me about ten minutes to download, rename, and move to a file. Then I'd have to email it to Travis.

Travis came by the house before his briefing and dropped off the Hawk in its Kleenex Box. He was wearing an old T-shirt with holes in it and had a couple days' growth on his face though he was wearing a fresh military-style haircut with clean "white walls" (the sides of his head shaved).

He had me move the money counter to the phone stand. He mentioned that the last time I used it, its vibration had caused some problems with the Hawk's picture quality and that as soon as I turned it off it went back to normal.

"I'll call you after the briefing and let you know when I'm in position," he said.

Pedro arrived at around five thirty and he had Skunk-head Omar with him. It was a while since I'd seen him. In fact, the last time was when Pedro had brought him out to do the paperwork for his .38 Super.

"He's the godfather for my daughter," Pedro said haltingly, searching for the English word for godfather. "I know him from where I grew up, maybe twenty years." That was a long time, especially considering that Pedro was only twenty-four years old.

Pedro placed a heavy plastic shopping bag on my living room table. "I got the money from Maria."

"How much did she give you?"

"There's $22,000 here—Maria counted it so it should be all right. That fucking idiot, Eduardo, he gave me an extra $2,000 for another two of those .38 Supers but he didn't leave any extra money with Maria to pay me for doing the paperwork so I'm going to keep the extra money."

I asked if Maria worked for Eduardo's group. "I would much rather work with her," I said.

"Nah, she's just his cousin."

I pointed at a DVD on the table. "Here, Pedro, I got you a present." It was a newly restored and enhanced version of the movie Scarface.

"Say hello to my little friend," he mimicked. "*Mira*," he said to Skunk-head, "Scarface!"

He pointed to the grenade launcher that Al Pacino was holding on the front of the DVD cover and laughed. "Hey, can you get me one of those?"

"No, I can't but that guy Dave probably can. Did you ever call him?"

He shook his head no.

Just as I had turned on the money counting machine, my cell phone rang. It was Travis and he wanted to know if Maria was coming. I told him no. He said the transmitter wasn't working. I went outside and took it out of my cargo pocket and looked at the switch. I turned it to the "off" position and then moved it back and the green light began glowing again.

I went back to counting the stack of money that Pedro had laid out on the table. It was mostly $20s and had already been arranged in bundles of $1,000. That made things a lot easier. There was $15K worth of $100 bills.

While I was counting money, Pedro and Skunky walked around the living room and picked up each weapon and played with it. For some reason, it was absolutely imperative that they insert a magazine in each rifle. I guess they wanted to see how the gun looked when it was loaded. Then they struck dramatic poses and pretended to fire the rifles.

While I counted, Pedro told me that Maria was pissed off with Eduardo too. Apparently he was supposed to pay her a commission for every gun he bought. She hadn't been paid anything lately. "Then today he calls her and says, 'Hey, come over here and pick up this money.' He's a loser!"

One of the stacks was short $100 and Pedro reached into his own money and took out a $100 bill.

"Make sure you tell Eduardo that he was short and owes you money," I said.

He just smirked.

Then it was time to turn my attention to Pedro's needs. "What can I get for you this evening?"

"We want ten of the cheap AKs."

I had already stacked them in the living room and recorded their serial numbers while I was waiting for Pedro to show up. I also knew that he was going to take the Colt Commander for his cousin José and had started to prepare the Multiple Disposition forms for the thirty .38 Supers that were for Eduardo. Everything was going to be in Pedro's name. He took ten of the cheap AKs, two Wiselite Generation III AK pistols, and a Yugo AK-47 rifle. Each time he wanted something, he recounted his money to see what he had left. He didn't want to leave with any extra money. This was the norm for Pedro—apparently he was instructed to spend as much of the money his uncle gave him as he could. When he realized he still had money to spend, he asked for two Rock River A2 carbines, so I had to go out to the storage area to get them. I opened each case and removed the price tags that I had placed on them for the gun shows.

After he had counted out the money, I asked if there'd be anything else.

"Yes sir, how much is that rifle for me?" he asked, pointing to the digitally camouflaged DPMS M4 carbine. It was a gun he had admired since he first saw it and I knew he was buying it for himself.

"Your special price is $1200," I said, discounting the gun $200 for him. Pedro started counting out the money.

I asked if the guns would be loaded together and Pedro said that Eduardo had his own guys for that. "We're going to take the Colts over to Maria's house now and Eduardo will come pick them up and then take them to be loaded. He's in a lot of trouble right now. He had all the money from the beginning and now the guys are saying, 'Hey where are my guns?'"

"That prick—he had all of the money from the start?"

"He's in big trouble. But he says he didn't want to buy all of the pistols until he could pay for the other guns he picked out. Remember? All of those other rifles and AK pistols. He's an idiot."

I nodded in agreement. This guy had caused me a great deal of distress.

We talked about the missed appointments and the fact that he turned off his phone when he was supposed to be meeting with us.

After counting his money again, Pedro asked if I had any more Romanian AKs and said that he would take one more. I ran back out to the storage area to get it.

Once outside I spoke to Travis via the transmitter.

"I'm out in the garage right now. I'm sure you can hear me because the transmitter is really heating up and my leg is sweating like hell. Eduardo is supposed to pick the guns up tonight around ten at Maria's house and take them to the loading place."

When I returned with the guns, Pedro told me he wanted to come back the next day. His friend, Omar, the skunk-head, was going to give me a cash deposit for ten of the Yugo AK-47s and would also take a couple of the AK pistols for use as samples.

I asked if his friend worked for José. "No," he said, "but he works for some of the same people. They are all friends."

"They don't shoot at each other?"

He laughed, "No, no . . ."

"But he lives here in Tucson?"

He nodded yes and turned and smiled at Omar who realized we were talking about him.

When we were finished, Pedro shook my hand and asked if I was happy. His concern seemed to be genuine. I think he was worried about the strain Eduardo's bullshit was putting on our working relationship.

"I am always happy when I have money in my pocket," I said smiling.

"Good, good," he said with the same facial expression as a puppy that has learned a new trick to please his owner.

While Pedro filled out the paperwork, I asked him if Eduardo was from Caborca too and he said Eduardo was from Magdalena. I was hoping that information would help Travis ID that guy, as they still hadn't been able to find anything on him.

Pedro said one of his friends had seen a guy at the gun show carrying a rifle and had bought it from him. The man turned out to be a cop and he was arrested. This was the same Tucson show where there was an abundance of ATF and TPD officers watching the crowd—especially Hispanic customers.

"I'm telling you—there's too many eyes at the gun shows," I said.

"That's why we're just going to do business with you, Mike."

I walked Pedro and Omar outside and immediately and reflexively looked up to identify the *wop-wop-wop* noise I heard above us. I spotted a helicopter and knew that we had air surveillance. That was great because there was much less chance of the stakeout getting burned by the bad guys realizing that they were being followed. Travis had said that the Department of Public Safety—Arizona's state police—was going to do the air portion of the surveillance. Neither Pedro nor Skunk boy paid much attention. Replaying my digital tape afterwards, the helicopter could be heard clearly. The chopper circled as it climbed for altitude.

I told Pedro to drive carefully and to use his turn signal so the cops would have no reason to stop him. Apparently the mention of police caused him some concern.

"That's why I don't want to deal with Eduardo no more. I don't trust him—he has too many troubles and I'm afraid."

"I stopped trusting him when he stole $5,000 from me. Maybe you can ask your cousin if Eduardo's organization has someone else here in town that is more professional. I don't mind working with them and I don't mind their money, but Eduardo is not a good businessman."

After he left, I thought about the ATF agents who would be following the guns to Maria's house and then to wherever they were going to be loaded and then to the border. It could be hours or it could be days. I almost felt as though I was the reason they were going to be stuck in cars for the next couple days. It had to be terrible, the temperature had already hit 100 degrees and they would probably have to go for a day or more without a shower or toilet facilities. Pissing in an empty bottle must get old after a very short time. So does sitting in the same car seat for hours on end. Those guys would really earn their money and then some in the next couple of days. So, yes, I did feel guilty that I'd have the luxury of nice meals, air-conditioning, showers, and fresh clothes.

The next morning Travis called around ten and asked if I had heard anything from Pedro. "We're sitting on Maria's house right now but we haven't seen Eduardo yet. I don't see how we could have missed him but I guess anything is possible. Would you mind calling him and just ask if he delivered the guns to Maria without any problems?"

Pedro said that the guns were dropped off and that he didn't think that there would be any problems. He told me that his guns, the ten Romanian AKs, were already in Mexico.

"You got them loaded that quick and shipped?"

"Yeah, yeah, they're already over there."

"That's great, that's what I like to hear."

We made arrangements to meet at five that evening for the next purchase. Before I put down the phone, I asked Pedro if Omar worked with his cousin. "No, he has his own people," he said, "but he's cool, he's friends with the Trujillo group in Caborco."

Obviously, Travis and the rest of the agents were still sitting on Maria's house waiting for Eduardo to come pick up the guns so I was alone again when Pedro arrived that evening with Omar and another man whom I guessed was between twenty-two and twenty-six years old, maybe five foot five and about 130 pounds with a lean, athletic build. He wore a baseball cap and had a mole on his right cheek, a mustache, and his hair was closely cropped at the sides. He moved among the guns, picking them up and handling them, but said almost nothing. "Hey, who is this guy?" I asked Pedro and he said he was one of Omar's employees.

I asked Pedro if he'd heard anything from Eduardo and he said he was going to go over and pick up the guns later that day and that I shouldn't worry.

Pedro gave me $3K as a deposit for ten Yugo AK-47s with a full stock. I told him it would be difficult to find them and that it might take some time.

I started counting the deposit he handed me with the money counter. Pedro asked me to get another Rock River A2 Carbine for Omar and I went to my storage area to get it.

Omar also picked out two AK pistols with the wood stocks and two with the black plastic stocks.

Pedro spoke to his cousin, José, while we were sitting in the living room. I asked how he was after he hung up. "The last time I spoke with him he said, 'Hey why do you want to put my name on a gun?'" said Pedro.

I laughed. "So, now he just wants his initials on it?"

Pedro nodded and asked how long it would take. I told him that it would take quite a while. I wanted to put this off as long as possible because I didn't think the ATF had any interest in going ahead on this deal unless they could put the full name of the bad guy on the slide. Apparently Pedro's cousin had already clued him in as to why this would be a bad idea.

Pedro asked for one of the Romanian AKs for himself. "Mike, what is my price? We are friends."

I sighed, "Yes, we are friends and your price is $450. Though I sold the other one to Omar for the full $500."

"Cool."

They ended up buying another $4,600 worth of guns plus the $3,000 deposit and that meant that I would need to do another deposit the next day.

I also told Pedro that I would be getting in some of the AR pistols for $1,000 each. "I think he will take all three," he said, pointing to Omar.

As I walked out with Pedro he asked me again if I was happy. "I'm always happy when I deal with you, Pedro." Just then my cell phone rang again. It was Travis. He wanted to see if I could get specific info about when Eduardo was going to pick up the guns and get them loaded. He was still sitting outside of Maria's home.

"Would you mind calling Maria and asking her if Eduardo picked the pistols up yet?" I asked Pedro.

"Sure, no problem. I will call her right now."

He dialed her number and let it ring but she didn't answer. "I'll call her on the way home and call you back, OK, Mike?"

"Let me know what Maria has to say because if we have to, I can drive my Suburban over there to get the guns. I get nervous with them sitting there too long." I tried to impart a sense of urgency to him as if I had a feeling of impending doom.

"OK, I will call you."

They were gone at 6:16 p.m.

About an hour later Travis called me again and asked me to call Pedro and see what Maria had to say. Pedro told me Eduardo had picked up the guns and that they were loading them right now.

I called Travis and he sounded skeptical. "If he's loading them right now, somehow we missed them. What's your opinion, Mike, do you think he's telling you the truth?"

"No, not at all. I think he's shining me on. He's telling me what he thinks I want to hear."

"Well, we're committed here. We're not going to break this surveillance."

"No, I wouldn't. Pedro probably never even called Maria."

"OK, Mike, good work. I'll keep you posted."

8

FAILED SURVEILLANCES

I WAS ATTENDING THE high school graduation of a friend's son a couple days later when Travis called to say that Eduardo had eventually come to Maria's house to load the pistols.

"I just wanted to say thanks Mike and good work. I'm glad that we stayed on the guns. It looks like it will pay off this time."

"Travis, are you serious? You've been sitting outside Maria's house since Tuesday night?"

"Yep."

"Oh my God, they don't pay you enough."

"Yeah, tell me about it. Stand by . . ." His radio crackled. It sounded as though air support was giving directions to agents on the ground. Lopez came back on the line and told me that they were "running with heat and were already halfway to Sasabe."

I could only imagine the excitement the agents must have felt at that moment. It looked like their long hours and uncomfortable conditions would pay off at last, and I have to admit I wished I was with them.

The following Monday was Memorial Day and Pedro called around three and said that he was just coming back from Caborca. He wanted to know if he could come out with Omar and pick up the AK pistols. "I think he wants some .38 Supers too."

They showed up around five thirty and Omar brought the employee who had been out with them the last time.

It turned out that they would not be buying the AK pistols on that trip. Pedro said that Omar needed the .38 Supers as sales samples and he picked out four blued pistols and three with stainless steel finishes. Pedro said that they would be out later in the week to get the AK pistols.

Omar also selected three Rock River rifles to be used as sales samples. One was the Entry Tactical—a high-end rifle comparable to the DEA carbine. That tidbit seemed to really impress these guys and, of course, I played it up at every opportunity.

I tried to make conversation with Pedro while he did the paperwork. "Did you see José this weekend?" I asked.

He nodded his head.

"Did you tell him how much I appreciate his business?"

"Yeah, we're going to make some more business. He likes doing business with you. Hey, did you find out about making that special pistol for him?"

"I'm still waiting to hear from that guy," I lied. "It's going to take a while."

"Cool, because I already told him that you were going to make a present for him. He's excited."

"Have you heard from Eduardo?"

"Nah, I haven't heard nothing."

"How about these guns? Will you load them tonight at your house?"

"No, these guys have their own people for that." He motioned towards Omar and his "employee." He finished the first half of the #4473 form and flipped it over to sign it.

Omar finished his purchase by choosing a Wise-Lite Generation III AK pistol and a Special Interest AK underfolder. They paid with all $20 bills and that made the counting process easier. I helped carry a stack of Colt boxes outside and was surprised to see that Pedro had not brought his truck but instead was driving a navy blue Dodge Caravan. I quickly noted the license plate and committed it to memory. I asked Pedro if he got a new car. "No, it belongs to them," he said, pointing to Omar. I hoped the plate number would help Travis ID Omar.

The next time Travis called he still sounded tired and I asked if he'd been able to get caught up on his rest that weekend.

"No, not really. I had to drive up to Utah for a family member's graduation."

I wondered where Lopez got his energy. He drove all the way up to Utah and back after spending three straight days in his car on stakeout. He's an animal, I thought!

But when I went to meet him at his office later that day, he was clearly dragging ass—to the point that he seemed mildly confused and outwardly frustrated.

He invited me to sit down and told me that he'd run the plate from Omar's van and it came back to a different name.

"What did his driver's license picture look like?"

"That's the fucked up thing," he said, clearly venting, "He doesn't have a driver's license, as far as I can tell."

I laughed. "Well, at least he registered his car."

"Nah, the registration is all jacked up too."

Lopez pulled a folder from his desk. It must have been four inches thick and he strained to pick it up. "Speaking of driver's licenses, I have one to show you." He flipped through the folder and I could see numerous aerial photos. Finally, he came to a driver's license picture of a heavyset Hispanic woman. "Is this Maria?"

"Yep, that's her."

"Good, OK, we have a good ID on her then." He flipped through some more pages and showed me yet another overweight woman. "Have you ever seen her?"

I shook my head.

"The car Maria drives is registered to her. I'm still trying to figure out what the relationship is between them."

Petey popped his head in Travis's office. "Keep up the good work," he said with a smile.

Lopez threw the file back on his desk with a thump. He stretched his legs out and sighed as he leaned back in his chair. "We don't know what we're going to do, Mike. We're supposed to have a meeting tomorrow to brainstorm but our surveillance didn't go the way we thought it would."

"Did they lose them on the other side of the border?"

"Shit, we didn't even get that far. After they picked up the guns, they started heading south real fast and then stopped and drove in circles for three hours. They stopped at an apartment on the far southwest side of town and then got up at 3 a.m. and started driving in circles again."

"What's the point of that?"

"Well, they know we can't keep a bird in the air that long without refueling. They probably got their experience smuggling dope. When you talked to Pedro did he say if he's talked to Eduardo?"

"Yeah, he called him on Friday."

"He wasn't hinked up then?"

"If he was, he didn't say anything to Pedro."

"Good, well we were wondering if they suspected anything. Now we know that these guys are just very careful professionals."

The time and effort he had invested in this investigation were taking their toll on Lopez. He sighed again and rubbed his knuckles. "Do you think Pedro would get hinked up if we popped Eduardo?"

"Oh yeah, without a doubt," I said. "He would definitely lay low if Eduardo got arrested."

"Damn."

"Did you hear on one of the recordings when he came out to buy some stuff? He said something like, 'I dunno what Eduardo is thinking. If I get arrested does he think I'll go to jail for him? I'll tell them everything I know.'"

Lopez sat forward in his chair. "I must have missed that. Maybe we should just jack Pedro? We could always tell them that we're investigating you and have your house and phone bugged."

"Pedro is an interesting guy. He tries so hard to please—I mean, he's almost like a puppy. Every time he comes out he keeps asking me if I'm happy. So, I'm sure that if you did bust him that he'd be trying to please you in the same way."

"You think that would work?"

"He's just got too much to lose here with his new house and wife and little girl."

"We'll hold that over his head, but there's no way that I can let him walk after all this. He's gonna have to do a couple years anyway."

I felt bad. No doubt the kid was wrapped up with some pretty serious shitheads but I liked him. He tried hard to please and he was always polite and courteous to me. Really, he was just starting out in life. He wasn't dangerous like some of these other characters, but the lure of easy money had clouded his judgment.

I had asked Lopez if he had enough to indict and convict peripheral players like Maria. He said they had way more than enough at that point. "She was actually helping them pack the load car, Mike."

"No kidding, did you get that from the air surveillance?"

"That, and I actually watched them from one of their neighbors' roofs. When they opened the gate for the load car, I started to walk through the neighbor's yard. I stepped onto the gravel driveway and it started crunching. I peeked over the fence and they were all looking hard, frozen in place, not moving. After a couple seconds they went back to loading the car."

"They heard you?"

"Oh yeah, but I could hear the plastic gun cases being bumped into each other so I knew they were loading. Their neighbor's house is vacant and I climbed up on the roof to watch them."

"Man you've got big balls! Did you have a night vision scope with you?"

"I was calling for one but we didn't get it in time. I had regular binoculars with me. But, sure enough, Maria would come out with a bunch of guns and they would arrange them in the load truck. Then they would shut all of the doors and go back inside. Then, a couple minutes later, they'd come out carrying a bunch of guns and open all of the doors again. Eduardo came by earlier in the evening and picked up one gun. Most of the other guys followed him but I stayed on the rest of the guns, fortunately. Eduardo came back for a little while and took off and then the load truck blew out of the gate."

Joey Pequeno walked past Lopez's office and saw me sitting there. He stopped and said with a straight face, "Hey Detty, we're going to take your guys out into the desert and beat the shit out of them." He was joking but he was obviously frustrated over the wasted manpower and uncomfortable conditions that went into the surveillance which had proved largely unsuccessful. I felt bad about the way things turned out and was hoping these agents wouldn't start hating me for these problems.

"This deal with our guys and all of the guns that they've bought from me . . . it's really just a drop in the bucket, isn't it?" I asked.

Lopez nodded.

How did these guys keep from getting discouraged? Maybe the occasional bust and seizure gave them the motivation they needed to continue. Maybe that's why it was so disheartening to hear Lopez talk about making arrests at that point. There wouldn't be any assets they could seize, and putting those players in jail would do nothing to stop the gun trafficking to Mexico.

Travis got out of his chair signaling the end of our meeting. He walked me to the security door and opened it for me. "We should be getting some cash in soon, Mike, and I'll get you caught up when we get it. Thanks for delivering that CD."

Based on Lopez's news I fully expected the investigation to be shut down soon.

Pedro called the following day and said that Omar was expecting to take a big delivery of cash and wanted to come out and buy a bunch of guns.

"How much cash?" I asked.

"He said he thought he would have enough to buy all of the guns you had in your living room."

Now it was starting to look like Omar was connected even better than Eduardo, and he was much easier to deal with. After I got off the phone with Pedro I called Lopez and relayed the news. He asked me when he wanted to do the buy.

"He's talking about coming out tomorrow but Pedro said that someone was going to deliver the money to Omar in the next two hours. I thought I'd call as soon as possible so you could see who brings the money."

"Thanks, I appreciate that, but we don't know where Omar lives. We still don't have a solid ID on him either."

I had forgotten that Lopez was sitting outside Maria's house the last time Omar came and bought some guns with Pedro. Of course, when Lopez gave me the go-ahead to sell those guns, we'd thought they were for Pedro. Neither of us suspected that Omar would be coming with Pedro that evening.

"Listen," said Lopez, "Jack is catching a lot of heat over the number of guns going south and we're going to have to do something about it. We're not having the luck we'd hoped for with our surveillances so we're trying to figure out an alternative. We're supposed to be getting some sort of tracking device from an aerospace company but it won't be ready by next week."

And it didn't really matter. Pedro called and canceled for the next day and I left for a week's vacation in Cabo San Lucas the following day. And Lopez had to go to California as part of a task force to crack down on illicit gun sales in Sacramento while I was gone.

The next time I spoke to Pedro was in June 2007. "Mike, we have a problem," he said.

I felt a tightness in my chest before he even finished his sentence and I was trying to imagine what the problem might be. Had Diego told Pedro about his kidnapping? Had someone finally Googled my name and seen all of my connections to law enforcement? Had one of the guys been arrested somewhere with my guns?

"Omar got arrested Friday night," he said.

"Shit, what happened?"

"I'm not sure. He got into a fight at a Mexican restaurant downtown. The police arrested him and then they deported him. He's in Mexico right now."

"Are you sure? He got arrested and they threw him out of the country? That doesn't sound right."

"Remember Fernando? The one who did the paperwork for Omar's pistol? Omar had the gun with him. Fernando was there and he told the police the gun was his own."

Pedro was obviously worried about this event putting a lot of heat on us. "Have they called you yet?" he asked.

"No, but I don't think it is a big deal. If they already deported him then they probably won't charge him with the gun. Don't worry about it."

After I hung up with Pedro, I called Lopez and gave him the news. "Sweet," he said, jubilantly.

"At least now you'll be able to ID him and you won't have to worry about shutting down his operation."

"I'll see if I can get the arrest report from the Tucson Police Department. Thanks Mike—good work."

Lopez called me the following morning, "A TPD guy came over with Omar's paperwork and asked if I wanted to put a hold on him. He hasn't been deported though, he's still here. TPD has a hold on him because they found him with a gun. There was also a domestic violence element to this arrest that's not entirely clear from the report."

"Pedro never said anything about that. Of course, he told me he was deported too."

"I'm trying to figure out how we can use this to our advantage. I wonder if I'd be able to flip him."

"What kind of time is he looking at?"

"An illegal alien in possession of a firearm is only two years."

"I wonder what he'd do if you cut him loose. Think he'd head over the border?"

"I'm not sure. I think I'll just go down and talk to him and tell him what he's looking at and then leave the door open to see if he wants to offer anything up. Let me email you his booking photo for an ID. Just drop me back an email with a yes or no, OK?"

When I received the email from Lopez with Omar's booking photo, I replied "Yes," that was him. Lopez subsequently spoke with the arresting TPD officers and found out that Omar and his wife were eating when Omar's girlfriend had confronted him and had started a scene. Omar dragged his girlfriend out to the parking lot where he'd held a pistol against her head and told her repeatedly that he was going to kill her. Travis and Mando talked to him and he was unwilling to cooperate and subsequently spent two years at a federal prison in Florence, Arizona, before being deported.

Lopez called me the following day. "Hey Mike, do you think Pedro uses two different cell phones?"

"I know he does, remember I sent you the other cell number?"

"Do you have it handy? I'm trying to get a court order for pen registers. That lets us know what number they are calling."

"Lemme turn on my Outlook and I'll get it for you in just a couple seconds," I said.

"And you think that is his work phone?"

"I think so. I tried to call him several times on one cell and while it was ringing my call waiting went off and it would turn out to be Pedro calling from his other cell. He carries both habitually."

At this point I'd been dealing with criminals for over fifteen months. I did what I thought was necessary to stay safe but there were very few nights of uninterrupted sleep. Little sounds would wake me and I would investigate, gun in hand. Everyone I dealt with knew that I used my home as my warehouse and that I had many guns stored there. I had hidden several loaded AR-15s around the house so I was never far from one. Sarge, my black Labrador, had died earlier in the year and now my Ridgeback-mix Morgan was on her last legs. I'd had both dogs for fourteen years. I had an alarm and

Despite some serious health problems, Detty chose to serve as a US Marine. He made it through Marine OCS and was commissioned a Second Lieutenant.

Detty makes his living selling rifles at Arizona gunshows. In 2006 Detty was approached by a young man with an illicit proposition.

Arizona ATF offices attend gunshows to promote their program, Don't Lie for the Other Guy, designed to deter straw purchase sales. Operation Wide Receiver was one of ATF's ill-conceived and mismanaged investigations.

Detty's fifteen-year-old Ridgeback mix, Morgan, passed away during Operation Wide Receiver.

Detty's new guard dog, Fudge, a chocolate Labrador, was allowed to sleep on Detty's bed.

After Fudge's premature death, Champ and Maya became the new additions to Detty's security team.

Maya and Champ made an awesome security team and would alert Detty any time someone was on the property.

Detty's security team was allowed an off duty swim each day to relax and play.

Detty would often set his living room up as a sales room before a visit from cartel buyers.

AK-47 variants were popular with the cartel buyers.

Colt .38 Supers were a common purchase among the cartel buyers.

Colt .38 Supers, AR-15 rifles, and AK-47 rifles and pistols were the most commonly purchased weapons by the cartel associates. Trujillo was often sent to Detty's house with a sack of money and instructions to buy as many guns as possible—most purchases ranged in size from $10,000 to $50,000.

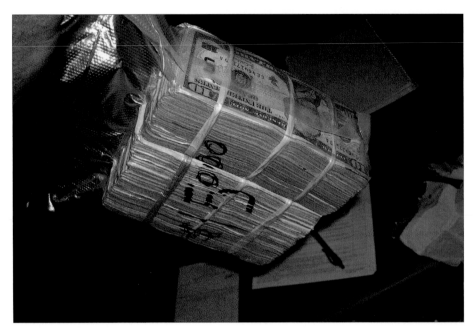

A vacuum-sealed brick of cash marked as $15,000 was $5,000 short and caused some significant problems.

A bank-quality money counter was purchased after Eduardo shorted Detty $5,000.

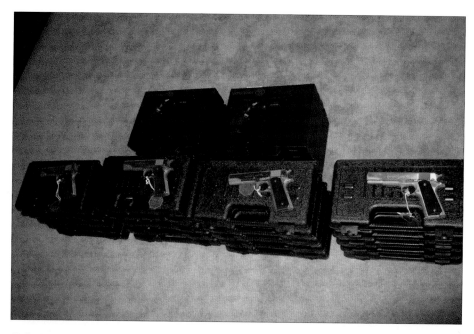

Colt .38 Supers and FN FiveSeven pistols for a purchase by Eduardo. It involved a three-day air surveillance in an attempt to follow the guns to the border.

Was Detty's ATF audit botched or was it an attempt to seize Detty's license?

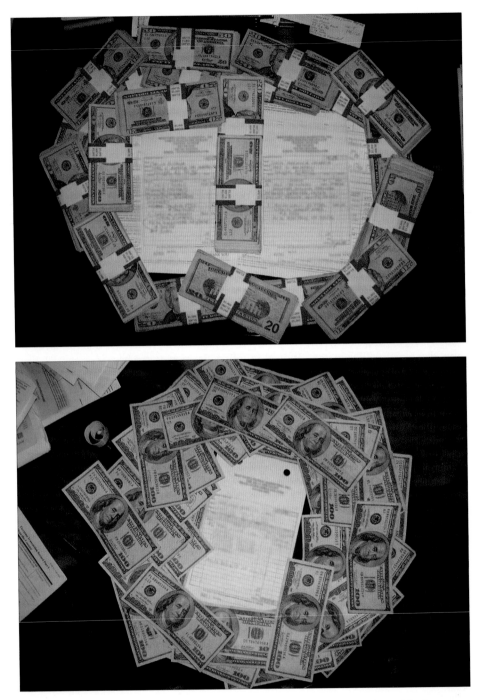

Detty would arrange the cash and receipts and photograph them for the ATF after a purchase. With piles of cash and guns stored at his home, Detty was warned frequently by ATF agents that he might become a target for a rip.

The Tucson ATF office had only one transmitter. It was of dubious quality and worked sporadically. Travis Lopez wrapped an old sock around the transmitter to keep it from burning Detty. The Kleenex box housed the Hawk video/audio recorder.

This clock radio was actually a covert camera. It was used to transmit and record a bad-guy purchase one evening.

For one of the purchases, this innocuous looking pick up was parked outside Detty's house. It contained electronic monitoring and recording equipment.

The AR-15 is a semi-automatic version of our military's M-16 and M-4 battle rifles.

An active competitor, Detty often practices shooting in the desert outside Tucson.

Detty writes firearm evaluations for a number of consumer and law enforcement magazines. (Photo by Alex Landeen.)

Besides working gunshows, Detty also writes for a number of gun-related magazines. He was on the cover of the March 2007 *S.W.A.T. Magazine*. (Used with permission of *S.W.A.T Magazine*, www.swatmag.com.)

CBS's investigative reporter Sharyl Attkisson was the first mainstream media journalist to report ATF's gunwalking policy.

Fox News's investigative reporter William LaJeunesse interviews Detty at his remote shooting spot and fires an AR-15, a gun commonly bought by cartel associates.

This custom built and engraved .38 super was commissioned by Detty when he was still proud of his involvement with federal law enforcement. Detty's pistol was engraved with a custom serial number, MAD DAWG 666. The inscription translates to "The most dangerous man is the one with nothing to lose." (Photos by Alex Landeen.)

security iron over the doors and windows but I was still in a constant state of alert and it was starting to have an effect on me.

I took Morgan outside to pick up my newspaper one morning and saw a navy blue van sitting in the same spot where Lopez normally parked his car when he was staking out my house. I could hear the engine was on and its tinted windows were up. Someone was sitting behind the wheel but I couldn't make out who it was. I stared hard at it for a moment while Morgan let out a throaty growl and the hair on her spine stood up. As I bent over to pick up the paper, I heard the van shift into gear and I started up my driveway headed for the flagstone walkway to my front door. I turned to look at the van—holding my breath, waiting for the inevitable attack—as it drove slowly past me and down the cul-de-sac. I still couldn't make out the driver. My pace picked up as I made my way up the walkway to my front door. Just inside the front door was a closet where I kept a loaded AR-15. I knew they'd have to have to turn around at the end of the cul-de-sac and come back and I'd use the ACOG scope on my rifle to try to read the license plate through my front picture window. As I walked through the front door, I heard my cell phone ringing and I ran into the bedroom to answer it. It was Pedro. I never did figure out who was in the van or even if it had anything to do with me, but it would be years before I went out to pick up the paper without a gun in my pocket. I never could shake that feeling of vulnerability.

Lopez had given me orders not to do business with Pedro until they had the tracking device ready to go. Mondays were always out because they couldn't get the off-duty TPD officers for surveillance on that day. According to Lopez we would be ready for business the following Tuesday. Pedro wanted to come out and buy some guns with one of Omar's associates. He said that they had $20,000 to spend and that he had at least another $10,000. As much as it hurt, I had to turn him down. "I've got some things going on tomorrow and the rest of the week for that matter. Why don't we plan on next Tuesday?"

"Tuesday? What's wrong with tomorrow" asked Pedro.

"Look, I've been thinking about this. I think the fewer times you come and the bigger the order, the less problems we'll have. I'm worried about my neighbor across the street causing problems for me. Also, it takes me a long time to set everything up in the living room for you guys to see. I don't want my girlfriend to know what I do."

"But these guys have $20,000 and I have at least $10,000."

"Do you think José can get you more money by next Tuesday?" I asked, pushing my luck.

"Oh, I dunno."

"It would be great if we could get the size of the order up."

Pedro was quiet for a moment, but when he spoke I could tell he was pissed. "Let me talk to those other guys and see what they say," he said.

I emailed the conversation to Lopez and he called me back.

"Yeah, that's a great power play, Mike. Right now he knows that you're calling the shots and that you'll do things on your schedule. Just let him know that you've been doing this for a long time and that you know how not to get caught. You've got these guys in your pocket. They're not going anywhere else so don't worry about losing them."

"I think this is the first time he's been pissed off at me."

"Fuck him, sucks to be a bad guy, I guess," Lopez said, chuckling. I have to admit that I laughed too. Sometimes it took a dose of Special Agent Lopez's rigid black and white world to put things in perspective for me.

Lopez called the following day to ask about the buttstocks on the AK-47 rifles that Pedro had been buying from me. "It looks as though I'll have the tracking device this Friday," he said. "The unit is about as long as two nine-volt batteries laid end-to-end."

"Some of the ARs have fixed stocks and some have a compartment in the buttstock for cleaning kits. It should be perfect for that device but I thought you said it was small enough to fit inside the receiver?"

"Well, even our technical guys seem to exaggerate. Pedro keeps mentioning the Yugo AKs. Will this fit in one of those?"

"We can make it fit for sure. Their stocks are a little more robust than the Romanian AKs and that should make them easier to modify."

"Will you be available tomorrow?"

"Sure, I can run one of the rifles down to you whenever it's convenient for you. With that tracking device, does an operator need to be somewhere in the vicinity to track it or can it be done from a computer?"

"No, we can use a computer to track it but the trouble is that it's not real time."

"But you'll get a list of GPS coordinates for everywhere the device goes."

"Right!"

The following morning I put the rifle in the car. I left the buttpad off the gun so I could show Travis how much wood he had to work with. Once I was curbside, I called Lopez and he came right down.

I opened the lift-gate on my Suburban and pulled the Yugo AK from the box and let Lopez examine it in the back of the car. He was careful to shield the gun from the many pedestrians walking downtown. The federal building in Tucson was close in proximity to a number of county, state, and courthouse buildings and there was constant foot traffic between the buildings.

He examined the buttstock. "I should be able to make this work." He put the rifle back in the box and put it under his arm.

"Did you get the subpoenas for the pen registers?"

"Actually we get court orders for those," he said. "It looks like we'll get everything we asked for."

"That's great. How's that work—do you get a computer printout or what?"

From the look on his face I could tell that it wasn't as simple as that, but he nodded. "Yeah, we'll get a computer printout of numbers they've dialed and the numbers that have called him and the duration of the calls, but one of the best features is that we can ping their cell phone at any given time and get a fix on their location." Lopez smiled. I knew that this development would be a huge help in the investigation since the physical surveillances seemed to always run into problems.

The next time Pedro called he sounded like he was in good spirits and not at all hinked up. He was pleasant and polite and asked me how my weekend had gone.

"Hey, I'm sorry I couldn't take care of you last weekend but my girlfriend was here the whole time and I don't want her to know what I do."

"No, it's OK, don't worry. Do you have time for us today?"

"No, today is bad. Why don't we do it tomorrow? Will that work for you . . . say around five thirty?"

"Yeah, that should be fine. We're waiting for more money to come from Mexico."

"Wait a second, is that money from Eduardo's guys or Omar's?"

"No, this money will be from Omar's guys. I'll have Omar with me . . . that's the small guy who was with the other Omar the last time he came over there."

"His name is Omar too?"

Pedro chuckled, "Yeah, uh-huh."

"Will this guy do the paperwork or are you going to do it for his guns?"

"I will do the paperwork for all of José's guns but we have a lady to do Omar's guns."

"Have I met her before?"

"No, but she works for Omar's people."

"You gave Omar his deposit money back, right?" After Pedro learned that his friend had not been deported, Omar had asked him to get the deposit money he'd given me for Yugo AKs back to use for a lawyer.

"Yeah, he has a pretty good lawyer and he needed to money."

"Do you still think that he'll get deported?"

"Yeah sure, but he knows his way back here," Pedro said with a laugh. "I'm also going to buy some guns for myself because I'm going to sell them over there in Mexico."

"You're going to sell them yourself? I hope you're being careful."

"Oh yeah, José helps me with it. I take some stuff for him and some stuff for me and I can make more money. He knows all of the cops so we don't have any problems."

"Good, be very careful."

"Oh yeah," he said trying to placate me. "I'm always careful. This Friday I am leaving for a week in Mexico. I'm making that house over there and I have a lot to do."

"What other kinds of guns should I put out for these guys?"

"I'm trying to tell them to take a lot of those AK pistols that you have too."

"OK, good." What a relief it would be to get rid of those. They had been bought and paid for a number of months ago. I had originally ordered them for Eduardo. Time after time they were supposed to be taken and then the plans changed at the last minute or the ATF would have me postpone the buy for one reason or another. It would be a huge relief to get rid of all of them as they did not move well at gun shows.

"You said this guy tomorrow has about $12,000 to spend?"

"He's got $15,000 with my money and the girl who's doing the paperwork's money, so maybe he will have eleven, twelve thousand to spend."

"I thought you said they had like $20,000?"

"Yeah, but during the week they spent some money. They want to get these guns first and then get some more later. They only want to buy what they can take in one ride."

He explained that he didn't want guns sitting around while they waited for another load car to take the next load. I knew this was bullshit but I didn't call him on it. He was just trying to justify the small order.

"Did you mention that Maria was waiting for Omar's guys to bring more money?"

"No, no," Pedro said emphatically. "Omar's guys are waiting for them to bring more money. Maybe sometime between today and tomorrow they will have more money."

"Cool, tell them to bring as much money as they can and I'll put everything on display in the living room."

"I called José right now and told him to send me more money so I can buy more things too."

"Have you heard anything from Eduardo?"

"No, not a word."

"I just think they were trying to scare him, you know."

"I'm sure they were. That's how they work. You tell him to keep his mouth shut and this will work out fine for him."

"Hey, I was wondering if you could give me a couple guns and then I can pay you when I get back from Mexico. You know, like give me credit."

"Let's talk about it when you come tomorrow," I said. Never gonna happen, I thought. Later when I relayed the conversation to Lopez, he said, "The answer to that would be no, for obvious reasons."

We ended the conversation by saying we would meet the next day at about five thirty and that Pedro would call me if there were any problems.

I called Travis who told me they had hollowed out the Yugo stock and got the tracking device in place but for some reason it wasn't working, "but don't worry, we'll get it figured out."

I called a very good friend of mine, Bryce Chandler, who was attached as an intelligence asset to a very elite military unit, and asked if he'd ever tried to place a tracking device in a gun.

Bryce replied, "Yes we have but have been largely unsuccessful. We found two complicating factors. One is that with a small unit you'll have very limited battery life. The other factor is that if you have to wrap the antenna around the unit to make it fit in the buttstock, it will never work correctly. We never did get it to work and had to find other ways to track the Taliban."

The next day Lopez called at about eight thirty in the morning. I was ironing a shirt to get ready for jury duty as I was supposed to report to the Superior Court at 11 a.m.

He wanted to know what time I could drop off the recording of the previous day's conversation with Trujillo and I told him that I'd be down sometime after 10 a.m. He told me that the tracking device was giving him fits and it looked as though he wouldn't be able to use it.

"Isn't there someone that you can call who can run a quick diagnostic on it?"

"No, it's working . . . it just doesn't work for shit. We definitely won't be able to use it for surveillance."

"What do other offices use when they need to track guns? There's got to be something better?"

"No other office lets guns go like we do, Mike."

He was referring to their policy of going after the high-ranking officers of the cartel instead of arresting the low-level mules that were doing the actual buying and transporting. Years later this policy would be called "gunwalking," or letting guns walk, and would become an issue of great controversy.

When I got to the federal building Lopez met me curbside to get the CD from me.

"Looks like we're going to buy that rifle from you, Mike. I'm still trying to figure out how we're going to do the bookwork for it."

"Hey don't worry about it. You don't need to do that. They'll never take the buttplate off that gun."

"No, we don't want to take any chances."

"I can always buy another stock for it."

"No Mike, Jack is adamant that we don't let this particular gun go."

"OK—he's the boss," I said. There was no sense in arguing further.

"Hey, do me a favor and give me a call when you're getting ready to leave the courthouse. I'd like to drop off the Hawk and the transmitter before our briefing. In the event that you get selected for a jury let me know and I'll run over and get you off the hook. We have too much manpower committed to this buy tonight for you to not make it on time."

On my way home, Lopez asked me to stop behind the Bashas Grocery Store near my house where they were having their briefing. When I pulled into the back of the parking lot I saw a group of guys gathered. All looked young and in shape and ready to rumble. Most sported high-dollar sunglasses, fresh haircuts, and untucked polo or golf shirts to cover their pistols. The guys on TPD that worked with the ATF were all selected for their capabilities and aggressive styles. There were no fat bodies or Barney Fifes among them.

I rolled down my window. "Hey, is this where the Gay Men's Support Group meets?" I asked one of the unfamiliar faces.

Travis was the only one who laughed. He pushed his way to the front of the small crowd.

"These guys gonna kick my ass or what?" I asked.

"Nah, they just don't know you," said Lopez as he handed me a wad of cash and a voucher to sign. "I got a little more for you this time, Mike. There should be $1,000 there." I took the $100 bills, folded them, and put them in my shirt pocket.

"Hey Mike," Petey Palmer yelled, "don't forget about that $600 you owe me."

"Was it only $600? I thought it was $700 but if you say $600 that's OK with me."

Now the other guys were smiling too because they understood who I was and that I was OK with the ATF guys.

I handed the voucher back to Lopez and he handed me the transmitter and Hawk in its Kleenex box. "They're both ready to go—just flip the switch." He said they were actually trying to get a wiretap on Trujillo's phone not just the pen registers. He spoke just loud enough for me to hear as he leaned in through the passenger side window. "I'm not supposed to say anything to you about this so keep it to yourself. I'll deny everything if you fuck up and say something." He made his point with an unsmiling stare.

"Sure, don't worry about it. Is there anything that I need to do differently when I talk to him on the phone? Anything I shouldn't say?"

"Nope, just keep playing the part of the dirty dealer. I was trying to get one for Eduardo's phone too, but he quit using that one phone he had."

Lopez gave me a quick list of things he'd like me to ask Pedro during the conversation. He asked me to leave the side door in the gym unlocked just in case there was trouble and said he'd be in to pick up the Hawk and transmitter after we were through.

Pedro showed up at 6:20 p.m. and I activated the transmitter, my digital recorder, and the Hawk in the Kleenex box. Pedro had driven separately in his truck and the new Omar had the old Skunkhead's blue van.

Along with them they had a new person, a pleasant young Hispanic lady named Julie, who would be doing the paperwork for Omar's guns.

They came in and looked around. After a few minutes I offered Julie a seat at the dining room table, almost directly in front of the Hawk. Omar looked around for a few minutes and made some selections. I followed him around the piles of guns with a notebook, adding together how much his selections would be. Pedro followed behind me, looking over my shoulder and interpreting for me.

He wanted eight of the Century Champion AK-47 pistols, four Olympic Arms Plinkers, a budget priced AR-15, and four Colt .38 Super pistols. I piled them on the tile entryway where I could record the serial numbers. He only wanted as much as he could put in one load car and he figured that would be about fourteen guns.

Omar asked in Spanish how my vacation was. Obviously Pedro had told him that I was unavailable and where I was. They talked between themselves about how nice a vacation to Cabo San Lucas would be.

Omar and Pedro continued to look at the rest of the guns while I took each one he selected out of its box and recorded the serial number.

When I was done, I sat down at the table and handed a clipboard to Julie. She started filling out the #4473 background check form. Omar started pulling cash from his pockets and piling it up on the table. Pedro helped count out the $50 and $100 bills into piles of $1,000 each.

I called in Julie's background check and it sailed through. I asked Pedro if he wanted to do the paperwork for his gun or have Julie do it. They talked between themselves and finally Pedro said that he would do his own paperwork. Most likely he was trying to save the money that she would have charged him. Tonight he was also there to buy guns for himself.

I counted out the money and it came to $12,000—still $400 short. Pedro handed me $400 from his wad and then Omar reached into his pocket and paid him the missing money.

"Hey, if you talk to Eduardo, see if he needs guns. As long as he shows up when he's supposed to and has the money with him, I'll sell him guns. But if he wants to play those bullshit games tell him to forget about it."

"I don't trust him," said Pedro. "Maybe I'll talk to him."

"I tried to call him about those shoulder holsters he ordered and his cell doesn't work."

"Yeah, he has a new phone number."

I picked up a pen, ready to write and not giving Pedro the option of not telling me. "What's that number?"

Pedro flipped open his phone and read me the new number.

I repeated it out loud twice as I wrote it down, knowing that Lopez would be ecstatic to get that number. If this was in fact a working number for Eduardo, he'd be able to get a tap on it.

Pedro wanted two Yugo RPK rifles, two Romanian AK underfolders, one AK pistol, and one of the nice Special Interest AK underfolders.

I asked if he had stopped by his uncle's house for money that evening and he looked puzzled. "Didn't you have to stop at your uncle's house tonight to get money to buy guns?"

"Oh, no I only do that when I'm buying guns for José. These guns are for me. I'm going down there on Friday for a whole week and I'm going to sell these guns and make some money for my house down there."

I was trying to see if I could get the name of Pedro's uncle for Travis so they would know which house to watch when the money arrived. "Normally you stop at your uncle's house for money? I met him once?"

"No."

"Didn't I meet him at a gun show with your cousin Antonio?"

"No, that was just a friend."

I gathered the guns and had Pedro pull the tags off of the trigger guards for the Century imported guns that had the serial number printed on them.

Morgan snuck up on Omar by the edge of the kitchen and dining room. She started to growl and he froze.

"She's a *vieja*—don't worry," I said to him. I turned to Julie and told her that she was fifteen years old.

"She's a good watchdog," said Julie. "She watches out for you."

I reminded Pedro that I still had all of the .38 Super magazines that I had ordered for Eduardo. "Do you need any?"

"Lemme call José and see if he needs any." He opened his phone and called but José did not answer.

I handed Pedro a necklace made from seashells. "When I was in Mexico I bought this necklace for your wife from a little girl on the street." It was made from sea shells.

"Thank you, Mike." I could tell that he was genuinely grateful that I'd thought of his wife.

"Back to business. You're going to take your guns down to Mexico on Friday, right?"

"Yeah, I'll be down there until the next Sunday."

"Are you going to come back with more money from José for guns?"

"Yeah, we're gonna have money here pretty soon."

"How about Omar's stuff? When will it go to Mexico?"

"It'll be in Mexico tomorrow."

"Good, OK. And we'll be working with Omar from now on?"

Omar looked at us intently. "*Entiendes ingles?*" I said to him. "You understand what we're saying, right?"

"*Mas o menos,*" he said, smiling. More or less.

Pedro told me that the guns he had bought would be sold Saturday morning. "José calls his friends and they come and they buy. One hour later they're all gone."

"Are you going to sell them on this trip or just work on your house?"

"No, I will sell them all Saturday morning and probably make $3,000 on each gun."

I smiled. "Hey, I finally talked to that guy who is going to engrave the gun for José. He's really backed up and it will probably be four months until he's ready for me. But I'll let you know."

Pedro told me that one of his cousin's businesses was a company that makes cinderblock and he was going to give him the blocks for his house.

"Where's this house at?"

"It's outside of Santana. In a little town called Ocuca. If you look on the map or Google it, you should find it."

"What's this Omar's last name?" I asked Pedro as we started carrying stuff out to the van and truck.

"Saldivar," he said.

Julie was already seated in the passenger seat of the van.

"It was nice to meet you, Julie. I hope these guys treat you well and pay you so that you come back. I always like when a background check goes through so easy."

"Thank you for making me feel safe."

"Oh, you're always safe here. No worries."

I said goodbye to Omar and he pulled out.

"Omar's stuff goes to Caborca too, right?" I asked Pedro.

"No, I don't need more competition. His stuff goes to Sinaloa. Only we sell to the guys in Caborca."

We stood at his truck and talked for a while. He told me how he put guns in vacuum bags and hid them in his gas tank. "They never stop me when I have my wife and baby with me. But when I'm by myself they always try to get money from me."

He told me that Omar's guys paid off the border guards. "We don't do that. Only if we get caught but then it costs more."

He said they currently had three load cars they used.

I said goodbye to Pedro and started back in the house. As I was coming up the walkway I could hear an engine roar as it rounded the corner and then accelerated down the street. Shit, what's this, I wondered. Were they taking him down early? I turned to see a red Z28 barrel up to Travis's stake-out car and then slam on the brakes as it pulled up even with him. It was Sharon's husband and he stayed parallel with Travis's window for a pregnant second and then slowly pulled into his driveway.

I came inside and turned off my digital recorder, the Hawk, and the transmitter, which by the way, was much more comfortable to wear thanks to a thick sock Lopez had taped around it.

Travis let himself in through the front door while I was busy organizing the money.

"I see someone gave you the evil eye," I said.

"Yeah, I guess that was your nosey neighbor's husband?"

"Yep."

"The wife came out about an hour ago."

"Did she talk to you?"

"Yeah, she wanted to know why I was parked on her property. I ended up telling her that I was law enforcement and we're doing an investigation a couple blocks away. She seemed satisfied with that and said I was welcome there anytime."

Lopez seemed pleased that I was able to get Eduardo's new number. He had also wanted me to get the name of the little town where Pedro was building his house. I showed him the piece of paper where Pedro had spelled out O-C-U-C-A. I made sure he had heard Omar's last name was Saldivar and he acknowledged that he had.

It was about 8 p.m. and Lopez collected the Kleenex box and transmitter and left. It would undoubtedly be a long night for them. For me as well. I needed to fax the Multiple Disposition form and #4473s, and my receipts. I also needed to do my own accounting work and log the guns out of inventory. I counted out all the money and got a deposit ready for the next day.

Shortly after Lopez left, I got a call from my neighbor, Sharon. She asked if I knew the person who had been parked on the edge of her property.

"I'm helping them with something," I said. "I'm sorry, I wish I could tell you more but I just can't."

"He told me he was a cop and working on an investigation a couple blocks away. But then we saw him pull into your driveway and stay for a while."

"Yeah, I know. Sharon. This is a project I brought to their attention and I'm helping them with it. I also know that last December you talked to a female agent parked on the side of your house. I just don't want you to think that your neighbor is a criminal."

"Oh no, Mike. I'm glad that you're helping them and thank you for being honest."

I think I got to bed after midnight and I didn't sleep well. I had a nightmare that I was on the rooftop of an embassy-type building that was under siege. At one point, I had a rifle and was shooting at people. As fast as I could shoot someone, three more people would appear. Then I found myself in a small room with doors on each side that I was trying to keep pushed shut with my arms extended. I could feel the wood doors bending, about to give way and my strength ready to give out. I cannot describe the overwhelming feeling of dread that I had—knowing that I had just seconds to live before I died a horrible death. I woke up drenched with sweat, covers thrown on the floor, and the sheet tangled around my neck, and Morgan staring at me with a very concerned look.

The following month Travis called to say he had emailed me a picture he wanted me to ID. We chatted until it showed up and I was able to download it. It was a booking picture of Omar Saldivar with a blue booking towel wrapped around his neck. "Yep, that's him," I said, "the mole on the right cheek and the unibrow are dead giveaways."

"Good, we've now got a positive ID on him. He has a felony conviction and is an illegal alien."

"What's his felony for?"

"Drugs."

"Go figure, dope and guns," I said chuckling.

"Yeah, go figure. Hey, are you going to be out and about today? Can you drop off the CD? The transmitter just isn't as good as your recorder."

I dropped off the CD a couple hours later and then drove over to the UPS center to ship a couple guns. Pedro called on my way home. "Omar is supposed to get $50,000 today," he said. "And he wants to buy more guns."

"I can't do it today and I'm not really sure about tomorrow either."

"But I'm not sure if he'll have the money anymore when I come back from Mexico."

"Yeah, I understand but I have some important stuff going on."

"Can I give them your number and have them call you?"

"Yeah, sure but the problem is that I don't speak Spanish."

"No, I know but Julie does and she can do the paperwork for them. That way I'll still get my money. Just keep track of how many guns you sell them, OK?"

"OK—go ahead and give them my number and we'll see what we can do."

I called Travis and relayed the news to him.

"That just might work, Mike."

"Really, you want me to sell to him?"

"Well, we'd have to do a traffic stop and take him down, but, yeah, as long as the guns don't walk."

"I'm here to tell you that if Omar gets popped, Pedro will never buy another gun from me."

"I think you're wrong. If it can't be tied to you, you can just say that the cops came and talked to you and that you did everything legally. After a little time he won't be scared anymore. If you don't mind, call him back and see if you can set up a buy for tomorrow at six. Also see if you can get some more info on Omar's boss and what cartel he works for."

I called Pedro but he feigned ignorance about the cartel his lifelong buddy Omar worked for. Remember, Pedro told me he had known Omar for almost twenty years and was his daughter's godfather. "You can ask Julie, she knows those guys pretty well," he told me. He was excited that he might have the chance to make some money before he headed south on his week-long vacation. I asked him how much money they paid him for each gun and he said he got $100 per gun.

Travis called at eight thirty and said that he was heading home from work. "I just can't think straight anymore. Have you heard from Pedro?"

"He just called five minutes ago and really didn't have anything to say other than he just called Omar and he said that he would have the money in like one hour. I asked him to call me back when he has the money. I also told him that unless he has the whole $50,000 that we'll do it when he gets back from Mexico in ten days."

"Ok, good. We got some pen registers for Pedro's personal phone, and we got a lot of numbers that he called while he was in Mexico."

We spoke about the wiretaps they were trying to get and Travis thought that he would have them by the following week. I asked if they had someone special who transcribes the phone conversations and he said that they used a retired, bilingual DEA agent who had special equipment to enhance the conversations so they got good usable info.

Then we spoke about the different players and their links to cartels.

"I guess that maybe when this is all done, I'll need to move," I said in a lighthearted manner.

Lopez paused for a moment and took a deep breath. "That's something I've wanted to talk to you about. If this goes down the way we'd like it to, there's going to be some serious heat on you. Are you prepared to move? Are you prepared to stop selling guns and do something else?"

I felt my lips go numb. I'd never allowed myself to imagine how the investigation might change my life.

I didn't sleep well at all that night. I couldn't imagine what my life would turn into. The thought of having to start all over again without being able to see the people I loved and cared about was unbearable.

Jack and Travis stopped by the following evening about forty-five minutes before Pedro was supposed to come. I activated my digital recorder to document the conversation as I realized it might have a great impact on my future.

Morgan barked at them as they came in and Jack bent over and looked at her. "Who is making all that noise?"

I grabbed her collar and tried to pull her over to him so he could pet her. "This is my security system." She didn't want any part of it and pulled away. I herded her out the back door.

Jack looked at all of the guns in the living room, "Wow!"

"Looks like a Third World arms bazaar, huh?"

"No, these guns are nicer than anything they'd have," said Jack. He turned to Travis. "Does Mike know what's going to happen tonight? Did you give him the lowdown?"

Lopez and I both said yes.

"After this goes down tonight you may start receiving a series of phone calls. We'd like you to record those calls."

I nodded again.

"But the real reason I'm out tonight is to talk to your neighbor because I want to be certain we don't have any fallout from our stakeouts. And we've also been ignoring the elephant in the room in terms of what is going to happen to you once we arrest all of these guys."

"My biggest concern is that I'll have to testify," I said. "Or it looks like it's getting ready to go to trial and they'll see all the CI references and be able to figure out pretty easily it was me."

"We're going to have to do it; the feds end up identifying anyway," said Jack.

"The feds will delay it a hundred times longer than the state," said Travis, "but it will still come out."

"We are months down the road from that," said Jack, "and it is not something that we can't address. And there are other issues to be concerned about and we'll move forward on that. But I'm not going to abandon you—you know that."

I was hearing doubletalk and I was getting frustrated. "I understand that, Jack, but I don't want to move, either."

"I know that, but we're going to have to make some decisions on how we process this. If this goes in the direction we hope it goes, this thing will never go to trial and will never have any discovery. They'll plea out on it. They will not have discovery unless and until the plea agreements break apart. They're not going to get discovery first and then pull you out. You know what I'm saying? So we have plenty of time to deal with that issue."

He sounded so cavalier about my future and welfare. He was doing nothing to build my confidence.

"They won't know who you are because in all of our reports we have you shadowed. It makes it appear that the CI and the FFL [Federal Firearms Licensee] are two different people. We structured that right from the beginning of this."

Not much of this was making me feel any better.

"I understand your concerns and I know that you don't want to move, and our position is that we don't want you to move. It's easier on everyone else if you don't move. But . . . if it goes down that road, we will have to do it and all the necessary things that a federal agency will do to keep a witness safe."

"And there are other things we can do to keep you safe without you having to move out of your house," said Travis.

"Look Mike," said Jack, "you're a big boy. If it comes to that at the end of the day and you need to move—you'd be a damn fool not to. But we're not even near that stage yet—not even close to it. You've received no threats and they think you're a stand-up guy, otherwise they wouldn't have all of these people coming through your front door."

"What's your experience with other cases that have gone down this road? I mean, I've taken some cartel money but they also got what they paid for. What they didn't count on, was that I would supply this information to you. Is this something they would kill someone over?"

Jack paused for a moment and let his chin fall into his hand, his arms crossed. "Right now, all you've cost the cartel is cash . . . and not a lot of cash by their standards. The reason that we haven't taken this case off is because we don't want these people. We want the people down in Mexico—the ones who are driving this train. If we can get to them, and it looks like there's a legitimate chance that it's going to trial, then you're going to move. I don't know if that is what's going to happen. We're several steps away from that. We're only eighteen months into this thing—we're really only at the beginning."

"We have other guys that have 'hits' out on them," said Lopez, "and they refused to move. They still even go to Mexico and back and they're still alive."

"It's all about targets of opportunity," said Jack. "I won't say that hit teams won't come into Arizona, but it's a lot less likely. If they kill a federal witness here, they will get the federal death penalty. It's not like in Mexico where they'll buy their way out of jail. It won't happen like that. This is all speculation anyway, because your case is specific to your case. But it's not something we haven't thought about."

We were all standing in the tiled foyer and even though the air-conditioning was running full tilt, I had cold sweat running from each armpit.

"We can also make it look like you got your license revoked too," said Lopez. "Technically you are breaking the law. They're filling out the paperwork and passing the check and the ATF happens to take the dirty dealer's license away—that may not look bad either."

"No matter what, these are discussions for down the road," said Jack. "We are months away from even having to approach those discussions. I'm going to talk to Dan tomorrow and let him know that you're starting to get concerned."

"Who is Dan?"

"Dan is the Assistant US Attorney—haven't you met Dan?"

I shook my head.

Jack tried to smile reassuringly. "Again, Mike, you don't want to hang your hat on this but we deal with many guys in the drug world that have had threats made against them and are told, 'we're going to kill you, we're going to kill you, we're going to kill you,' and they don't come into the US to do that. In fact, we have one guy who travels back and forth regularly to Mexico who ought to be in the WitPro program and he should be dead. I begged him four times to go into the witness protection program and he refused to do it. He's an action freak, a dope, he just likes to do that. But I wanted to come out here and talk to you and let you know that I understand your concerns. The actions that we're going to take tonight and that we've repeatedly taken throughout this case are to prevent anything from coming back to you."

"In our interviews we always ask them about you," said Lopez. "If we get to the point where they give you up, we question them at length about you. Everyone from Rodriguez to everyone else thinks you're a suspect. Anyone who is arrested is going to be led to believe that you are a suspect."

"We'll talk again," said Jack excusing himself. "I have to jump over and talk to your neighbors before our evening starts. Good luck tonight and we'll meet next week, OK?"

"What did you think about what Jack said?" Lopez asked as Jack walked across the street.

"I was hoping to hear something that would make me feel better, but I've got to tell you, Travis, I don't feel much better after talking to Jack."

"When we got started with this, I don't think that you realized the magnitude of what you were getting into."

His words started to piss me off. If I'd had any real warning from these guys that I would have to be relocated, I would never have gotten involved. But I listened patiently without cutting him off.

"I don't think that we knew the magnitude of it either," said Travis. "At first it was just selling Diego's buddies a couple AKs and then it was ten of this and that. Then Eduardo got involved and then it was big buys once a week and now Omar and his guys. We didn't see it coming."

And, of course, that was true. It was a slippery slope and at what point did I or the ATF realize that this was going to turn into a major trafficking case, and at what point could I have extricated myself from this mess?

"You're one of the best CIs we've ever had. Your motivation isn't all about money and you're not doing it because you're being forced to. You're a patriot and you believe in our country and our system. We never have to waste our time encouraging you, and the information that you get for us is always of the best quality. You have no idea, Mike, how much I and the rest of the guys in the office respect you for what you've done."

Lopez had done more to motivate me in just seconds than Jack could have done in hours. Knowing that my efforts were appreciated made the crazy risks worthwhile.

9

MI VIDA LOCA

SPECIAL AGENT LOPEZ had told me before he left my house that his cell phone wasn't working, so when Pedro called and said that he'd be twenty minutes late, I had to walk out to his car to let him know.

I brought my laptop into the dining room to do some bookwork while I waited for Pedro. I was so engrossed in my spreadsheets that he walked up to my front door unnoticed by me. Shit! I let Pedro in and grabbed Morgan's collar to take her out the back door. Once outside, I activated the transmitter and my digital recorder. When I came back in, Omar and Julie were at the front door. Omar shook hands and made a point of looking me in the eye and smiling when he crossed the threshold. Julie was her usual bubbly self and I invited her to have a seat while the guys picked out what they wanted. I still had not activated the Hawk in its Kleenex box. Did I dare do it now with everyone here? The wet bar was covered with a mirrored wall and I wondered if they'd notice. But I really didn't have a choice as there was now a Kleenex box with wires and a toggle switch hanging out.

I walked over and pulled a Kleenex from the box and started cleaning my eyeglasses. I flipped the small switch and tucked the wires into the box as nonchalantly as possible. I turned around slowly, still wiping the lenses. Julie smiled sweetly—she was oblivious to what I had just done. All the electronics were now activated and I hadn't lost anything meaningful because of the delay. I was lucky that time and realized I would have to be much more careful in the future.

Pedro and Omar walked among the piles of guns and talked between themselves while Julie and I made small talk while sitting at the dining room table. Omar pointed to the stacks of ten Rock River AR-15 carbines and spoke in Spanish.

"He wants all of those," said Pedro. He asked if I had more.

"How many does he want?"

"He says at least ten more."

Omar also wanted all of the .38 Supers that I had left. They had me do some quick math to see what the total came to. Pedro had not yet started picking out guns for himself and after a while it became apparent to me that Julie was going to do the paperwork for all of the guns and that Omar would just pay for Pedro's guns, rather than give him a cash kickback. A little later, Pedro put one of the Rock River Entry Tactical rifles aside saying that it was for his cousin José.

With the selections now made, I tallied the order and it came to $33,994. Omar had brought a stack of cash in a Big Lots shopping bag. I had Julie and Pedro separate the denominations and count the money out into stacks of $1,000 which I then confirmed with the counting machine and banded. This took at least a half hour and with just one exception the count by my two "friends" was correct. While we were doing the counting, Omar went outside and came back in with a large black nylon case. Inside the case were two other similar bags. He started opening the blue plastic Rock River Arms cases and removing the rifles' uppers and lowers and placing them in the bags along with the magazine that comes with each gun. Pedro asked if there was anything I could do with the cases because Omar wanted to leave them with me.

"They have no value. I really can't give him anything for them."

"Oh no, no he just wants to leave them here."

"Sure, no problem. I'll take care of them."

When he had finished filling the bag, he strained to lift the strap onto his shoulder—its weight nearly pulled him over—and took it out and put it into the blue van. He repeated this process until all of the guns were loaded and then joined us back at the dining room table.

Julie seemed to be very happy that evening. She told me that she was going to use the cash they were paying her to buy the piece of land that she had her trailer parked on in Naco, a small border town in southern Arizona.

She was a pretty young woman, albeit a little heavy, and her impoverished lifestyle must have made it very difficult to say no to the easy money. She seemed to be a genuinely nice person and someone I would have liked to be friends with in any other setting.

I had finished counting the money and was now completing the #4473 Julie had filled out. After I got a "proceed" on her background check, I finished filling out her receipt. I asked Pedro when these guns would be loaded and he asked Omar in Spanish.

"*Esta noche*," said Omar. I gave Omar a thumbs-up sign, which he returned.

"Yeah, don't worry, Mike," said Pedro, "these guns will be in Mexico before you wake up tomorrow morning."

Julie, still smiling, got up and thanked me, and then she and Omar said goodnight and turned towards the door. As I walked with them, I noticed that Pedro was lingering behind. He was not going to leave with them. It worried me—Omar now had the weapons, and the cash was still sitting on my dining room table. Was this the night Pedro had been ordered to kill me? He seemed nervous.

"Do you remember the first time I came out here with Diego?" Pedro asked me. "The guy that had the T-Bird with the NY Yankees logo on it—he's my nephew. I was talking with him last night and he said that Diego's thug roommate, Santos, told him that Diego got stopped by the DEA or something and that they asked him all sorts of questions about guns."

"What?" I looked at him with disbelief. "No, oh shit no." I pretended to get angry and I clenched my teeth and raised my voice.

"But Mike, I think he was just making a joke. It's been a long time since Diego has been around and nothing has happened yet."

I took a deep breath. "No, it does make perfect sense. Think about it, he knows that you're still buying guns. Why wouldn't he come over and ask for his money?"

"I dunno. I think they were kidding, you know, joking."

"That little prick. If he's working for the cops I'll fucking shoot him!"

Pedro looked down at his feet. He wasn't a killer and didn't want to be responsible for someone else's death, even Diego's. But for me, this development was perfectly choreographed and would draw any suspicion regarding future arrests away from me and put it on Diego.

"Look," I said slowly, as if I was trying to formulate a plan that would save us both, "call your nephew tomorrow and see if you can get any more information. Find out if Diego is still in town and where he's living. Do you know if he's still working at the same place?"

"Yeah, I think so. I know where he lives—in a trailer park by the airport."

"That fucker," I snarled as I slapped my hand on the table.

"I'm sorry Mike, I'm sorry."

"Well, there's nothing we can do about it now. Let's see what your nephew has to say tomorrow and then we'll make a plan. But this worries me a lot."

"Yeah, me too, I didn't get much sleep last night."

"Shit." I tried to look disgusted and would not look Pedro in the eye. He wore the look of a child who knew he was in trouble and kept looking down at his feet, ashamed. I intentionally said nothing that might ease his discomfort.

Pedro started gathering up his guns. He had two .38 Supers and a couple AR-15 pistols. He started to pick up a Rock River Entry Tactical AR-15 rifle but the case was empty.

"This one is supposed to be mine too," said Pedro.

"No, Omar already packed it. Remember I handed you the case and said to put it where it's separate from Omar's stuff? He must have packed it with his stuff."

Pedro opened his cell phone and called Omar, who had now been gone for less than ten minutes. He talked briefly and then closed his phone.

"Is he going to come back?"

"No, I'm going to go over to his apartment right now to get that gun. It is for José."

I helped Pedro carry his load out to his truck. "Give me a call tomorrow about Diego, OK? I'm very worried about this."

"I'm really sorry, Mike." He said that he would call me the next day with more news. But I knew that there would be even more news to come that evening.

I walked back inside and turned off the Hawk and the transmitter. I also turned off my digital recorder and installed the ear mic so I could record the phone conversation I knew I would be receiving shortly from Pedro.

Lopez walked through the front door a few moments later.

"They stopped Omar but he bolted. They're still looking for him right now. But they did get the girl."

I could tell that he was excited.

"If Pedro comes back, try to turn on your transmitter and the Hawk, OK?"

"He's heading over to Omar's right now," I said.

"Are you shitting me?"

"No, Omar accidentally took one of the rifles Pedro bought for José."

"Oh shit. Well, this may add some validity to things. Let's see what happens. Is there anything else important that I need to know about?"

"He told me that his nephew told him that Diego was stopped by the DEA and asked a bunch of questions about guns."

"Seriously?"

"Yep," I said.

"That's beautiful," said Lopez. He obviously realized the implications and timing of this news. "I'll probably send one of the other guys over here to pick up the Hawk and transmitter later, OK? And make sure you record the conversation if he calls. If you don't mind, could you please burn a CD with tonight's meeting?"

I downloaded the conversation and burned it to a CD for Lopez. Then I started doing the paperwork that always followed one of these huge transactions. I had to complete and fax the Multiple Disposition form to the ATF West Virginia office and the Tucson office and I also had to complete the back of the #4473 that Julie had filled out. Then I had my own inventory and detailed sales ledger to complete. I also needed to take some digital pictures of the money, the bag they brought it in, the #4473 form, and my receipt. I took high-resolution pics so the agents could blow them up and read the serial numbers. It was just an extra measure that would cover us if a piece of evidence got destroyed or lost.

About ten minutes after Lopez left, Pedro called me. "Mike, you're gonna be mad. I just went by Omar's apartment and there's a bunch of cop cars there. I almost got caught."

"Do they have Omar?"

"I don't know."

"Did you see his van?"

"Yeah, I saw the van in the parking lot. I could see that they had Julie. But I couldn't see Omar. I called him a couple times and he didn't answer his phone."

"Goddammit," I growled. "Don't call him anymore. If they have him they'll get your number on his caller ID."

"I'm going to throw this phone out anyway. Wait, hold on. Omar is calling me right now."

I stayed on hold for approximately four minutes. Fuck it, I hung up and started on my paperwork again. I knew he'd call back.

A few minutes later my cell rang and I activated the digital recorder again.

"They didn't get him. He ran through the wash."

"Where's he at right now?"

"I think that he's like at Golf Links and Prudence."

"Are you going to look for him?"

"Yeah, I think I'll go look for him right now."

"Pedro, be very careful," I said sternly. "If you see the helicopter with its light, don't go anywhere near there, *entiendes*?"

"I understand. What should I do with the guns in my car?"

"Go home and hide them at your house. It will be tomorrow before anyone comes to see me. At this point there is nothing to tie Julie to you. Do you understand? You didn't do any paperwork tonight so there's no reason for them to arrest you."

"That's good. Julie doesn't know my last name."

"Good, I'm sure you won't have any problems tonight. Call me tomorrow and let me know what's going on, OK?"

"I'm really sorry about this."

"It's OK, Pedro. I know how to talk to these cops when they come to see me. I did everything legally and Julie passed the background check."

After I hung up, I called Mando on his cell phone, knowing that Lopez's phone was not working. I told him what Pedro had said.

Lopez called an hour later. "Good work tonight. We have Julie in custody and she's cooperating. Omar got away but we're not too terribly concerned. I haven't talked to Julie yet. They took her downtown and she has no idea I've been watching her all night."

I put the cash in the safe and finally took off the Kimber pistol that I'd worn all evening and rubbed my back where it had made an impression in my skin. Next to my nightstand was a loaded AR-15 carbine with a tactical light attached to it. It was about 1 a.m. before I fell into a restless sleep. What if Omar realized I had set him up? What if he thought he could get the cash he spent here tonight plus the rest of the guns before heading back to Mexico? Even though Morgan is still a very good watchdog she doesn't hear like she used to. I'm going to need a couple really good dogs in the near future.

The next morning Pedro called at eight and I was still in bed. I turned on the digital recorder that I had left next to my cell phone.

"Omar is already in Mexico," he said. "One of his people came and got him and they went straight to Mexico. I'm leaving later today."

"Call me on Monday. Try to have a good weekend and I'll let you know if there are any problems."

Lopez called me at about 11 a.m. to tell me I'd done an outstanding job the night before. He said he finished interviewing Julie at about two in the morning and he only got to bed around three and was up again at six thirty.

"Oh shit, you must be tired," I said.

I heard him yawning. "Tell me about it." He paused for a second before adding, "I have to tell you, Mike, these guys are very afraid of you. They think you're some kind of badass."

I waited for the punch line, thinking that Lopez was setting me up for a joke. Nothing followed so I asked, "Why are they afraid of me?"

"I guess you've got a good line of shit. Apparently Julie and Omar spoke between themselves on the way over and Omar told her he wanted to do everything he could not to piss you off. You talk tough and you're very believable. Yeah, they're very afraid of you."

Lopez explained that the only reason they did a formal interview with Julie was to throw any suspicion off me. It should have lasted no more than twenty minutes instead of two hours. But after an hour she still hadn't given up any information and Lopez started to get frustrated. He raised his voice and told her all the charges she was facing and she started crying.

"She was sobbing. She said, 'I'll tell you everything, but please, please don't tell Mike. He'll kill us all.'"

Imagine that, I thought—I'd gone from a mild-mannered gun dealer to a rogue international weapons dealer who frightened even cartel associates. I was living *la vida loca!*

I had created an alter ego that these people believed and as far as I could tell, never suspected. I was a dirty gun dealer so obsessed with money that I had absolutely no compunction about selling guns to *narcos*. I had welcomed these criminals into my home and treated them like my best friends. It was a character so far removed from who I really was that it was laughable.

The fact that I was able to hide my contempt for these people and all that they stood for was unbelievable, even to me. I was the kid in high school who never tried pot, the college student who never drank, I never cheated on my taxes, and I always drove the speed limit. Yet somehow, I was able to play the part of a sinister underworld gun dealer convincingly.

My work with the ATF had given me a sense of purpose and I felt as though I was involved in something that would be monumentally historic. The fog of depression that had hung on me so long had finally lifted. And I have to admit that I was enjoying this work and seemed to be well suited for it. The positive feedback that I received from Lopez and the other agents was all I needed to push myself a little harder. I followed orders like a good Marine and never lost sight of our goal to topple a powerful cartel—even if it meant placing my personal welfare secondary to accomplishing our mission.

Jack Hinkley's plan to shut down one of our peripheral players was a success. Omar would never buy guns from me again and I have no idea if he ever had to pay a price for losing that load of guns. I hadn't heard from Eduardo for a while and I was unsure if I would hear from him again. But, understandably, there was some fallout from the justice department regarding the number of guns that were being allowed to cross the border. When Pedro first started buying guns, Lopez would occasionally mention that the Mexican authorities were cooperating on the case. But by the end of summer 2007, he never mentioned them again and I never questioned him about it. As a confidential informant it was not up to the ATF to brief me or include me in case updates. There was no need for them to give me any information other than what I absolutely needed to know to aid their investigation. In fact, doing so could have created a huge liability for them. So, I never specifically asked them about the *Federales* but did make note of any information I could gleam in casual conversation. I was hoping that Jack and Travis would be able to fill in all the gaps for me when the case was over. In the meantime, I tried to work on my journal every day and included as many details as I could remember of my conversations with Pedro as well as with Travis.

It was still too early to arrest Pedro and his friends. The wiretaps for his phone had still not been approved and it was my understanding that this was critical to working their way up the cartel ladder and taking down a kingpin.

Pedro stayed in touch after Omar lost his load of guns. Lopez had me tell him that two agents came out and made copies of Julie's paperwork but that everything had looked legal and they didn't expect any problems. To my surprise, Pedro told me that his cousin José wanted him to start buying guns again and was ready to send him some money. My suggestion was to wait a couple weeks to make sure we weren't being watched and Pedro thought this was a good plan.

A few days later I went down to the federal building to meet with Lopez. He opened his top desk drawer and gave me a stack of bills that had been paper-clipped together. "I'm paying you through July 20, that's $800, and then another $600 for the rifle that we tried to put the transmitter into." I put the money in my pocket without counting it.

I signed the voucher and checked that I had the serial number for the rifle so that I could log it out of my books. Lopez's desk was piled high with papers. I noticed that my file was on the floor and was nearly as thick as any big city phone book. A pair of leg shackles lay next to it. As we talked, I watched a lightning storm as it moved past Picacho Peak, miles and miles away but clearly visible from the eighth-floor office.

"Well, I guess it's a good thing that things are quiet right now. I've been working on the affidavit for the wiretaps and it's sixty-one pages long." He pointed to a thick stack of papers on his desk and rolled his eyes. "It has to go to Washington for approval and then comes back here and a judge signs off on it. At this point, it looks like it shouldn't take long to get the approval. They'd rather we do this than let guns go to Mexico."

"So, once the taps are in place, things should advance pretty quickly, huh?"

"Yeah, I'm thinking that you'll be able to get two more buys out of these guys before we wrap them up. But these taps should give us all of the missing pieces we need."

"I asked Pedro to talk to José to see exactly what they need. But I'm going to talk to you before I order anything for these guys."

"We should be ready to go within a few weeks."

I walked through the security checkpoint in the lobby of the federal building and out into a summer monsoon. The wind was picking up and fat dirty raindrops stung my face as I walked to my car which was parked by the fountain in front of the building. I glanced at my reflection in the windows.

My limp was so noticeable that there was no way for me to hide it. I looked up at the sky and to the east the clouds were black and foreboding—I was about to drive headlong into the storm.

About a month later, Travis called at eleven and asked if I could call Pedro and just give him a heads-up that we wouldn't do any buys for a week or two. I tried calling Pedro on both his cell phones, but he didn't answer. I didn't bother to leave a message but I was a little worried. Had his cousin given him advice to ignore me?

About a half hour later Pedro called me. I hurried to get my digital recorder activated before I answered.

"I just wanted to let you know that those two ATF agents from Tucson came by to see me at the Phoenix show," I said. "They were asking about Julie. You know, has she tried to contact me? Have I heard anything from her? But I don't think I'm in any trouble. These guys were laughing and joking around. They spent some time looking at my guns and wanted to know if I could get them discounts."

"Everything is OK?"

"Oh yeah, these guys are stupid. I think the smart guys go into the FBI and the ones that are left over go into the ATF. Let's give it another week or so before we do anything, OK?"

"Cool, Mike, when is the next gun show?"

I walked over and looked at the calendar on my refrigerator that lists all of the gun show dates. "It looks like the third week of September there is a gun show at the Tucson Community Center."

"Maybe I'll buy just a couple there?"

"No, Pedro there are too many eyes on us there. If you need something come get it at my house OK? But let's wait for a few more weeks."

"Oh, okay Mike. No problem. I'll call you soon to see how things are going. José will need some guns soon."

"Tell José that I got in some of those FN Five-seven pistols he was asking about."

The FN Five-seven pistol is one of the common "bad guy" guns. It is a lightweight, polymer-framed gun with a magazine that holds twenty rounds and could easily be retrofitted to hold thirty rounds of ammunition. They are accurate and have very light recoil. The round it fires is a small-diameter, lightweight bullet which travels at hypervelocity. With the right ammunition, it will sail through bulletproof vests designed to stop traditional handgun bullets. For this reason, the Mexicans nicknamed them the *Mata Policias* or Cop Killers.

I downloaded the conversation and emailed it to Travis. A couple minutes later I got his email response.

Got it . . . thanks for talking up ATF . . . There is always some truth in sarcasm. Take care and I will keep you posted . . . later, Travis.

It was only about forty yards from my front door to the end of my driveway but it seemed like the longest walk ever to pick up the newspaper. It was the first time in fifteen years that I'd made that walk alone. The day before I had to put my dog Morgan down. She was the last remnant of the family I used to have, and I had never felt more alone. I busied myself with picking up dog toys, her bed, food bowls, etc. I cleaned them all and put them away in case I got another dog. With the company I was keeping, I felt I needed one.

A few days later, I adopted a beautiful chocolate Labrador from a local rescue. Fudge was about four years old, short, muscular and had the classic blocky face. They'd been having trouble adopting him out as he had a pronounced limp—the result of a bout of Valley Fever. But his eyes shone with intelligence and I couldn't understand anyone underestimating this animal because of a limp. In that regard we were alike and, to be perfectly honest, I took it as a sign that we were meant to be together.

When the rescue came to do my home inspection they brought him along. As soon as he saw the pool he ran straight for it and made a huge belly flop. We bonded immediately and were best friends in no time. He was wonderfully protective of his new house and let me know whenever someone was near.

I introduced Mando to Fudge as my new guard dog on one of his visits. "Labradors aren't known for being terribly ferocious," he said, rubbing Fudge's ears.

"It's not his job to attack anyone. He only has to let me know when someone is here. I'll handle the rest."

Mando laughed. "Yeah, I can only imagine."

A few days later Lopez called and said they had everything in place and were ready to flip the switch. "The phone company is already set up and we just have to do a couple things internally before we're ready to go. Basically, we're going to have you call him and tell him that you can't do the buy tomorrow. Hopefully, since his load car is leaving Thursday, that will set into motion a bunch of phone calls. Thursday night is when we'd like to have the actual buy."

Well, finally things were rolling again. Lopez told me that he would call back later and have me phone Pedro Trujillo.

At 12:30 p.m. Lopez called and told me that he was ready for me to call Trujillo and put him off until Thursday. I called his first number and had to leave a voice mail message for him. Lopez told me to try his other number.

I told Trujillo that I had to be up north the next day and that the earliest I could accommodate him would be Thursday evening. He called back around five and said that he had talked to José and that Thursday was okay. Lopez's plan had worked, now he had the phone calls between the major players and would be able to match up phone numbers.

Later in the evening, as I drove home from dinner out, Pedro called. He told me that he had just spoken with Eduardo and that he wanted a bunch of guns. "He wants .38 Supers."

"OK, I've got ten here right now. I think half have blued finishes and half are stainless steel."

"I think he wants like thirty, Mike."

"I can get him thirty. If he wants the ten I have, bring him with you on Thursday night. I can order the other guns for him but it's going to be like before—he needs to give me half down as a deposit."

"Uh, okay Mike. I'll let him know."

I smiled. This was exactly what Travis had wanted when he asked me to start bringing up Eduardo's name again in conversations with Pedro. But Pedro was so turned off about dealing with Eduardo that he'd resisted calling him. Earlier in the day I'd asked Pedro if he had talked with Eduardo and told him that I had his shoulder holsters. Pedro replied that he would buy them from me, presumably so he wouldn't have to deal with Eduardo. But I was sure that Pedro could use the money since it had been almost six weeks since we'd done business. Eduardo paid him a $100 commission for each gun that he bought from me. This was the news that I needed, especially since Pedro intended a relatively low-volume purchase for Thursday.

I quickly dialed Travis Lopez's cell number. It was eight thirty in the evening and I was worried about bothering him but knew that he'd want to know about Eduardo. I told him what had happened.

"Excellent," he said, "that's what I was hoping for. Good work as usual, Mike. It looks like everything is going to work out fine. I'm getting ready to leave in the next hour but I'll be in touch tomorrow."

"Are you serious? You're still at work?"

"Yep, I'll be heading home soon. I'll be in touch tomorrow."

Around seven thirty the next morning I received an email from Lopez thanking me for the conversations that I had emailed him. What hours that kid worked!

Pedro called later that evening just as I was about to turn off my computer. He said he would be getting the money from José's people the next day at about noon and would call me when he had the money.

"Eduardo says that he doesn't need any guns now. I think he's scared. I think Maria told him about Omar and now he's afraid something will happen to him."

"Does he still want his holsters?"

"I think I'll take his holsters. I'll pay for them."

"OK, well fuck him then. That's okay Pedro, don't worry about it."

We hung up and I downloaded my recorder and emailed the conversation to Lopez with a brief synopsis.

I received an email from Travis after my morning swim with Fudge.

Thanks Mike . . . we did intercept that one . . . but please continue to send me the recordings . . . thanks and we will see you later . . . someone will be coordinating with you on the equipment. Travis

In the afternoon Mando dropped off the Hawk and transmitter. I invited him in and gave him a soda and we shot the shit for a while.

I expressed my concerns about Pedro possibly getting cold feet and maybe deciding not to come out that night. Eduardo's input might have been all it took to scare Pedro from doing further business.

"Don't worry about it. We've got tons and tons of information, more than enough to get indictments on everybody involved in the case. But I'm worried about them trying to rip you. If they've already decided they're not going to use you anymore, what would stop them from ripping you for $50,000 worth of stuff?"

"Yeah, I think about that too. But I just don't think Pedro is capable of doing it even if José called him and told him I was an informant and gave him orders to kill me. The kid just doesn't have it in him."

"That would be his mistake if he tried," Mando said with a grim laugh. "Don't worry though, we've always got at least four guys with M4s and raid shields outside when you do these deals."

"Yeah, I know but I think that the shooting will be over long before you get inside."

Arroyo laughed again. "Well, we'll get inside as soon as possible so we can drag them outside so they don't ruin your carpet."

I looked at the mauve carpet that had looked so stylish when I bought the house fifteen years before. "Nah, take your time, it needs to be replaced anyway."

Mando told me about the night Omar was arrested. "I was on the tail and once we got around Prudence Street, I radioed the Tucson Police Department guys in a marked unit and told them to get behind them. We had him dead to rights on a failure to yield. They lit him up and I saw him start to slow down. I knew that he was going to bail—I'd seen it hundreds of times when I was a border patrol agent. I pulled around and in front of their van and pulled into the parking lot. Then I heard the radio call that he had bailed out and jumped over the wall into the wash. I was walking back towards the lights and here comes this chubby little Mexican girl running down the sidewalk. I stopped her and asked her what her name was. She stammered and was unable to come up with a name so I put her down on the curb." Arroyo chuckled as he mimicked the waddling motion of a fat girl running.

"Travis did the interrogation that night and I gotta tell you, he's a natural. He was getting so pissed off at her. It took him almost an hour of solid hammering before she flipped and started giving up names. She gave up Joaquin and Omar first. Travis asked her if she was absolutely certain that she had told him everything she knew when she pulled your receipt out of her bra. Travis was ready to explode. She started crying and said, 'Please, please don't let Mike know I told on him—he'll kill us all.' That girl is scared to death of you."

It was funny to hear Mando's account of the story. I had thought that maybe Lopez had embellished it a little. Before Mando left I gave him a stack of gun and police magazines that had accumulated on my dining room table to read during his stakeouts.

But Pedro never made it that night. He called and let me know that he did not yet have the money. He said that someone in Tucson owed his cousin a large sum of cash and that they were supposed to deliver it to him soon.

I lost track of the number of times Lopez had me call Pedro over the following ten days to see if he had gotten his money yet. Each call would generate a series of calls from Pedro to his cousin and those calls not only gave the ATF the details of the drug dealers in Tucson that owed José money, but also the inner workings of his organization. The ATF found out that José was cash poor as he had harvested his last crop of marijuana but had not yet brought it to market.

Finally Pedro got some money and we arranged to meet at 6 p.m. By six thirty Pedro was still a no-show. I stood by the front window, determined not to let him catch me by surprise so I could turn on the Hawk video and transmitter. Around six forty I was just about to call Pedro when Travis called.

"Pedro and Maria are on their way. Maria was having a little trouble getting the money. They were talking about bringing Eduardo with them but from what I heard it doesn't look like he'll be coming."

That made me happy. I wouldn't have to deal with that little asshole that night, but I'd still be getting his money. As I was talking to Travis, I saw Mando drive by. He made a couple laps through the neighborhood and finally parked where Lopez normally parked. A little later he sent me a test text message on my cell. It would be a prearranged signal that he was having trouble hearing me through the transmitter.

"Travis, I'm sure that you would have told me, but have you ever heard these guys talking about ripping me?" I asked.

"No, nothing even close Mike and of course we would tell you. To be honest, these guys love you and don't suspect a thing. They were trying very hard to get the money tonight just to save face with you."

Pedro and Maria pulled into the driveway in Pedro's blue pick up at about six forty-five. I hadn't seen Maria since Eduardo had come out for the first time. She was carrying a big leather purse with a shoebox wrapped in a plastic grocery bag. Fudge met both of them at the door and promptly shoved his muzzle into Maria's crotch. Then, excited to have company, he ran in circles in the living room bothering both of my customers for attention. Pedro walked over to the dining room table, lifted his shirt, and withdrew a stack of bills. "I have a problem, Mike. José needed some of the money so I had to give him back $2,000. Now I have a little more than $10,000."

This was a perfect segue way for me. Lopez had wanted me to talk about the guys who owed José the money. "What's going on with those guys? Did they finally give José back his money?"

"No, I think that this money came from Mexico, not the guys in Phoenix."

"José hasn't got his money yet? Does he need me to talk to those guys? I work cheap." I smiled and pointed my finger like it was a pistol.

Pedro shrugged his shoulders and diverted his eyes. "I'll ask him, but only he knows what's wrong with those guys. I got this money tonight from my uncle."

Maria sat down at the table as Pedro pointed out the ten Colt .38 Supers that she would be buying. Lopez had asked me to get her to make a statement saying that the guns she was buying were for Eduardo.

"I have Eduardo's shoulder holsters too."

"Oh, OK," said Maria.

I looked directly into her eyes. "You're buying these pistols for Eduardo, right?"

"Oh yeah, they're all for him. Pedro doesn't want to do the paperwork for us so I'll do it."

Great, that's exactly what Lopez needed. She just implicated herself on audio and video tape.

I handed her the clipboard and gave her some simple instructions to complete it. She gave me her driver's license and I started a receipt for her. Pedro asked if he could start his paperwork.

"What's the matter? Are you in a hurry?"

Maria started laughing. "He's a big pussy! He's afraid there are police outside watching him."

I laughed too. "Well, if they come through that door without knocking, I might get scared and accidentally shoot one or two or three of them." I watched her smile turn into abject horror. It was as if all the blood had drained from her face. She quickly looked down at her clipboard. I could tell my comment bothered Pedro as well.

"So you haven't heard nothing more?" he asked me.

"No, not since those two guys came to see me at the Phoenix gun show a couple weeks ago. I told you they were joking around and asking me if I could get them discounts on guns. I don't think we'll have any more problems. Have you heard anything from Omar?"

"Omar is in Mexico."

"I know but they have phones in Mexico."

"No, I think he panicked. Maybe the cop was just behind him and he didn't use his turn signal; he thought that they were following him."

"How about the other Omar? Have you heard from him?"

"He's still in jail."

"He's up at Florence right?"

"Yeah."

"Have you been to visit him?"

"No, not yet, but I will. He's stupid though, Mike. He held that gun against the girl's head, that's why he was arrested."

"Are you serious? I thought they found the gun when they arrested him for the fight."

"No, he held the gun against her head."

"He's getting out of prison next year," said Maria.

I turned to her, "Are you related to Omar?"

"No, but he's married to my sister-in-law."

"Do you know his girlfriend?"

"I've only seen pictures of her and heard about her," she said, exhorting a catty chuckle.

"See, Pedro," I said, "women are nothing but trouble. Be happy with your wife."

Pedro looked a little embarrassed.

They both finished their paperwork and I called in the background checks and finished their receipts.

Maria's purchases were simple. She would take the ten Colt .38 Supers and one Micro Galil AK pistol. It wasn't so easy with Pedro. He knew that he needed the seven FNH Five-seven pistols and, of course, his pimped out Taurus 9 mm that I had special ordered for him. But he had to count and recount his money. Finally he decided on two of the AK-47 underfolders priced at $800 each.

Pedro had stacks of money rubber-banded into $1,000 increments. The trouble was that each stack was made up of different denominations so I had to separate the bills and then run them through the money counter. Fudge stood with his paws on the pedestal and tried to bite the money as the machine spit it out—his fat brown tail swinging from side to side. Maria and Pedro laughed at his antics. "He likes money, Mike!" said Maria.

Eventually I had all of Pedro's money counted and strapped. He had brought $10,200 with him and that covered his purchases. Maria's money was easier to count as it was all $20 bills that had been rubber-banded into stacks of $1,000. "These stacks are coming out perfect," I told her. "Eduardo must have found someone new to count his money."

She laughed. "Yeah, me," she said, implicating herself again. Maria had brought $11,000 but did not have enough left over to pay for the shoulder holsters. "Maybe Eduardo will come to the gun show to get them," she said.

While I counted the stacks of money at the wet bar, I used one of the stacks of money to push the Kleenex box into a better position to video Pedro and Maria as they sat at the dining room table.

Once all of the paperwork and money counting was finished, I sat down at the table and asked Maria how quickly she'd be able to get her guns to Mexico.

"They'll be loaded tomorrow," she said.

"And when will they get down to Mexico?"

"Tomorrow, it only takes a couple hours to get down there."

"You're not going to load these at your house, are you?"

She looked as though I had punched her in the stomach. "No, no, of course not," she stammered. "Eduardo has someone to do that for him." Of course I knew this was a lie because Lopez had told me in May that he watched her from a neighbor's rooftop loading guns into a car in her backyard.

Pedro told me that he would wait until Friday and might actually take his guns down himself. He also asked me if I could deliver the guns to his house next time. "José is afraid that I will get stopped and lose all the guns and his money. I can come over here and do the paperwork and give you the money but then you can bring the guns for me to my house. Is that OK?"

"Yeah, I don't have a problem with that. I will do that as a favor for José."

We carried the guns outside to Pedro's truck. Fudge followed us thinking he was going to get to go for a ride. When Pedro opened the passenger side door, Fudge jumped in and sat in the child's seat. He resisted my efforts to pull him out so I let him sit in there while I talked to the two.

"Okay Pedro, make sure that you use your turn signals and drive the speed limit so you don't have any problems." I noticed that he didn't seem to be paying attention, his eyes locked on the pickup truck parked on the side of my house.

"Whose truck is that, Mike?" asked Pedro warily.

"That belongs to my friend. He's in Baghdad right now doing contract work. The last time he came home on leave his wife gave him divorce papers. He didn't have anywhere else to park it." Of all our conversations, this statement was probably the only truthful one I had made all evening.

Pedro continued to look at the truck. Was he thinking that someone was in it watching him? He seemed extra paranoid.

We loaded the guns in the bed of his truck and said goodbye. I watched as he left. He sat at the end of my driveway eyeing Mando's car for what seemed hours before he pulled out onto the street and left.

There was no doubt that he was rattled and I had to remind myself that the last time he was at my house was the night that Omar and Julie were stopped.

I went back inside and photographed the money with the receipts. Mando rang the doorbell and came in.

"Hey nice work, Mike. I could hear about 90 percent of your conversation inside but when you came outside it was crystal clear."

"Is it just a matter of range?"

"Yeah, we could use an amplifier but basically we're relying on the transmitter for your safety. We'll use the Hawk and your recording for information."

Mando grabbed the Kleenex box outfitted with the Hawk and the transmitter that I'd had in my cargo pocket.

"Lock up tight behind me. I want you and Fudge to be safe tonight," he advised.

I took the money and put it in one of my gun safes and then put Fudge in his crate. I was hungry and left to have dinner at a nearby Mexican restaurant. Just after nine when I returned home, my cell phone rang—it was Pedro. I hurried to the couch to get my digital recorder and struggled to get the ear mic inserted before I answered.

He sounded frantic. "Someone followed me to my house from your house tonight."

"What did you say?" I fumbled with the mic and tried to get the recorder activated.

"On my way home, a gray Dodge Dakota followed me."

"They followed you all the way to your house?"

"No, not all the way, but for a long time."

"Well, the easiest way to tell if you're being followed is to drive into a cul-de-sac and see if they follow you out."

"That's a good idea but I don't know if he was just following me or some guys just said, 'Hey, let's follow that car.'"

"That doesn't seem very likely. Did you ever do that when you were a kid?"

"No, maybe it was just a coincidence. Maybe it was a couple trucks that looked alike?"

Pedro had an odd way of getting very upset about something and then convincing himself that it wasn't as bad as he thought. Like when his nephew had told him that Diego was arrested by the DEA and was now working for them. He had called me all excited and then by the end of the conversation had said that he thought the kids were just joking. Or when Omar was stopped by the cops, he said that Omar had panicked and had probably just forgotten to use his turn signal or something. Now he was saying that the car following him home was probably just a random follow-up.

"Yeah, it's probably just a coincidence," I said. "Cops don't use pickup trucks for work. They almost always use a four-door car in case they arrest someone, they can put them in the back. But I'm more concerned that it might be someone who knows what you do and that you have money and guns."

"I don't know anyone with a Dodge Dakota. Tonight I got the money from my uncle, the same as always."

"If someone was going to rip you they wouldn't use a car you recognize. Can you think of anyone who knows when you get a bunch of money that might try to rob you?"

"I don't know, I will have to think about that. But they didn't follow me all the way to my house."

"Did you get the guns unloaded?"

"Yeah, they are in my house right now."

"OK, give me a call tomorrow and let me know if everything is alright."

I hung up with Pedro feeling a little pissed. This was the second time since I started working with the ATF that a tail was spotted. They were supposed to use a rotating tail with different cars taking turns behind the target. Their ineptitude was amazing especially since I was the one who would have to pay the price for their recklessness. Honestly, I didn't know why they even bothered to follow him. They knew he usually drove from my house straight to his house.

I sent Travis an email asking if he needed me to save the shoebox Maria had brought her money in. I also asked if the Dodge Dakota was one of his guys. I attached my phone conversation with Pedro. He called me a half hour later. It was indeed one of his guys and they called him off the tail a couple blocks before Pedro got home.

"I like how you turned that around on him," said Lopez. "Now he's thinking one of his own associates is going to burn him. I also like how you told him that cops can't use pickups because they don't have backseats. I broke a rib laughing at that one!"

But, just like with the case of an agent shining a flashlight on the license plate and setting off my motion detector lights while I was inside alone with bad guys the first night I met Pedro, there was no apology for their careless work.

I was working a gun show at the Tucson Community Center and late in the afternoon I saw Eduardo and his very pregnant girlfriend making their way towards my tables. I activated my digital recorder before saying hello.

Using his girlfriend as an interpreter, he asked if I had the shoulder holsters that he'd ordered from one of my friends. I told him they were at home.

He asked if I could bring them the next day and I said I would. He turned and spoke rapidly in Spanish to his girlfriend—so quickly that I was only able to understand a couple words.

"He says that he wants to order thirty .38 Supers but his people won't give them the money for a deposit because you had some problems. They're afraid they will lose their deposit."

Trying not to lose my composure, I replied, "*El problemo no es mio.*" I shook my head. "Look, Omar's problems had nothing to do with me. If Eduardo wants more guns then he'll have to give me a deposit. If he wants thirty guns he's going to have to bring me a deposit for $15,000 before I will order them. I'm a businessman, if I don't have a guarantee that he's going to take these guns, then I won't order them. That would be a three-year supply of guns for me." She nodded politely but did not bother to repeat the information in Spanish.

I was disgusted by Eduardo's bullshit. He was obviously trying to place an order without giving me a deposit and was using Omar's problems as an excuse. Yet he had no problem sending his own cousin, Maria, out to buy more guns just a couple days earlier. It made me wonder if he was planning to rip me.

He made his way around my tables and looked at the different styles of AK-47s. He asked how many I had in each style and then said, through his girlfriend, that he would have Maria come out that week on Thursday or Friday to buy twenty rifles. He explained that the rifles had to have the slant muzzle brake on the end for his people. Again, he wanted to buy stuff in stock so he wouldn't have to give me a deposit.

"*Maria es mi prima,*" he said.

I nodded that I understood that she was his cousin. He went on to say that she had bought the ten .38 Supers for him when she was out at the house earlier in the week. He came all the way around the tables to the front where I had the AR pistols. He wanted to know how many I had and then asked if I could send an email with pictures of this gun and the FNH 5.7 pistols. I asked his girlfriend to write down her email address and I then asked her for Eduardo's cell phone number. Travis had asked me to try and get it. Eduardo's girlfriend looked at him quickly. "Why do you need that?"

"I'll need to call him and let him know when I have the guns for Maria."

She spoke to him in Spanish and he told her to give me her cell number. They said that they would be back the next day and I shook hands with Eduardo. I offered my hand to his girlfriend. "I'm sorry I didn't introduce myself earlier. My name is Mike."

"It's nice to meet you, Mike, my name is Charlene."

On my way home I received a call from Lopez. "This investigation has taken a turn. To be honest, I don't agree with it but we're going to try to tie Eduardo and Maria into this deal."

"Why would that be a problem?"

"I just want to arrest Pedro. We've got way more than we need to convict him and I'm not sure what else we need. I'm getting bored with this case. Now, the AUSA wants us to get more on Eduardo and Maria."

I could understand Travis's frustrations. He'd been locked in the listening room since they got the wiretaps rather than out in the field. For a guy like him, that was tantamount to torture. But arresting Pedro, Eduardo, and Maria was a far cry from taking down a cartel. These were the people who Hinkley characterized as mules and I couldn't see how they could climb the ladder to the kingpins by arresting these three.

Travis asked if Charlene was wearing a wedding ring and I had to admit I didn't notice one. I promised to look the next day when they came to pick up the holsters. I told him about Eduardo wanting thee Supers but not wanting to leave a deposit.

"What an asshole! I guess he won't get the Supers then, huh?"

"Not from me." I told Lopez that I had made a tape of the conversation and that I would download the conversation and put it on a CD and give it to Mando when I saw him at the gun show in the morning.

Eduardo showed up towards the end of the day. I had his holsters and the four .38 Super magazines that he had asked me to bring. Each of the Colt pistols came with two magazines but he didn't know that. I took each extra magazine from the pistol box and sold the extra magazines to him at a later date.

I told him that I needed to run to the restroom and left. While I was there, I activated the digital recorder and returned. Just as I got to the tables, Mando called me on my cell and asked if that was Eduardo at my tables. He was up in the blacked-out office that looked over the show floor and had told me earlier that he wanted to get some more pictures of Eduardo.

I lifted the grocery bag with the three holsters and four magazines onto the table. "He just wants the one holster for himself today," Charlene told me.

I was about to explode. "You're fucking kidding me. Are you serious?"

Charlene recoiled and Eduardo got that same stupid look on his face again. I'd had it with his bullshit but I regained my composure quickly.

He looked through the three holsters for a left-handed one for himself. He didn't stay long to chat—he knew I was pissed at him. Every time I had to deal with that guy I ended up aggravated. I hated him but I couldn't let my personal dislike of this criminal screw up the investigation.

A few days later I worked late to finish an article to submit to my publisher in the morning. It was close to ten when I decided to run out to get something to eat. I put Fudge in the backyard and went out to the garage.

My Suburban took up every inch of garage length so my practice was to hit the automatic door opener and walk around the back of the car to get into the driver's seat. The garage door was about halfway up when I got to the car's rear passenger quarter panel and was hit with a tremendous surge of adrenaline and the hair stood up on the back of my neck. I didn't understand what caused it but I didn't hesitate—I ran to the driver's side door, ripped it open, retrieved my Kimber .45 pistol and Surefire flashlight from the console, and ran back to the now-open door.

As I neared the door I could smell the lingering odor of Old Spice aftershave. That was what had set me off.

Just as I spun around the corner, I heard Fudge give an alert bark from the back yard. Whoever was there had just run past him and was most likely now on Fort Lowell Road which my backyard butts up to—maybe 150 yards uphill. I realized I'd never catch him by running through the thick tangle of cactus and mesquite so I jumped in my car and drove up to Fort Lowell Road at least hoping to get a license plate number or see who it was. But the person was gone before I got there.

What was their purpose? Was it a scouting mission to test my alarm or had I unwittingly spoiled a planned rip? Why had Eduardo asked so many questions at the last gun show about how many of each style of rifle I had? Was this Eduardo's bodyguard—the guy that had reeked of Old Spice at that first meeting? What would have happened if I hadn't opened the garage door when I had?

I went back inside, put a .45 on a belt holster, and donned a vest that held multiple AR-15 magazines, a first-aid kit, flashlight, and my cell phone. Then I made a sandwich and as I ate it, I moved through the house with my carbine slung around my neck and blacked out all of the lights. That night, Fudge slept on my bed and we got up several times to walk through the house and yard. I woke up in the morning still fully clothed with my AR-15 draped over my chest.

10

TURNING OFF THE TAP

FOR A COUPLE weeks Pedro called wanting to buy more guns but wasn't able to get the money. With the wiretaps in place, Lopez was able to learn a great deal about the inner workings of Pedro's cousin's marijuana enterprise and before Pedro even called me, Lopez had already learned that he was going to get the money that day.

Pedro and I agreed to meet at 5 p.m. and shortly before he arrived, Mando came to my door with the transmitter and Hawk in its Kleenex box.

I had already laid out the pistols that Pedro wanted on the living room floor. I took the phone stand into the dining room and put the money counter on top of it.

Pedro came to the door alone. He was carrying a paper sack that looked weighty. He had a hard time looking me in the eye. I think he knew I was mad and was looking to make amends for the weeks of putting me off.

I extended my hand and greeted him. He smiled and walked over and put the money on the dining room table.

"How much did you bring?" I asked.

"I'm not sure Mike, maybe $35,000."

I acted annoyed, putting my hands on my hips. "I thought you were going to bring $10,000 extra."

Trujillo hung his head, "I think my uncle is spending the money on other things. Last year he said he lost some money and then suddenly he was driving a brand new truck. José had to confiscate it from him."

"Did you get the money from your uncle today?"

"Yeah, but he's in trouble with José."

Pedro took out several bricks of money that were rubber-banded together. I picked up one of the bricks of twenties, removed the rubber bands, and placed the bills in the money counter.

Many of the bills were in small denominations. I had over $2,000 in $5 bills. These well-worn pieces of currency weren't crisp enough to work well in the counting machine and so I had to count them several times. The largest bills were $20s and I wrapped them in $2,000 bundles.

I held up some of the $5 bills. They were limp as toilet paper. "Do these guys own strip joints or something? Where do they get all of these $5s?"

Pedro laughed. "No I don't think they have any places like that in Caborca."

"Does this money come up from Mexico or from somewhere up here?"

"It comes from somewhere up here, I think."

"Oh, I understand. Stuff is sold up here and that's where this money comes from."

Pedro nodded.

"What's going on? Why are you guys having so much trouble getting money?"

"Oh, it's just the time of year," said Pedro.

Lopez had told me that October and the next couple of months were especially difficult for them because they were harvesting their marijuana crops. They still needed to process the crops, get them into distribution, and then sell them. Everyone in this business is cash-strapped at this time of the year.

"I gotta tell you, Pedro, I'm a little worried. I think I might have to start getting deposits from you. If you stick me with one of these orders it could put me out of business."

"Oh no, Mike, please don't worry. We won't have no more problems. I promise."

I gave him the stink eye to make my point. Of course, it was just acting on my part, as I already knew it would be my last buy with Pedro.

My cell phone rang. The Caller ID said "Restricted" so I excused myself to the living room to answer it.

It was Lopez. "Hi sweetie, how is everything going?"

"Everything is great, how are you?"

"Mando wanted me to tell you that the wire is down. Do me a favor and flip the switch off and then turn it back on."

"OK Susie, I'll take care of that. Don't worry."

"Alright, Mike. I'll talk to you in a little while."

I pulled the transmitter part way out of my cargo pocket, just far enough to see the switch, and turned it off and then on again. The green light started glowing. I went back into the dining room and finished counting the money.

I asked Pedro how Maria liked her job.

"She likes it OK, I guess. A lot of our people work there. My sister, Maria, and another couple cousins all work there."

"That's a neat company. I did some consulting work there a few years ago."

"Yeah, I guess it's OK. Maria needs work because her husband is in prison in Oklahoma. He got caught dealing drugs. Nobody liked him because he was always short on money."

"Did he sell for the guys in Caborca?"

"He sold for everybody, but after a while no one wanted to do business with him because he never paid them for the stuff that he sold."

"Sounds like Eduardo."

Pedro laughed and nodded in agreement.

"That sucks," I said. "Maria has some kids, doesn't she?"

"Yeah."

"Are they babies?"

"No, I think one is like eight and the other is six."

By now, I had finished counting the money and we stacked it. I separated enough piles to cover the thirty pistols he had ordered. Then I made a separate pile of cash to let him know how much extra he had to spend.

"How much are the regular AKs? $500?"

"Yep."

"I'll take four of those."

Fudge followed me into the gym and I'd started carrying all four back into the dining room when my cell phone buzzed. I had a text message. "The wire is down again." In the privacy of the gym, I removed the transmitter from the cargo pocket of my pants and flipped the switch to the "off" position and held it for a few moments. A red light blinked a couple times and then stopped. I flipped it back to the "On" position and the green light blinked. The entire time I worked with the ATF we always used the same transmitter which seemed to work, at best, sporadically. I guessed the agency had better things to spend their money on than something that could protect a CI.

I went back into the house and stacked the rifles next to the pistols. "What else, Pedro?"

"I want one of those nice AKs—you know the American-made one." He was referring to the underfolders that I got from JKF. He also wanted an AR pistol and I returned to the gym where I took the guns from a box along with a thirty-round magazine.

After recording the gun's serial number on Pedro's receipt, I set it down. He pushed another $1,000 bundle across the table to me and laughed. "I have $6 left."

"When are you going to take these guns south?" I asked.

Fudge kept dropping his toy in Pedro's lap. I noticed that Pedro didn't want to throw it because it had dog slobber all over it but he was trying to be polite. "Some will go tonight; they'll be in Mexico before you wake up tomorrow, and I will take some when I go tomorrow evening."

"God, you make me nervous when you do that shit. I wish that you'd just pay someone to take them for you."

"I'll be alright. It's no problem."

"You going to load the cars at your house?"

"Yeah, I feel more comfortable doing it there in my garage." Pedro looked at the door and swallowed hard. "I guess it's time for me to go. I hope there won't be any problems."

I could tell that he was still a little paranoid. I helped him carry the guns out to his pickup. He glanced around nervously while I looked over to Mando's car. Maybe it was just perception on my part but Pedro had the look of a condemned man. He acted like he didn't want to leave.

"Be careful," I told him. "Use your turn signals and drive the speed limit. You won't have any problems. Give me a call when you get home so that I know you're safe."

After he left, I went back inside and turned off all the recording devices. I was arranging the piles of money on the table so that I could take a picture of the cash when Mando rang the doorbell and Fudge pushed his way past me and launched himself into his chest. He bent to give him a rub and came inside.

"Did Pedro give up any good information?"

"Yeah, he said that some of the guns are going south tonight. He'll take the rest of them tomorrow when he goes down. He also said that Maria's husband, his cousin, is in prison in Oklahoma for selling drugs."

"There are a couple federal penitentiaries in Oklahoma. Travis may already have that information. I'll ask him about it."

Fudge kept bringing his stuffed duck to Mando and dropping it at his feet and he would obligingly throw it for him.

I took the transmitter out of my pocket and handed it to Mando who stuffed it down the hole in the Kleenex box. I winced when he did this; Travis had mentioned to me how hard it was to get the Hawk positioned correctly to video through the pinhole.

"You going to make it home tonight, Mando?"

"I doubt it. We need to sit on those guns until they hit the border. Then we'll have ICE take them down. Thanks for everything, Mike. I'll be talking to you soon."

And he was on his way for a surveillance that would go through the night and into the next day.

An hour or so after Mando had left, Travis called.

"Hey, Mike, I just wanted to say thanks. It looks like everything is going to script and I wanted you to know that we could have never made it this far without your help. It isn't often that we let a civilian get this deep into an operation and or have an investigation last this long. Everyone in this office appreciates your hard work."

"Thanks, Travis. That's really nice to hear—you know I'm glad to help."

"I'll keep you posted on the bust and let you know when it happens so you can prepare for Pedro's call. Try to act pissed off at first but then try to calm him down. We don't want him dumping his phone or fleeing for good to Mexico. You know how to talk to him. Keep him a little optimistic. Somewhere down the road we'll give you the message that will sound something like, 'It's getting too hot for me. It was a nice ride while it lasted but I don't want you to ever contact me again.'"

"OK, I understand."

"Right on, bro, I'll give you a head's up when I know something. Have a good night and thanks again."

The next day Lopez called at about nine in the morning. "I just wanted to let you know that that load never went last night. In fact, it still hasn't left."

"Hmm, I wonder if they're going to wait until Pedro leaves and drive together?"

"That could potentially screw things up."

"You'd have to arrest Pedro then, wouldn't you?"

"No, not necessarily, we could just wave Pedro through. Hey, did he mention last night that he got his money from his uncle this time?"

"Yeah, I asked him specifically and he said yes but that he was in trouble with José. He told me that this uncle has lost money before and that José had to confiscate his brand new truck."

"What a dumbass!"

A little while later, Lopez sent me an email that said the quality of the Hawk's audio was not great and he wanted to know if I could deliver a CD of the meeting made from my own recorder? I told him I'd be there after one.

When I entered the antechamber, I saw Travis heading into his office with a fist full of cash. I pressed the doorbell and he rushed out. "Your timing is perfect," he said as he handed me the cash. He put the voucher on his desk for me to sign. My eyes quickly searched for the amount on the paper and it read $1,500.

"I was just heading out the door to join the surveillance," he said. "That load car never left last night so now it looks like they'll leave this afternoon. We'll follow it all the way down to the border and then ICE will do a random inspection on it."

I looked at Travis—his pupils were like pinpoints yet he acted like he was full of energy. But he was also jittery. It seemed like the kind of energy you get from caffeine, nicotine, and sugar. He had a wad of tobacco in his mouth. I asked him if he got any sleep the night before.

"Yeah, I left here around midnight and got up at about five."

I felt a couple fingers in my back and heard Jack Hinkley say, "Give me all of your money." I turned and Hinkley extended his hand to shake. He also looked tired and a little disheveled. I guessed he must have also been out all night on the surveillance. "Has Travis given you the game plan? Do you know what to do?"

Travis said that he had already briefed me but Jack felt it necessary to rehash the material. He had just started, when he received a cell call. He looked at the caller ID. "I have to take this." He stepped into the hallway for his phone conversation.

"He's going to tell you the same things I already told you, so just pretend like it's the first time you've heard it," Travis said, rolling his eyes. Then he started laughing. "We were just laughing about you. I was telling Jack how you were selling the bad guys back their own magazines that are supposed to come with the .38 Supers."

I batted my eyes. "Now that you know me as well as you do, why would that surprise you?"

"Oh it doesn't buddy, believe me."

"I hope that you don't mind, but I took the sock off the transmitter and rewrapped it. Mando put new batteries in it and when he was finished it looked kind of monkey fucked."

Lopez shook his head, "You know, it's the little shit like that that gets on my nerves. It's always the little things . . ."

"That's OK, I fixed it. I'm sure Mando has plenty of redeeming qualities that make up for it."

"Oh yeah, Mando's a good guy. Don't get me wrong. But we work in such close quarters . . . I'm sure I get on his nerves too sometimes."

It was easy to imagine—the office space was designed for one person but had two desks crammed into a ten-foot by eight-foot space.

Jack came back into the room from the hallway. He was still speaking on his cell phone. "We're planning on having ICE stop them at the border and take them down. Mike Detty is here. Geez, it's not bad enough that he robbed those poor Mexicans of all their money but now he's down here with his hand out again." Jack laughed good-naturedly and I extended my hand, palm up and he slapped it. He was apparently talking to an assistant US attorney assigned to the case.

Jack ended his call. "Look," he said to me, "sometime later today Pedro is going to realize that his load car has been taken off. When he calls you, I want you to get pissed off. Forget about his problems. Ask him if his driver knows your name. Ask him how his guy could be so stupid as to get caught.

But after a while, I want you to tone it down. Take on a paternal tone—you know how to talk to this guy. Tell him that you think it's going to be OK."

"Is there any chance that the ICE guys will miss him?"

"Oh Jesus Christ," said Lopez, not relishing that possibility. "Sure that can happen. Stranger things have happened in this case but I think that we'll be able to get him stopped. That's why we're following him down to the border."

"Any idea on when you'll bust Pedro?" I asked.

"No," said Lopez, "it could be anywhere from two weeks to two months. We don't want to rush it because we'll still be getting good intel from his phones."

"Well, I'm sure that once you get him in custody he'll roll for you in record time. Even if it means his cousin will kill him."

"Yeah," said Lopez, "I expect he'll flip easier than Diego."

"Yeah, Travis had a really hard time with that interrogation," Jack said with a chuckle.

"I told him that we were investigating gun trafficking," said Lopez, "I asked him if he knew any dirty gun dealers. He squirmed around and looked at the floor and said, 'Ah geez, he's such a nice guy. I hate to give him up. His name is Mike Detty. I can take you to his house if you want.'"

All three of us laughed hard.

"Pedro will have the opportunity to help himself out after we arrest him," said Jack. "We took a vote yesterday as to whether or not we should arrest him. It was 7 to 1—I voted not to arrest him."

For a moment I thought he was serious and then I realized he was pulling my leg. If only it was that easy—let's take a vote to see who we're going to arrest.

"How about Eduardo?" I asked. "Anything new with him?"

"Well," said Lopez, "the good thing is that his girlfriend works at the university so she'll probably have her baby at University Medical Center. Then we'll be able to get Eduardo's information off the birth records."

"Yeah, Charlene sent me an email a couple days ago asking for my cell number."

"We have her email address?" Jack asked.

"Yeah, Mike forwards all of their email communications to me."

"That's great," said Jack. "When we get the warrants to go up on their phones, we'll be able to see who she's emailing too."

It was rewarding to see Jack and Travis so excited about the upcoming arrest. Their script was playing out exactly as planned. Despite the obvious repercussions for me, I was excited too and somewhat relieved to see this case coming to a conclusion.

I was at home working on my notes when I received this simple text message at 6:45 p.m. from Lopez. "Got him."

I went to bed around midnight without hearing from Pedro. It was the first night since the previous spring that I turned off the air-conditioner and slept with the windows open. Fudge launched himself off the bed several times during the night and started barking. The first couple times I took my Surefire flashlight and rifle to investigate. I couldn't find anything and I wondered if he was barking at coyotes. In any event, it was a restless sleep.

The next day was a beautiful day in Tucson and the weather had finally broken. Fudge and I spent a couple hours enjoying the pool and Jacuzzi. It was about 2 p.m. when Pedro finally called.

I turned on my digital recorder and listened to his breathless explanation of what had happened. He told me he saw in his rearview mirror his guy being pulled over for a secondary inspection.

I played the conversation exactly like Lopez and Hinkley had told me. I got mad, asked if his driver knew my name or anything about me, and then took a protective tone telling him that things may not be as bad as they seemed. By the end of our conversation, I'd managed to calm Pedro down and told him that it would be weeks before any law enforcement came out to see me. He promised to call me when he got back to Tucson the following week and I told him I'd let him know if I heard anything.

And that is how they turned off the tap on the flow of guns that crossed the border—at least from this investigation. Pedro would call me several times a week in the following month or so and ask if I'd heard anything.

"Maybe we'll get lucky, Mike. They still haven't called you about Omar's gun, right?"

"That's right. We may never hear another word about this."

I'd forward these conversations to Lopez. At one point he emailed me back, saying, "He definitely turns to you for comfort. He has got to be the most optimistic person in the world."

On October 15 Lopez called to tell me they had just intercepted an interesting conversation between Pedro and his wife. "He apparently thinks there was a camera somewhere in his garage."

"What? Are you serious?"

"Yeah, I guess he thinks that's the only way that someone could have figured out what he's doing."

I smiled. Apparently I was a better actor than I gave myself credit for. For someone to suspect that government agents had surreptitiously slipped into his garage and secreted a bug, instead of suspecting a middle-aged gun dealer who still wore a military haircut, was astounding.

"Do you suppose he's tearing all the drywall out of his garage right now looking for that camera?"

Lopez barely laughed. "I don't know. But if he calls you, try to turn it back on him and ask him a lot of questions about the guy that got arrested. Tell him that shit only happens on television. He is definitely getting hinky."

This poor kid was coming apart at the seams. The anticipation must have been eating Pedro alive. "I bet that when the handcuffs get slapped on him it'll be the first time he'll be able to truly relax since they took out his load driver. He's trying to reassure himself, but I think that he's had the feeling for quite some time now that his luck was going to run out."

And it wasn't just Pedro's luck that was waning. My nemesis, Eduardo, was beginning to experience some bad luck too, though it had absolutely nothing to do with me or the ATF.

Mando called me one day while I was driving to a gun show in Phoenix. We talked about guns for a while and then he asked if Travis had told me about Eduardo's problem.

I wondered why Travis hadn't filled me in but that was his nature. He told me what I needed to know but was guarded even about that.

"One of Eduardo's neighbors at the leased property noticed a horse trailer out by the guest house. The neighbor had no idea that the house has been rented to Eduardo and Charlene. She reported a suspicious vehicle to the sheriff's department. As a deputy walked up to the trailer, two guys bolted through the door and into the desert. When he looked inside, he found about three thousand pounds of drugs."

"The leafy kind or powdery stuff?"

"It was pot. We figure he lost between five to six hundred thousand dollars. Retail would have been around a million. I guess it's just a cost of doing business."

"Is Eduardo hanging out in Mexico?"

"Nope, he's at home."

I couldn't believe that because they knew Charlene leased the property and it wouldn't take long for the sheriff's office to get back to her. "I would have thought that he'd be laying low in Mexico."

"Nope, it's business as usual for him. Just goes to show—most people think these kind of stash houses are only on the south side. But it can happen in any neighborhood."

It boggled my mind because that neighborhood was very close to mine. It was an upscale area with many houses costing between half and three-quarters of a million dollars. Those families had absolutely no idea that Mexican cartels were using their neighborhood as a staging point to spread their poison throughout the United States. They lived their American dream completely oblivious to the fact that a criminal drug trafficking organization was pursuing their own perverse version of the American dream just down the block.

As oblivious as the neighbors were of this cartel presence in their neighborhood, Eduardo was equally unaware of those watching him. He had yet to suspect that he was being watched, followed, and listened to.

I was driving home from a business appointment in Phoenix when Lopez called me. "I'm on a surveillance right now and thought that I'd take the opportunity to call you with an update. Have you talked to Mando today?"

"Actually Mando came out to my house with Joey Pequeno."

"Did he say anything about Eduardo?"

"No, not really. I told him that I was waiting to hear from you about what you wanted to do regarding the next buy and whatever email you wanted me to send."

"What we're thinking right now is that we'll let this wire expire in a couple weeks and not do another buy. We have a couple reasons for doing that but probably the most important is that if we do a gun buy and he gets busted, you'll be the last person he sees before getting arrested and we want to insulate you from that. I'm not sure if Mando told you, but he lost a shipment of pot at the property Charlene leased."

"Yeah, he told me. But how is it that Eduardo hasn't hightailed it back to Mexico? Doesn't he know that someone will come looking for him?"

"Based on his phone conversations, he thinks someone followed him up from Mexico. He doesn't have a clue but he's not really hinked up too badly. But we were on surveillance of his house yesterday and we saw a sheriff's office guy go up to the front door for a knock and talk. Fortunately, he and Charlene weren't at home."

"Why wouldn't he think that was going to happen? I mean Charlene signed a lease and a huge load of pot was found on their property."

"Well, apparently the lease was an unwritten thing and the owner was out of town. The sheriff's office finally got hold of the owner and that's why they were doing a knock and talk. But we got hold of them and let 'em know that it would screw up our investigation."

"Looks like you had luck on your side for once."

"Yeah, no shit. By the way, they found his Beretta and shoulder holster in the trailer. What type of shoulder holster was it?"

"It was a left-handed, black leather Aker holster."

"Yep—that's what was recovered. We have a bunch of text messages between him and Maria saying how he had to run through the desert and almost got caught."

"That's a nice piece of evidence, huh?"

"Oh yeah! Now we have drug charges that we can lay on him."

"Are you glad now that you didn't arrest him a couple months ago like you originally wanted to?"

Lopez paused for a moment. "Hmm, maybe only in the regard that we can now load him up on drug charges. I'm not sure that what we've gathered in the last couple months has been worth the wait. I can't wait to get off these fucking phones and back into the field." And then he added, "I'm going to tell you something but I want you to keep it to yourself, OK?"

I sensed that I was being sworn to secrecy and was about to learn a piece of information that Lopez probably shouldn't share with me. "Sure," I said.

"Eduardo is banging Maria."

The news took my breath away. After all, they were cousins. I laughed. "Get the fuck out!"

"I'm telling you straight."

"Travis, I've got to tell you—I've sat a couple feet from Maria and as a bachelor, I looked at her from every angle, and there was just no way . . ."

"I know what you mean. That day she came up to the office with Omar's wife I got a pretty good look at her. Ughhh!"

We both laughed at their expense. Eduardo's girlfriend, Charlene, was an attractive woman in her early twenties and this news would devastate her. I heard the crackle of a radio and then Lopez spoke for a few seconds before coming back on the phone with me.

"Before I go, I want you to know that I've put you in for a reward. If we can bust these guys and confiscate some dope money, it will be a substantial amount. I mean, don't expect a ridiculous amount—I didn't want these guys to laugh at me when I put in for it. But I think you'll be happy."

"Ah, that's great Travis. I really do appreciate it." I was afraid to even ask or get my hopes up after my experience with Jodi.

Earlier, I had spoken with an assistant US attorney who told me they gave six-figure rewards to drug addicts who don't give them information anywhere near as good as the information I was giving them. And they didn't have to assume the risks I'd taken either.

The money would be a Godsend to me. I had just found a surgeon who was doing complete ankle replacements and she thought I was the perfect candidate. But it would involve six months of recuperation for each ankle. There was no way I could go that long without working—I just didn't have the savings. Maybe I could live on this reward money while I recuperated from the much-needed surgery on my ankles.

Lopez also said that they might have me disappear from the gun show circuit for a while. At least until the heat was off me. He said the government would take care of me during that respite. I allowed myself to fantasize briefly about a life without pain and the ability to be as active and productive as I used to be.

Lopez interrupted my day dream, "I have to apologize for the last couple of months. Our budget is tapped out and we have some CIs who didn't get anything. But we want to make sure that you're taken care of. If we can confiscate some money from these guys then it won't come out of our budget."

"I only have one favor to ask of you."

"What's that, Bro?"

"I want to see the video tape of Charlene's face when you play the recording of Eduardo and Maria having phone sex."

Lopez laughed. "Maybe we can interview her in the room with cameras. This will destroy her—she is so whipped on that guy. She's head over heels in love with him and he's out fucking Maria. In fact, he's been fucking Maria since after the baby was born."

"Didn't you tell me a while back that you were going to have a marked Tucson PD car stop Eduardo for his ID?"

"Yeah, we did. They stopped him and he didn't have any ID on him so they followed him back to his house and he showed them some sort of Mexican identification. His real name is Eduardo . . ." Lopez paused, he was obviously weighing the risk of telling me his last name. I said nothing . . . waiting . . . "His last name is Quijada."

That was big news to me. In all my conversations with Pedro I'd never heard him slip and mention that name.

At a gun show in January 2008, I noticed a couple of Hispanic gentleman looking at guns and speaking in Spanish. The shorter and much pudgier of the two, who looked to be in his early thirties, pointed at numerous guns. I didn't think much of it until his partner came back a little later by himself and told me that he needed to buy several guns. He was young and had his hair pulled back into a ponytail. He wanted two AR pistols and an AK pistol and a Beretta .380. I nodded and handed him a clipboard and asked him for his driver's license. I asked him if he would be paying cash and he said yes.

It was obvious to me what was going on. I casually asked if the guns were for him. "Yes, these are all for me." I learned his name was Jorge Perez and he completed the #4473 in a very short time.

I called it in and there was no delay in getting a proceed response from NICS. I wrapped the two AR pistols in butcher paper and packing tape. I told him that his neighbors would think that he brought home some fresh fish. He chuckled at that. I told him I wanted to do everything possible to keep him from getting any extra attention. I leaned forward and asked in a hushed voice, "How many guys do you have here with you?"

"Three counting me."

"Good, listen I can only make these recommendations but it is up to you whether or not you want to do them. I would suggest that you split up the guns between yourselves and leave separately. That way you won't attract any attention."

He smiled and nodded. He reached into his stylish leather jacket and removed a wad of $100 and $50 bills and paid me the $3,200 owed.

I put a business card in with each gun. "Look, if your guys need more guns just call me at this number. I'll take care of you at my house so that there aren't so many eyes on us, OK?"

"I'll definitely be calling you," Jorge said with a smile. "Thanks for your help."

The following day I passed the paperwork on to Lopez and the day after that Jorge Perez called me and said that he needed at least another dozen guns. A day or so after that I got a call from someone named Manny identifying himself as Jorge's boss and asking me to come to Nogales Sonora for a business meeting. "Mike," he said, "I'll guarantee your safety and I'll make sure you have a good time. I have some beautiful women here that want to meet you."

It was after hearing this recording that Jack Hinkley requested I come down to the federal building for a meeting.

On February 7, 2008, I drove down to the federal building for my appointment and arrived about fifteen minutes late. Travis was printing some papers at the glass window next to the antechamber. He opened the door and welcomed me in. I could see that he had a picture of Jorge Perez sitting on the printer's tray already.

"Man, it seems like a hundred years since I've been up here," I said.

"Yeah, no shit, huh buddy?"

Lopez took me into his office. Mando was on the phone but quickly ended his call and came around the desk to shake my hand. The small office became cramped with all three of us standing when I felt another body trying to squeeze past me. It was Jack and he had grown a goatee since I'd last seen him. "Hi Mike, we're going to have a meeting in just a minute and go over some things, give me just a minute, OK?"

I nodded as Jack took Travis's arm and led him out of the room. I guessed that Jack was already trying to steer the conversation. That was fine by me, I accepted that there were certain things I needed to be aware of.

In their absence, I chatted with Mando about the SHOT show. The Shooting Hunting Outdoor Trade show was an annual industry get-together with firearms manufacturers. It was a chance to see what was new in the industry and visit with old friends. I had been in Las Vegas the week before and Mando was unabashedly envious of my trip. I had someone take a picture of me standing next to a rack of Perazzi over-and-under shotguns—the cheapest of which cost $188,909. Mando wondered out loud who could own such a gun.

"Someone like Pablo Escobar or a sheik," I said.

"Yeah, you're probably right. I don't think anyone ever shoots these guns. They're for show."

Lopez motioned for us to follow him. I passed Petey's office and he let out a whoop and waved. I found a chair in the corner of Jack's office and Mando and Travis settled in. I noticed that there were still no pictures on the wall and asked Jack if he was getting ready to leave.

"I can be out of here in five minutes Mike. I like it like that. That's why I never put up any pictures. I could literally fill a box in five minutes, leave my gun and badge on the desk, and I'm out of here."

Mando and Travis chuckled. Of course, Jack was kidding but in a way that one could tell that he fantasized about it. I noticed the coffee table in front of me had seven huge three-ring binders stacked one atop the other. The stack had to have been twenty-four inches high.

Jack pointed at the binders. "There's the fruit of your labor, Operation Wide Receiver."

It was the first time I'd heard this investigation called by its code name. I learned later that Jack named it in tribute to Lopez—the rookie agent who played college ball but also ran the largest case ever handled by the Tucson office.

"And those are just the phone logs. Believe it or not there's twice as much material that isn't in here. We're getting ready to put it all on a hand truck and wheel it across the street to the AUSA."

"It seems like this case went on forever and it's still not over," I said.

Jack nodded. His facial expression changed and he looked down at his desk. I could tell that he wanted to be serious. "Mike, I want to tell you that we appreciate everything that you've done for us. I know that sometimes we go too long in saying this but there is not one agent in this office, one person in the Tucson Police Department that has been involved with this case and the agency itself that doesn't appreciate and admire what you have done. Without sounding like Pollyanna, I can tell you that everyone respects you for the danger that you've placed yourself in and the way that you've handled yourself throughout the case. You have earned the respect of veteran agents, me, and the bureau too."

I felt my cheeks blush. Jack was very good at back-patting and I knew that it was merely a motivational thing on his part but his words did move me. He had said the things that I'd often wondered about. Was what I was doing being appreciated by anyone or did these people consider me to be just another expendable CI? If what he was saying was true then it felt like my efforts had been worthwhile.

I smiled and looked Jack directly in the eye. "Thanks Jack, that really does mean a lot and I appreciate you saying that." The tone had grown too serious so I looked at the other two agents and said, "By the way, how do I rank as a CI?"

Before the other two could answer Jack snapped back, "Just average." We all laughed.

"This last case was very important to us," said Jack, "and we think that we can do some real damage to the cartel with what we have. But first and foremost is your personal safety. We don't want to do anything that will increase your chances of being hurt or becoming a target of violent action. You're just getting too hot and, believe me, we don't want you to have to move. We don't want these new guys to find out where you live. With that in mind, Travis and I have sketched out a scenario for this new case."

"What Jack and I planned on doing," said Travis, "was having you make an introduction to the new guys. At some point we'll tell them you don't have the juice to get them the numbers they want but that you have a friend who might be able to help them."

"Yeah," said Jack, "we'll tell them that this kid, Travis, used to work for you and that you taught him the ropes but that what they want is very dangerous and that you're too old and too close to retirement to help them. It's our hope that they take the bait and that will deflect suspicion away from you."

I looked at Travis, smiled, and said in a paternal tone, "You OK with this? Have you talked with your wife about going undercover?"

He nodded and smiled. I chuckled. "You haven't even told her yet, have you?"

"Oh no, I told her and she's fine with it."

"God almighty, she must hate my guts—all the shit that I've got you into."

"Yeah, Mike Detty—Shithead Magnet. Don't worry about my wife, she's a very cool lady."

We all shared another laugh. "Well as long as we have Mrs. Lopez's approval," I said, "I suppose that we're good to go."

We discussed my original meeting with these new guys and subsequent phone calls while Mando took notes for the Report of Investigation. All investigations had a starting point and this was it for the new case. There was much discussion about how to hide my involvement and how they were to write their reports to protect me—excluding both my name and my CI number.

I asked Lopez if he had found a property for the warehouse. He told me that he had and it was right off the freeway. "The bad guys should like that for access. Just load up their trucks and get on the highway."

They did in fact lease a warehouse and outfit it with secreted video cameras and microphones. The ATF even issued Lopez a conditional federal firearms license so that sales wouldn't have to be routed through my company.

After meeting with the Tucson ATF office, I received a couple weeks of phone calls and requests for pricing on guns and was given some unbelievable anticipated quantities from Manny. Several times we were supposed to meet and on each occasion our plans fell through.

And then nothing. Weeks passed without communication and Lopez finally had me try to call Jorge. There was a recorded message with a woman's voice asking to leave a message. Mando explained that dope dealers often give their phones away to anyone on the streets when they suspect problems. Apparently that's what happened with Jorge. I also tried calling Manny and received a message that his phone was out of service. I'd never hear from either of them again. Perhaps they were smart enough to Google my name?

It seemed unfortunate that so much time and money had been spent getting ready for an investigation that went nowhere. But that didn't mean I was having problems finding criminals or them finding me.

There are few women who attend or work at gun shows, so when an attractive woman comes into a show she gets a lot of attention. When she wears tight fitting jeans, high heels, and a low-cut blouse, she'll get even more notice.

I saw Bambie when she first walked into the gun show. Heads turned wherever she walked. Eventually she found herself at my tables. She picked up one of the AK-47 pistols and asked the price.

"That model is $600."

"Wow, that's a good price. I may need to buy two," she said. "Will you give me a discount?" She leaned forward and put her hands on the table, letting her ample breasts nearly spill out of her top. "I'm sure there's something we can work out," she said. Her lack of subtlety flummoxed me.

"Are you sure that an AK pistol would best suit your shooting needs?"

"Oh yeah, I already bought a camouflage outfit. I think it would be cool if my shooting buddies saw me show up tomorrow with one of these in each hand."

I laughed at the mental picture she created. "What type of work do you do?"

She smiled, batted her eyelashes and said, "I'm a dancer."

"Where do you dance? I'll come watch you sometime."

"I don't dance at a club. I do private dances. Maybe I can dance for you sometime?" She let her gaze drop from my eyes to my crotch and let go a throaty purr.

For a moment I was powerless—her dark eyes had me captivated. She shifted her weight from one hip to the other and I made an audible gasp and she giggled.

She cocked her head slightly. "Let me look around. I'll probably buy these two guns, OK?"

I nodded, still unable to speak.

After a half hour or so I wondered if she had left and asked one of my helpers if they had seen her. He turned and pointed and said that she was sitting down at Estevan's—another gun dealer—tables. I could see her long styled mane cascading down her back.

Minutes later she was back at my tables ready to do business. I handed her a clipboard with a #4473 to fill out. I learned that she was forty-two years old and was born in Cuba but was now an American citizen and her last name was Dominguez.

After I finished the receipt, called in the background check, and collected the money, she asked if I had a business card. I handed her one from a stack.

"That's my personal cell phone number and email address. You'll be able to reach me at either."

"You'll be hearing from me. I still want to dance for you."

After she left I walked down to Estevan's tables and asked if she had bought guns from him also. Estevan told me that her boyfriend had filled out paperwork for an AK-47 pistol but his background check had been a deny. I was unaware that she had been there with a man—I didn't see them walking together and he was not at my tables with her.

I had already planned on forwarding Bambie's information to Lopez but now I knew that it had been a straw purchase. On my drive home from the gun show Bambie called me and wanted two more guns just like the other ones she'd purchased. She wanted to come to my house to pick them up.

"Please let me come out tonight. I'll give you a freebie."

I wasn't sure if I had heard her correctly or not. "I'm sorry, what did you say?"

She paused for a moment. "I'll give you a freebie."

Of course, I already knew that she was at the show with someone who couldn't legally purchase a gun and I couldn't let myself get set up to be ripped. There was no way that she'd be coming to my house.

"Sorry, Bambie, but all of my inventory is at the show. I don't have any more guns like the ones that you bought but I'll have more coming in a week or so."

She promised to call me later in the week and on Monday morning I forwarded her information to Lopez.

On March 12, 2008, Bambie and I arranged to meet at a closed tire center behind Park Place Mall on Tucson's Eastside around 4:30 p.m. I'd had a Marine lunch with several other guys who were also in the Marine officer program, at the University of Arizona, some twenty-five or more years earlier. We'd eaten at La Placita Village in downtown Tucson and the federal building was just a block or so away. I walked over to pick up the transmitter from Lopez. There was no need for the Hawk but I would use my digital recorder to record our conversation.

I got to Park Mall right around 4 p.m. and beat everyone else there. Travis called me while I was on my way. He told me to meet him at the old Firestone tire shop that was on the southwest side of the mall. He also said a Tucson Police Department undercover officer would meet me there as he was still a few miles away.

Lopez must have developed some very important information on Bambie's boyfriend because he told me that if he showed up, they would take him down in the parking lot. "Mike, if we do that, we're going to take you down too, OK?"

"That's fine—I think it will make things look better. Should I take off my gun?"

"No, absolutely not! You need to be able to protect yourself. This guy is a serious Shithead. He just got released from prison a few months ago. Just do what you need to and when we get to you, put the gun down and put your hands in the air so we can see they're empty. We'll introduce you to the troops but we don't want one of the TPD guys accidentally shooting you. But, you feel alright having her boyfriend get in the car with you?"

Of course I didn't, especially after what he just told me, but I couldn't tell Travis that. "Sure, you guys will be pretty close. I'll be fine."

I had already put on my Kimber Ultra .45 in its Fobus paddle holster. It was in the small of my back. My outer shirt covered it. But after he told me about Bambie's boyfriend, I took the Kel-Tec P32 in its paddle holster out of my console. I put it butt-forward on my left side. Even if this guy grabbed my right arm or incapacitated it, I'd be able to get this pistol in action with my left hand. While I waited for Travis, I rearranged my truck—folding down the rear seat behind my driver's seat. That way I wouldn't have to worry about this felon being directly behind me out of my view. He'd be forced to sit behind Bambie and that would make me a whole lot more comfortable.

A couple minutes later my cell phone rang and it was Trevor Summit, the TPD officer. He asked me if I was wearing a green shirt and khaki pants and explained that he was in an old gray Mustang with blacked-out windows that had just driven by. He pulled in next to me and got out.

Trevor had a goatee down to his chest and long hair. He looked much younger than he was. He was athletic-looking and seemed pumped about the evening's activities. "Travis told me what you looked like and gave me a pretty good description, but your 5.11 pants gave you away."

I laughed as I shook hands with him. "Yeah, I have a military haircut and wear clothes like these. You'd think these guys would have a clue, wouldn't you?"

"Nah, that would be giving them too much credit." We both laughed.

We stood and talked for a while before Travis showed up. Trevor was a former Marine and U of A student too. He seemed like a genuinely nice guy. I'm sure that the reason he was so friendly was because Travis had already put in a good word for me. He told me to wait around after our transaction was done so that he could retrieve the transmitter and give it to Travis later. He also gave me advice on what to do if they took down my car.

"Mike, as a guy that has been taken down, and as a former SWAT officer, the best advice I can give you is to relax and go with it. Don't fight it and you won't get hurt. Our guys will know who you are and won't purposely slam you on the asphalt. I'll be watching things from the surveillance room. You should move your truck. I can tell right now that this tree right here will block the view from the video camera."

I saw Mando drive by in his tinted-out car and then saw Travis in his Jeep. Trevor hurried to get to the surveillance room and I got back in my car. I never did have a face-to-face meeting with Travis at Park Mall but he called me several times. He had me move my car a couple aisles away and positioned his Jeep so that he could watch my truck through a heavily tinted side window. I backed into a spot without any cars on either side of me. Once I was settled, I heard him contact the other agents and officers on his radio and then he had me get out of my car so they all could see me and know that I was a "friendly."

"If something bad happens, Mike, just yell help and we'll get to you. Petey, Joey and I will be the ones that come running—just so you know."

At about four thirty-five Lopez asked me to call Bambie. A guy answered my first call and was muttering as he handed her the phone, and then it was disconnected. I called back again. This time she answered and I told her that I was out and about—currently at Park Mall and had her guns with me. She told me that she needed to go to the bank and that it would take her between a half hour and an hour to get to me.

"Well, I can't wait an hour Bambie. How about if you can't make it in forty-five minutes, we'll do it some other time because I have other things to do."

"Oh no, I can be there in forty-five minutes. Please don't leave without me."

I relayed the information to Travis. They had units outside her house and I could hear his radio crackling with news of people leaving the house and vehicle descriptions. At this point all we could do was sit back and wait.

About a half hour later Bambie called me to tell me that she was about twelve minutes away. I asked her what she was driving and she said an older Pathfinder that was tan. I asked her if she was coming by herself and she said that she would have the kids with her.

I was relieved. It looked as though I wouldn't be thrown face down into the asphalt that evening.

A few minutes later, Bambie called me. Apparently she was unfamiliar with which way was north or south and was driving around Macy's looking for me. I finally saw her and waved until she saw me and pulled up next to me. She had a boy that looked to be about nine and a little girl of maybe eleven with her. Both shot poisoned looks at me while mom pulled up next to me. Bambie got out and ran over to my car, admonishing the kids that she didn't want to hear a word from them while she was with me. She opened my passenger side door and leaned in—almost as if she was going to kiss me. She was wearing a gauzy top that could barely contain her breasts. I extended my hand and shook hers.

"Do you have my guns? Are they the pretty ones with wood like the others?"

"Yep—they're exactly like the other ones that you bought the last time."

"Can I see them?"

"Sure," I said. I exited my driver's side door and moved to the back tailgate where she met me. I opened the box and showed her the guns.

"Good, they're beautiful, and the magazines? They are in here?"

I showed her the thirty-round magazines and the instruction booklets that were packaged with each of the Century International Champion AK-47 pistols.

We got back inside my car. "OK," she said, "what do I need to do? Fill out another paper?"

"Yep, I'll have you fill out the same paper as before and then I'll call in the background check."

She filled out the #4473. It was easy to see that she had done this many times before. She answered the questions without reading them.

"OK, I have to ask you this," I said. "You are buying these guns for yourself, right?"

"Yes, they are for my personal collection," she said in a manner that seemed too well rehearsed.

"OK, now that we have that out of the way, I want you to know that what you are doing is OK with me. If you need more guns, that's fine with me. But I need to know where they're going so I can try to smooth things over if the police ever come to me."

She was adamant. "No these guns are for me only. If I sell them to someone, I will do all the paperwork to do it legally."

"Alright, that's cool, but if your guys need anything just make me a list, OK?"

"Do you have three of those guns?"

"Nope, just the two that you looked at."

"But you have more right?"

"I have more but not exactly like those. The other ones I have are more expensive but they are nicer."

"When we're done here, can I come over to your house to get it? Please."

"When we're done here, I have to drive over to the west side of town. Sorry."

"How about tomorrow?"

"I might be able to do it tomorrow. Give me a call around noon, OK?"

"No, you call me around noon and we can meet here." She smiled and cupped one of her breasts. "When am I going to dance for you?"

"Oh we'll do that soon enough." I laughed to myself knowing that we were being videotaped and how Trevor Summit must be laughing up in the surveillance room.

Once she finished the form, I used my cell phone to call in the background check. She was one of those people that required a "further review" before clearing—probably because she was born in a foreign country. Still it only took a couple minutes to get her cleared. She had started counting out the money—all in $20 bills—while I was still on the phone with NICS.

"Mike, please take $100 off of the price, OK?"

"I'm sorry I can't. I just don't have the margin to discount, sweetie. But you're going to get this money back anyway when you dance for me."

She smiled and batted her eyelashes. "You can't give me $100 right now so I can go shopping for something today?"

"Sorry babe, I just can't do it."

Once I had the money, I walked to the back of the car again and got her guns for her. She picked up the box and carried them to the back of her

Pathfinder. I helped her open the door as she struggled with her keys. I told her that I would call her the next day.

"We can meet here from now on," she said. "Like we're doing something illegal." She gave a hearty laugh and then said, "You're cute!"

"So are you," I said as she pulled out.

I pretended to be dialing a number on my cell phone while she drove away. I watched Petey, then Joey, and finally Travis pull out after her. I sat for a few minutes until Trevor Summit came to pick up the transmitter. He was also in a hurry to join the chase. It made me wonder exactly who Bambie's boyfriend was and what he had done. It was neat to see those guys get so excited. I think for the most part they were all adrenaline junkies that needed a regular fix of adventure. To be completely honest I felt the same way.

The next day Travis called at about 8:00 a.m. on his way to work and he really sounded tired.

"Hey man, did you get any sleep last night?" I asked him.

"Not enough, that's for sure. We ended up taking them down at her house. We've got her, her boyfriend, and his brother in custody."

"Good! Is everybody safe?"

"Yeah, things went exactly as planned. It couldn't have worked out better."

"You didn't shoot the kids did you?"

"No, we didn't shoot the kids," said Lopez, laughing. "I told her that she'd have to call someone to come and get them and she said that she didn't have anyone. I told her I would just have Child Protective Services come and get them. Guess what? She found someone right away."

"I'll be out and about today. Is it OK if I come down and drop off the #4473 and CD? My fax line is still screwed up."

"Oh, that would be great. In the meantime can you email me the firearm's information?"

"Sure, it will be waiting for you when you get there."

At about 11:30 Travis called me again. "It hasn't been a good morning, Mike."

"Uh-oh, what's wrong?"

"Ah, this fucking assistant US attorney is causing problems. They put the guns in the trunk of the boyfriend's car last night and we had to obtain a search warrant to get the guns out. Now the assistant US attorney refuses to seal the search warrant, which means that your name will be out there."

"Are you fucking kidding me?"

"I'm serious as shit. I'm sorry, Mike."

I felt that sinking feeling again.

"I wanted to run this past you but I can't make the decision for you. Either your name gets exposed as the informant or we drop the charges and cut this guy loose."

"That's it? There's no middle ground? What does Jack say about this?"

"Oh, he's really pissed. In fact he's on the phone right now trying to get some answers. Would you like me to have him call you?"

"Yeah, I think that would be a good thing. I mean, I just don't understand enough to make a decision on the fly."

"Hey, no problem, Mike. I'm sorry about this and I just want you to know that whatever you decide I support you on."

Less than five minutes later Jack called. "I can't apologize enough. This is not the way this is supposed to work and for the life of me I can't understand why it's happening this way. What I can tell you is that I have already called the assistant's boss and they have already made one change. We need them to make another to protect you and I'm still waiting to see if that will happen."

"I just don't understand this, Jack. I'm putting my neck way out there and brought you a good case and the assistant US attorney doesn't care if I get shot? Does she know who I am? Does she know that I'm not just some dirt bag trying to get my sentence reduced?"

"I made that very clear to her. As it stands right now, we have been successful in sealing the search warrant. We also want to take your name out of the reports and we're waiting to see if that will happen. The way it reads right now, it would be too easy for them to figure it out."

"I'm going to have to rely on your judgment on this one. I mean it doesn't make sense to let me get shot on this deal when we still haven't got our indictments on the other case that we've worked a year and a half on."

"I understand and agree with you wholeheartedly, Mike. Let me call you back in a few and see if we get the changes we need. We wanted to be aboveboard with you and let you know exactly what's happening. Believe me, you won't hurt anyone's feelings if you tell us to drop the charges."

"I wish that I could say that I'm not worried, Jack. But we both know this is a dangerous guy and that AUSA is putting me at risk for no good reason. It wouldn't be logical for me to assume this risk for this case."

I felt better after that phone call. Jack seemed to be going to bat for me. It just seemed so senseless for our team to put me in a position like that. I had never met that assistant attorney nor did I know her name but I had already developed an intense dislike for her.

Jack called again a short while later. "I just wanted to let you know that I've got you on speaker phone with Travis here in my office. I spoke with the assistant's boss and he agrees with us and has decided to make the needed changes. As it stands right now, the search warrant is sealed and as far as the reports are concerned we call you the FFL [Federal Firearms Licensee] and they read as though we questioned you about who bought the guns and you provided us with documentation. I really don't think this will come back to you. He's done prison time and has been out a short period but this will send him back for significant time. This really is an impact crime, Mike. If you hadn't come to us with this information this guy would have continued to buy guns all around Tucson and do who knows what with them. Taking this guy out of his game is very important and this is a good catch. I'm glad that we were able to make them see things our way."

"I guess when I brought this one to you I was hoping that it would turn into something bigger. Do you have any indication that Bambie or his little brother will give up info that will turn this case into something bigger than a "felon in possession" case?"

"Last night when we took them down his little brother invoked his right to a lawyer right off the bat," said Travis. "But it is my impression that he's just afraid of saying something in front of his brother. We're going to bring him over a little later to see if he'll talk."

An hour or so later I went to the federal building to drop off the CD and #4473 and rang the bell to get in. Travis opened the door and greeted me with a sheepish smile.

"Why is it that you always have trouble with women?" I asked.

"Fucking cunt," he said referring the assistant US attorney. "I just can't figure out what she's thinking."

"Does she know me? Maybe I went out with her once?"

"Nope, she's just being a cunt. I told her that there was no reason for the search warrant not to be sealed and she was like, 'Oh right, like these guys don't know who snitched them out.'"

"Are you serious?"

"Believe me, when we interrogated these guys they had no idea. The chick started flipping out and screaming and when she did, I opened up my cell phone and said, 'OK, that's it—arrest the gun dealer.' Then she really started screaming. She has no idea that you're the guy that fingered her."

"What about her boyfriend?"

"He's convinced that they were watching him all day and that it has something to do with a rape investigation. He thinks that somehow we just stumbled across the gun buy."

"Sweet! Now you said that he was in the parking lot while she bought the guns?"

Lopez nodded.

"That's scary. How far away was he? Should I have noticed him?"

"No, in fact if our guys hadn't followed him from home we wouldn't have noticed him either. He was about one hundred yards away from you, close to Macy's. When she finished with you she was on the phone with him and he was right behind her on the way out. By the way, if either of these people call you, put it back on them. Tell them that the cops stopped you and handcuffed you for a couple hours before they let you go and that they took all of your paperwork."

Mando, Petey, and Joey walked into the office and broke into smiles when they saw me. "There he is," said Petey, "the most dangerous person in Tucson."

I was sitting down between Mando's and Travis's desk and with them in the room, it was really packed.

"None of these guys have heard about this morning's developments," said Travis.

The three looked at him quizzically while Travis explained that the AUSA steadfastly refused to seal the search warrant until Jack called her boss and straightened it out.

The four of them all shook their heads.

"The problem is that they think we work for them," said Travis.

And I could see that would be a tough attitude to deal with. When you have a title like "Assistant US Attorney" it would be easy to see ATF special agents as submissive minions. She apparently had the need to assert herself. So what if it gets a CI killed?

"That's quite a woman you brought us, Mike," said Joey Pequeno.

I laughed. "Did you hear her telling me she wanted to do a private dance for me?"

"Is that what she was saying? I heard her whispering something but I couldn't make out what she was saying."

"Yeah, you'll have to look at the video; she was cupping her boob and telling me what a good time we were going to have."

"Holy shit, you're a nut," exclaimed Pequeno.

"She was a trip to interview," said Mando. "She talks a mile a minute."

"She was like that all night long, ranting, raving, and laughing hysterically," said Travis. "She thought it was all a big joke. Typical fucking Cuban attitude. 'Why are you picking on me when you could be out arresting real criminals?' I have to tell you, Mike, after they got her out of her street clothes and into a T-shirt and scrubs, her tits were hanging down to her waist—not a very good look."

"I don't care," I said, "I still want to see them. Did you have the feeling that her behavior was chemically influenced?"

Mando and Joey both nodded. "Oh yeah, without a doubt," said Lopez.

"Then she should be having a pretty bad day today, huh?"

The other four nodded again.

I recognized her purse sitting next to Lopez's chair. "Did you find anything interesting in there?"

"No, nothing really, other than a receipt from Estevan's Guns. She went there a couple days after the gun show and they sold her the same AK pistol her boyfriend got denied for."

"Seems to fit the classic definition of straw purchase, huh?"

"Guess who'll be getting an audit," said Lopez. "As a matter of fact we've already been watching Estevan for a while."

I wish that I could say that this was the last time that an AUSA from the Justice department threatened to expose me as an informant. Sadly it was not.

11

JUST WHEN I THOUGHT I WAS DONE

PRESCRIPTION DRUGS THAT I'd been giving Fudge to treat his Valley Fever and allergies had burned a hole through his stomach lining. He was slowly bleeding to death and it was agonizing for both of us. By the time his vet figured things out and performed last-minute surgery, it was too late. I was alone again and heartbroken over losing that wonderful dog.

Beyond losing a cherished friend, I'd also lost an invaluable piece of my security system. Without those extra sensitive ears and sharp eyes, I was on my own and needed to be vigilant.

Within a week my contact at the Lab Rescue called and told me that they had a one-year-old male chocolate Lab in Phoenix they wanted to drive down for me to look at. He was badly underweight and had been picked up roaming the streets. The humane society was having trouble adopting him out as he wasn't a puppy, and the Lab Rescue stepped in when he was scheduled for euthanasia. His name was Champ and it looked as though he was also part Irish Setter. He came into my house, ran circles through the rooms, came back to me, gave me a lick, and climbed into my lap. It wasn't until the rescue ladies left that I discovered he wasn't house broken.

It didn't matter—I was happy not to be alone anymore. He was house broken in a week and I let him start sleeping on the bed with me so I would wake if he jumped off to investigate a noise in the night. He became my brown shadow. But he was also unlike any other dog I've owned. He didn't like to play. Champ wouldn't chase a ball and ignored Fudge's old retrieving dummies. He was a great companion but he needed a doggie buddy to play with.

A month after Champ joined me, I called the Rescue again. I told them I was looking for an older, more mature female. Bigger, if possible, and maybe even a little alpha so that she could teach Champ some doggie manners. I was in luck. They had just received five-year-old Maya from a family going through a divorce. She was as white as a polar bear and big, weighing over one hundred and ten pounds. She possessed all the traits I was looking for and then some. Their personalities complemented each other and together they made an awesome security team. Nothing got past those two and I was starting to sleep better at night even though Maya also slept on the bed and snored worse than me.

I'd still not heard anything from Lopez regarding when Pedro Trujillo might be arrested. It had been almost six months since his load car was taken down at the border. Lopez blamed the AUSA on the case, mentioning that he was promoting himself for an appointment to US Magistrate rather than working on getting the indictments for the case. I'd never met this AUSA but I hated him for letting the case go so long without prosecuting it. Jack Hinkley had told me, "We handed them this case on a silver platter with a nice ribbon tied around it. There was nothing left for them to do other than convene a grand jury and issue the indictments."

But for me, it was business as usual. There never seemed to be a shortage of those wanting to make easy money by taking guns to Mexico.

In May 2008, I was at a gun show at the state fairgrounds in Phoenix when I was approached by a young Hispanic man towards the end of the day. He wanted to know if I would eat the tax on a sale if he bought two rifles.

"I'm sorry, I just don't have the margin to eat the tax," I said.

"Well, would you be willing to take $10 off each rifle if I bought two?"

I learned that he was twenty years old and his name was Gilberto Moreno. As he completed the paperwork for two of my cheapest rifles, he added, "Hey, you know what, Father's Day is coming up. Let me have another one of those rifles."

As soon as he said that, a young man filling out a background check on the other side of my display said, "Yeah, that's right. Let me have another rifle too."

As one of my workers grabbed another rifle for his customer, I asked the young man in front of me if he knew the other buyer. "Yeah, that's my friend Miguel Sancho, we both played high school football together."

Both background checks went through without a problem. A third individual showed up just as I was completing the sale. He was carrying two long gun cases that he had purchased from another dealer. Before they left, I motioned to Gilberto to come closer, and spoke to him in a hushed tone.

"Look, it's no secret that there are cops out in the parking lot. If they see three young Hispanic guys carrying six rifles to your car, you'll get some unwanted attention."

Gilberto nodded and looked at me intently.

"I'd suggest you leave some of these rifles here and walk out separately—one at a time with not more than one rifle. Sit there a minute and look around before coming back in."

His eyes grew bigger and he smiled a toothy smile, "Ah, I knew it. You're cool. Thanks man."

I leaned over my tables and handed him a business card. "Look, if you need five or ten or even twenty rifles give me a call, OK? We'll do it at my house in Tucson where there won't be a lot of eyes on us."

The next day a very similar-looking young man came to my tables and said he'd like to buy an Olympic Plinker Plus. I handed him a clipboard with a #4473 form and he handed me his driver's license—he was obviously familiar with the drill.

His name on his driver's license was Antonio Moreno. "Is Gilberto your brother?"

He nodded and smiled. The resemblance was unmistakable. They were handsome kids with million-dollar smiles, well built, muscular and athletic, and clean-shaven and had no tattoos. They were also articulate and polite and I had to assume were the product of good parenting. It was a damn shame they were getting involved in obvious trafficking.

As Antonio was filling out the form, he said, "You know what? Father's Day is coming up—why don't you give me two of those?"

I laughed to myself and wondered how many times he and his brother had used that same line this weekend.

I thanked him and gave him the same safety speech I gave his brother. I also gave him a card with my number and email on it. Sadly I knew that I would be hearing from those kids again.

Early Monday morning I made a call to Lopez and explained what happened. He asked me to fax their paperwork and said he would check to see if they were already being watched. If not, he'd open the investigation.

Lopez called me later in the day and reported that the Moreno brothers and Sancho had been buying guns all over the Phoenix valley but nobody had reported them. I was relieved when he told me I would not have to work with the Phoenix ATF office again.

Antonio called me around 9:30 a.m. and asked if he could come to my place and pick up "at least five more guns." Now I was in a quandary. He said that he was just leaving Mesa and that would put him here in two hours. I took a deep breath and told him to come on down and call for directions when he got into Tucson.

I called Lopez as soon as I hung up with Antonio and explained the situation. To my relief he was OK with what I had done.

"Just hang tight, Mike, and I'll see if I can round up the troops."

Lopez called a while later and told me that he was in position. I looked out the window and could see him sitting in his Jeep at the usual spot.

"I don't have a transmitter for you today so if you have a problem, just run out the front door or something."

I wondered if the hunk of crap transmitter had finally given up the ghost. It still amazed me that they couldn't find the money to buy a handful of new transmitters.

While I waited for Moreno to arrive, I set out some guns in the living room on display. I put out the most popular guns that Pedro, Eduardo, and Omar had been buying.

I called Antonio at about twelve thirty to see where he was at. He told me that he was "sitting behind a huge accident on I-10 and that he would call me as he got closer to Tucson. I relayed that info to Travis—afraid that he'd be upset with me and my spur-of-the-moment surveillance with tardy criminals.

About half an hour later Antonio called me and I gave him directions to the house. He called once again when he was about to turn onto Ft. Lowell and then again as he pulled into my driveway. I turned on my digital recorder, put it in the knife pocket of my 5.11 pants, and walked out to greet them.

Antonio and Miguel were in a white late model Pontiac—not something that I would have guessed these youngster gun traffickers would drive but I could see that it was in good shape and well taken care of. Its windows were darkly tinted.

Inside I showed them the collapsing stock of the M4 rifles and explained that this seemed to be a very desirable feature for my customers "down south."

"In fact," I said, "the Olympic guns were not that popular with my other customers south of the border. They're just too cheap."

"These guns aren't going south," said Miguel. "They're staying right here in the state."

I looked him in the eye and held the stare momentarily. "That's a shame," I said, shaking my head slightly. "These guns can't come back to me if they make it to Mexico. The *federales* don't cooperate with the ATF. If these guns turn up here, it could be a huge problem for me. Look, I've been playing this game for a long time and I've never had a problem so I must be doing something right. I'm cool with it. In fact, I have other customers in Phoenix that never buy less than twenty rifles at a time."

Sancho looked away quickly but said nothing. He was being very careful, trying to choose his words precisely. He didn't want to admit to anything or give away any information.

"Look," I said, "talk to your guys and see what kind of guns they want. Right now it is getting harder and harder to get guns." I pointed to the stack of Olympic Arms Plinkers. "Those took me six weeks to get in."

Antonio seemed very surprised. "I've seen some other guys at the gun shows with those rifles."

"They get them from me," I said matter-of-factly. "That's why they are more expensive on the other dealer's tables."

Moreno knew I was right and that their prices were quite a bit more expensive. I explained to him that I get the best prices by buying in distributor quantities.

"Where are you guys going from here? Nogales?"

"No, we're heading back to Mesa from here," said Moreno.

"Oh," I said feigning surprise. I let it go at that, I didn't want to push them too hard on our first meeting. I helped them carry out the eight rifles and put them into the back seat of the Pontiac.

As I handed a rifle case to Sancho, he said, "Do you know who is sitting over there in the silver Jeep?"

My heart leapt into my throat. I looked over his shoulder directly at Travis to let him know that he had elicited some attention sitting there with his windows rolled up and engine idling.

"That car belongs to the house right there. They have like six girls and they're all home from college right now."

Moreno popped his collar. "Really? How do I look?"

I laughed. "Dude if you want to poke a fat red-headed chick then you look fine."

They pulled out of the driveway as I hurried inside. I opened the closet door just inside my front door and grabbed an AR-15 carbine with an ACOG scope and moved just a few feet to my picture window. The chevron aiming point bounced with every heart beat as I watched as Moreno pulled his car up even with Lopez's. I held my breath, would the door pop open with Lopez drawing down on them? Would their door open for a confrontation? After several seconds their brake lights went out and they continued on slowly around the bend.

I dialed Lopez's number. I heard the familiar crackle of the radio before he even said hello.

"Did they spot me?" he asked.

"They asked about the car. I told them that it belonged to the neighbors. Did they give you a bad look?"

"I don't think they saw me. I slid down pretty far in the seat."

"That's good." Just then I noticed a white car coming back behind Lopez's Jeep. "Look out they're on your six."

After a few seconds, Lopez said, "Nope that's not them." It was an older couple driving slowly through the neighborhood. My heart rate finally started to slow. I put the carbine back in its rack in my closet.

An hour or so later Lopez called me to say they were driving fast and erratically so they decided to call the tail. They were, however, heading south not north back to Mesa.

The next couple weeks I received a few phone calls from Antonio asking if I'd received any more of the cheaper rifles. At one point he called and asked if I could get a .50 Barrett rifle for him. The .50 Barrett rifle fired the same bullets that the US fighter planes used in their machine guns during WWII. It was a popular rifle with military snipers who have used it to make kills more than a mile away and its devastating power is enough to disable any vehicle. At the time they retailed for about $8,500 each.

But he never did order one from me. I left for a week's vacation in Cabo San Lucas and when I got back Antonio called me and said he needed guns right away. Lopez had already told me he was taking some time off on Wednesday so we would need to do it the following day. When I forwarded the digital conversation to Lopez he said that it was perfect timing and he wanted to put a tracking device on their car.

Just before Antonio was due to arrive, I backed my car out of the garage in an attempt to block Antonio from parking his car where it would be visible from my front room so that Lopez could attach the tracking device without being seen.

Lopez had brought Doug Molson with him. He was the one who called me the night Rey Ayala got busted. I remembered that Travis had told me that they both went through their initial federal law enforcement training in Glynco, Georgia, together. He looked to be about forty, thin and athletic, and also a dog lover. That was a good thing because Champ and Maya swarmed them both trying to crawl into their laps. All I could do was swat at them and apologize.

The plan was for them to wait in the gym when Moreno came and to attach the tracking unit a couple minutes afterwards. One of them would be the watch—if one of the two came out of the house and headed towards the car, he would intercept him and ask if I was at home and pretend to introduce himself as a new neighbor.

We went into the gym where I unlocked the side door and the security steel door. Doug had brought a laptop computer with him and I noticed that Lopez had a small protective case that held the tracking device. Molson went outside to orient himself and test the gate to see how loud it was.

At about seven forty-five Antonio called and said that he was having some problems with the heavy traffic and that he would be late. I told him that I absolutely had to be out of the house by ten and that if he thought he'd be later than that that we would have to scrub it for the day.

"Hopefully I will be there by nine forty-five," he said. "I'll give you a call when I get to the edge of town."

I hung up and gave the bad news to the two agents. Travis immediately got on his radio and told the rest of the agents that they were going to be late. I had thought that Lopez and Molson were alone and asked Travis how many people were out on this job. He did some quick adding and said there were seven other agents.

Lopez left Molson with me and went out to talk to some of the other agents. We had almost two hours to kill. Doug showed me the tracking unit that attached with magnets and took maybe thirty seconds, at most, to attach. He then opened his laptop to show me how it worked.

"The tracker uses GPS and pings the cell towers it passes," he said as he showed me the route they had taken from the federal building downtown.

He flipped between a map that showed the street names to one that showed geographic landmarks like the Agua Caliente Wash near my house.

I noticed that along the route there were a number of closely grouped pings. "I guess there are a lot of cell phone towers in that area."

"No, we were actually adjusting the pings—we can do it anywhere from every fifteen seconds to once an hour. Right here, we had it set at fifteen seconds."

I was thoroughly impressed with their cool gadgets. Lopez came back and we sat in the living room where I would be conducting the deal. Lopez had brought a new Kleenex box in which he had cleverly and neatly cut a flap at the bottom of the box where the Hawk's switch could be activated. He placed it so it was facing the table where I would do the paperwork. He left the transmitter on the table for me. It was the same old worn-out unit that never worked properly.

Just then Moreno and Sancho pulled into the driveway and the two agents hastily made their way into my gym. Sancho carefully inched his car around my Suburban and parked it directly in front of the garage. I activated the transmitter and digital recorder and walked out to meet him. Lopez had asked me to check the car to make sure that no one else was in it.

Miguel and Antonio met me and followed me inside. They both looked much bulkier, like they had gained some weight and been lifting weights non-stop.

"You look like you've been working out."

"No, I wish. I haven't worked out in over a year."

I had the seven rifles they requested laid out on the floor inside with the cases open so that they could see each rifle was complete. They looked at them quickly and said that they liked them.

"How did your guys like the last guns?" I asked Miguel.

Both kids bobbed their heads and said that they were fine—no problems.

"Right now I have enough money to buy six rifles," said Miguel.

"Just six?"

"If I can get these six now, I guarantee that I will come back for ten more."

"OK, I have them—it's not a problem. But I'm going to be out until about four today."

"That's OK," said Antonio, "we'll come back sometime between four and five."

I nodded in agreement and asked who would be doing the paperwork. Miguel took the clipboard from me and started filling it out.

I took his driver's license and completed the receipt. Antonio sat on the couch against the west side wall. I was afraid that he might be able to see the guys in the driveway and asked him if he wanted to join us at the table. He waved me off and continued to play with his cell phone. It didn't take long to complete the paperwork.

Sancho struggled to pull a fat roll of bills from his pocket. They were all $100 bills.

"How many do you have there?"

"Go ahead and count them—there should be forty-eight."

I pulled the cover off my electronic money counter. It elicited an exclamation of "Cool" from both kids. It counted their bills in just a second.

"Yeah, I had to buy this counter last year. One of my customers thought he'd be cute and short me $5,000."

"Man," said Sancho with conviction, "the last thing you do is screw around with somebody's money."

I smiled. "I was going to shoot him but then his boss sent him back to buy a bunch more guns. He's an asshole but he hasn't shorted me since then and I got my money."

Sancho and Moreno looked at each other. I would have loved to hear their conversation about this topic when they left.

I started to close the rifle cases but Sancho told me they didn't need them. "Can we leave them here?"

"Sure, I'll get rid of them for you."

With that he started to grab a couple rifles, and I worried that it might be too soon. Had Travis attached the tracking device yet?

"You know, let me go out and take a look around. I have one neighbor that is a real busybody and it could be a problem if he is out doing yard-work. Give me just a second, OK?"

I walked out the front door and out to the garage. Lopez leaned around the corner and held his hands up as if to say, "What's going on?"

Just then I heard my front door open and turned to see Miguel heading towards me. I gave a quick hand signal for Lopez to hide again and started talking to Miguel in a loud voice.

"I don't see him out here, Miguel. We can probably load those guns without any problems."

Sancho got his cell phone out of the car and followed me back inside. My cell phone started ringing and I answered it at the threshold as Sancho and Moreno started gathering up guns to take to the car.

It was Travis and he said that he had not yet put the tracker on. My wire wasn't working and he couldn't hear anything in the gym.

"Can you keep them in the house for another couple minutes?"

"No, I don't think so Susie," I said. "I'm just finishing up with my customers but they're going to come back for some more stuff between four and five today so we'll have a late dinner, OK?"

Lopez understood what I was trying to tell him and hung up. I picked up the last two rifles and carried them out to the car. Sancho had laid them on his back seat.

"Miguel, do you have something to cover those rifles with?"

"No, we don't need anything. We're going to get rid of them real quick. Don't worry."

I turned on my paternal gun trafficker role. "You guys be careful, go the speed limit and use your turn signals, OK? If you have any problems call me as soon as possible so I can get my act together."

I dialed Lopez's cell as soon as I had closed the door behind me. He was walking into my living room by then.

"The fucking wire was down, Mike. I couldn't hear a thing. I never got the tracker on the car," he said, clearly frustrated.

"Shit, I'm sorry, Travis. I turned on the transmitter when they pulled into the driveway. I saw the green light go on."

"We even tested it earlier and Mando said that he could hear it loud and clear."

I asked Lopez if it was the same transmitter I used each time or if they had a bunch of similar units.

"Nope, we just have that one," said Lopez sounding disgusted.

"Shit, why can't Jack get the office a new one?"

"I don't think Jack has any control over that. Budgets are tight everywhere."

"I know, but this one could actually get someone killed. Remember that night when you had to call me twice to turn it off and on again?"

Lopez sighed. The last thing he needed was a CI telling him the equipment he was using, which he had no control over, was screwed up. He was upset and understandably so. We missed an opportunity to get a tracker on the car which would provide invaluable information.

"The good news," I said, "is that they said they would be back later to buy ten more rifles."

Lopez's radio started crackling with agents and TPD officers giving the directions of Sancho's car. Lopez keyed his mic. "Keep it loose guys. I didn't get the tracker on it. I repeat, I did not get the tracker on the car but they are coming back this afternoon for more rifles."

I didn't hear anything from Moreno or Sancho and around 7 p.m. Lopez called and said that he was going to call it. He instructed me to tell them I had made other plans and couldn't accommodate them if they called later that night.

But I never did hear from those goofy kids again anytime soon. A week or so later Lopez called me and told me that Moreno was driving Miguel's car and was stopped on I-19. His registration had expired so they impounded the car.

"The good thing about this, Mike, is that we can go put a tracker on it before he picks it up and we won't need a court order or warrant."

Probably two weeks after that Lopez called to tell me that he and Mando were on their way over to the impound yard to install the tracker.

Other than the occasional call from Lopez to see if I'd heard anything, things were very quiet. I did not hear anything from Moreno and wondered if they realized that they'd been tailed. Or maybe something I said or did scared them? I remembered having the same types of doubts with Trujillo and it always turned out that the problem was not with me.

In July Lopez called while I was finishing the loading of my trailer for the big Ice House show in Phoenix. "If you see Antonio or Miguel at the show and they want to buy guns tell them that there are just too many eyes on you there at the show and that you'd rather do it at your house," he said.

The agents had worked a gun show in Tucson the weekend earlier hoping that Moreno and Sancho would show up. They were grumbling about having to work two weekends in a row.

We had a busy Saturday at the show and like most Sundays, sales started a little slow but picked up around 11 a.m. Sometime in the early afternoon I saw Antonio Moreno talking to some kids who looked to be about his age. They were looking at my .308 rifle rack, and Moreno pointed at a couple different rifles. I watched him for a few moments and then finished what I'd been doing. When I turned around again he was still standing in front of my rifle racks. I walked over to shake hands. He looked surprised—almost as if he didn't know that he was standing in front of my tables. I asked him what had happened—he was supposed to come back with Miguel the day they came to my house.

"We went on a little vacation," he said.

I tried to act perturbed. "You guys should have at least called. I thought something was wrong."

"Nah, we had to take a vacation."

"Where's Miguel?"

"Shit, I haven't talked to him in like two weeks."

"Is he in trouble? Can you get hold of him if you need to?"

"Oh yeah, there's no troubles—I just haven't spoken with him."

"Okay. Do your guys need anything today?"

"Nah, I think they're good right now. I'll give you a call," he said as he walked away. His cohorts melted away into the crowd and I was pissed that I couldn't get any good information out of him.

Maybe fifteen minutes later a kid asked one of my sales people if he would give him a discount if he bought more than one .308 rifle. "I'll let you handle this one," he said sensing that this might be one of my traffickers.

The kid asked about buying two different styles of .308s and what discount I would give him. I think I minimally discounted them by a total of $50 and as I was doing the paperwork he said he would take a third rifle if I would throw in a scope. I had an old display scope that I didn't mind throwing in. It was of dubious quality and hadn't cost me much. While he filled out the paperwork, two more Hispanic kids reached into the rack and picked up .308 rifles saying that they wanted to buy them. One of my sales people wrote up their orders.

While I prepared his receipt, I asked Jon Rutgers, my purchaser, how long he had known Antonio.

"Who?" asked Rutgers, feigning ignorance. "I don't know who you are talking about."

To me he seemed very disingenuous, almost unbelievable, but I didn't care. I had thought this kid was Hispanic based on the way he looked and dressed but when I looked at his #4473 he had filled out the White/Caucasian box on the form. He had a very dark tan and was slight in build, maybe five foot eight, and 120 pounds. When it was time for him to pay, he pulled out $20 bills to pay for his purchase.

The other two kids also paid with $20 bills. I found out that they were brothers with the last name Montenegro. In a heartbeat, my sales had just increased over $5,000.

Early Monday morning, I faxed the three .308 purchasers' information to Lopez. He was out of the office for training but called me the next day while I was working out.

"I hear that you sold a lot of .308's this weekend?"

I chuckled. "Yeah, I wish that I could tell you conclusively that these kids, Rutgers, and the Montenegro brothers are connected. I thought I saw Antonio talking to them and pointing out rifles and then they walked away when I shook hands with Antonio. I can't tell you definitively if they were the same kids that came back later and bought the rifles."

"It was a good call on your part. Now we have all of their info from the #4473. We do know they are connected because we have Moreno crossing the border at Douglas in a car registered to Rutgers's sister."

"So, they are connected? Bingo!"

"They were pretty busy at the Phoenix gun show. Each of these kids made multiple purchases."

Lopez told me to contact him if they called and needed rifles. A week or so later Lopez called me from Phoenix. He was on a stakeout. "Can you remember of Rutgers has a tattoo on his arm or not?"

I honestly could not remember one and relayed that to Lopez.

"Hey no problem man. We're just up here watching these guys. They've been really busy. Each of these kids has been buying guns at different gun stores. There's been a lot of activity." Lopez broke off and said that the subject was now northbound on the radio. It was obvious that they were following someone. There were several more exchanges before Lopez came back to his cell phone. "OK Mike, I'll be in touch—thanks for your help!"

In August I was back at the Coliseum at the Arizona State Fairgrounds for a gun show when a group of Hispanic men in their early twenties checked out the .308 rifles. Their lack of firearms experience and their badgering to lower the prices made me wonder if they were connected with Moreno in some way.

Fredrico Iglesias was interested in a DPMS 24" .308 rifle with a 10X scope and bipod. He was a big guy, six foot three and about 305 pounds and looked as though he might have played football. He was polite and frequently called me "boss." He asked me to show him how to take off the bipod and scope and then asked to fill out a #4473 background form to purchase the rifle. We removed the scope and bipod again and I bagged them for him. While I worked with him, one of my helpers wrote up another young Hispanic man, Michael Montoya, for a Rock River .308 rifle.

I asked Fredrico if he knew the other kid and he said that he'd never seen him before. But still I wondered because I had seen them talking with each other before they approached my tables. After Iglesias finished his #4473 I called in his background check. It was a "delay" and he seemed surprised, telling me that he'd never had any legal problems. I gave him the NICS phone number and told him to try to call them and see if he could straighten things out. Our other customer apparently passed the background check and left with his rifle.

I took the rifle that Iglesias wanted back out of its case and put the bipod and scope back on it for display. I walked out of the exhibition room to use the restroom and saw Iglesias standing there eating some jerky. I thought that I saw Antonio Moreno standing with the rest of the group and I noticed that Fredrico intentionally placed his body between me and the rest of the group, blocking my vision. I stood and spoke with him for a few moments. When I finished, I walked down the circular hallway and as I passed the first alcove from the snack bar I saw Antonio Moreno talking with a small group of kids. I passed by without acknowledging them and continued on without looking back. Once I was in the other hall I looked around and reached into my pocket for my cell phone. Lopez sounded tired when he answered the phone.

"Hey Travis, Moreno is here at the gun show."

"Oh shit, is he really?"

"Yeah, two of his guys just tried to buy .308s. One of them, Fredrico Iglesias, got delayed. The other one, Michael Montoya, got his rifle."

"OK, let me make some calls and see if we can get things rolling. I'd like to take these kids down today."

Lopez called me back about ten minutes later. "It doesn't look like we'll be able to deal with these jokers today, Mike. I can't get enough people together for this. Do me a favor and call me later and let me know how many guns they bought from you and if Moreno ever actually comes and talks to you."

Not long after I got back to my tables a young Hispanic man came up and started to ask me about the gun that Fredrico had attempted to purchase.

I recognized this kid as one of the group that had hovered while Lopez filled out the form. He said that he would like to buy the gun and I invited him to sit down behind the table and fill out the form. I asked him for his driver's license and he handed me an Arizona identification card. His name was Gilberto Moreno.

"Oh shit, Gil—no wonder you looked familiar. You've bought guns from me before."

He nodded his head and smiled.

"Hey, what's your shithead brother up to these days? I haven't heard from him, in fact, the last couple times I tried to call him he hung up on me."

"I doubt he hung up on you. He likes you, man. He's over in New Mexico right now working."

"What kind of work is he doing in New Mexico?" I asked trying to sound unsurprised since I knew that he was really out in the hallway.

"Demolition. We have a neighborhood of like thirty houses that have to be demolished. He doesn't get good phone reception over there."

"Oh . . . I was calling him to see if he needed anything special for this show. I thought if he needed a bunch of .308s I would pack some extras in the trailer. How many do you need today?"

"I'll take the one with the long barrel and also that one right there," he said pointing to the Rock River LAR-08. "You'll throw in a free scope, right?" He looked me in the eye and flashed his Hollywood smile.

He was a handsome kid and so was his brother, Antonio. It seemed such a waste to see these kids, who could be successful at anything they applied themselves to, go down this road of easy money.

"I can't throw in a free scope but I'll do the best that I can for you," was my earnest reply.

After he completed the form, I called in his background check and to both of our surprise he was delayed. Back in April his background check went through without any problems.

"I don't understand this. I haven't been in any trouble," he said, seemingly pleading with me.

"I wish I could sell you these guns but I can't unless the background check goes through."

"Would a Failure To Appear be reason enough for my check not to go through?"

"Oh, shit yes, especially if they issued a warrant. Did you get a ticket that you didn't take care of?"

"I was driving on a suspended license."

I started laughing—how could anyone be so stupid. "Just some advice. You should probably do whatever you need to do to get this cleared up or it will follow you around forever."

Just then one of my workers came up to me. "There's a gentleman up there who wants to buy two DPMS A3 Lite rifles if you throw in a scope."

I looked up towards my rack of economy rifles at the far end of my island of tables. There stood another Hispanic kid with his hat on sideways.

"Explain to him that our economy guns have very little profit and I can't afford to throw in a free scope."

"That's one of my dogs," said Moreno.

I told Moreno to wave him over.

He nodded, stood up, and had a private conversation with his friend. Gilberto said goodbye to me and said that he'd talk with me later. After he left, his friend said that he would take the two original guns he was asking about and also the gun that Moreno had attempted to purchase.

I handed a clipboard with a #4473 to the kid and asked for his ID. He was Aldo Montenegro and he and his brother had bought rifles from me at the last show. I didn't recognize him because one of my helpers had written them up. But now that he was sitting in front of me, I recognized him from the crowd that had gathered in the morning when Fredrico was trying to buy a rifle. He was also in the hallway speaking with Antonio.

Montenegro's background check went through without a hitch. He ended up buying the two DPMS AR-15 rifles and we added the DPMS 24" .308. I threw in an old electronic red dot sight that I had managed to find in one of the bins and Aldo seemed OK with that.

Aldo paid me with $20 bills that he carried in his front pocket. He struggled to carry all three rifles and left.

On the drive to dinner, I called Lopez and told him about the day's events. He seemed surprised that Gilberto Moreno came back delayed.

"Yeah, he said something about a Failure to Appear."

Lopez laughed. I told him that Aldo Montenegro ended up buying his guns for him. "I asked Moreno about Miguel and he said that they haven't heard from him for a while. I'm thinking that he might have been kicked out of the club."

JUST WHEN I THOUGHT I WAS DONE

"Sure sounds that way. He hasn't bought any guns lately. I'd like to know what happened with him."

"Yeah, it would be interesting, wouldn't it? Of course when these kids get popped, suspicion will naturally fall on him. Maybe it is fortuitous?"

"That's true, huh?" Lopez chuckled to himself.

In September 2008, Travis asked me to meet him down at the federal building to give me a voucher. He was delayed and so I girl-watched while I waited for him. I loved going downtown. Between the courts and county, city, and federal buildings there were many beautiful women dressed to kill walking through the professional plazas. I didn't mind waiting at all.

When Lopez finally came out of the federal building he was on his cell phone and I could see that he was holding the voucher in one hand. He hung up as he neared my Suburban and put the phone in his pocket. I rolled down the window and he reached through to shake hands.

"Sorry it took me so long. Today has been pretty hectic," he said. I noticed his hair had been freshly cut very close to his scalp although he had let his beard go for a couple days. His shirt was clean and pressed; it was worn untucked and loose fitting enough that it would not restrict his movements.

"It doesn't look like they let you just ease back into things when you get back from a trip, huh?" I said.

Lopez handed me the cash and then the voucher and a pen. I signed the voucher without checking the amount and pocketed the cash. I counted it later and it was ten $100 bills.

"I'm going to leave within the hour to go find Ira Goldblatt," he told me.

"Ira Goldblatt? I thought that was a forgotten deal."

"Oh no, we wanted to wait a while because we knew your name would come up on the other cases. But now his time has come. Either he'll give up his Tijuana connection or he'll go to prison tonight."

"Don't they go to jail first?"

Lopez smiled. "Feds take 'em straight to federal prison. We'll offer him the chance to talk, if not, fuck him. You were asking about Moreno the other day and I meant to tell you there was a seizure of guns in Agua Prieta and we think that's scared them off buying. None of their guns have showed up yet, but they might in the future."

"Do you think that they'll stay scared or that the greed will get the better of them and they'll start up again?"

"In Mexico there are some pretty hefty punishments for trafficking. It wouldn't surprise me if they've been scared into stopping."

"But you have enough to arrest them, right?"

"Oh, fuck yes! We've got plenty. We'll probably roll up Sancho first and see if he'll give us what we need. He hasn't been part of the buying for some time and will probably be able to give us the best info."

"Sounds like he is ripe to flip."

I asked about the influx of agents. Lopez said that there were now ten new agents in the office.

"You probably won't work any less hours but your office will handle a lot more cases," I said with a laugh.

Lopez looked a little queasy. "I'm hoping that after we get these current things settled our hours will be more reasonable. But, I've got to get running, Mike. I'll let you know how things went with Goldblatt."

There seemed to be a difference between the Wide Receiver and this current case and I wasn't quite able to put my finger on it. Maybe it was because the ten young subjects did not have the same type of cartel connections that Trujillo did. Or maybe it was just a simple case of burn out. But the lack of enthusiasm on this case, compared to Trujillo's, was palpable. The same seven agents had worked on Wide Receiver for over a year and a half and the case had still not made its way to court. The same players were still walking the streets and as far as I could tell our efforts had done nothing to slow the cartels from importing their drugs into the US, let alone putting one out of business. Even more sobering was that I'd heard nothing about Mexican authorities rounding up these weapons like Hinkley had told me they would.

Things were picking up for me business-wise. With eight years of George Bush as president and two wars, it became obvious to me by spring of 2008 that our next president would be either Hillary Clinton or Barack Obama. With the economy heading south it looked as though our country was due for a change. I took my life savings, profits from the bad guys' sales, took out a second mortgage on my house, and poured all of that money into inventory by early summer 2008 when rifles were still available. I was ahead of everyone else in this regard and by the end of summer 2008, I was the only dealer at gun shows that still had a good inventory of AR-15 rifles on display. For the first time in my adult life, it looked as though one of my gambles would pay off.

A few days later Travis called to say they were going to round up Moreno and his gang that week. "I just wanted you to be aware just in case there is any kind of fallout. But to be honest, these guys have been buying from everybody in the valley and not being too inconspicuous about it. I don't think they'll have any reason to suspect you."

"Have you heard anything else about Trujillo's case?"

"Not a word. I'm starting to think it's a dead issue. I've called over there several times and offered to come over and present the case to them and still have not received a response. I'm the only one that can get an indictment."

"What a shame, Travis—all that time, money, and man hours for nothing!"

"Something else I haven't told you is that it looks like I am transferring to Albuquerque in February and this has to be taken care of before then. They won't even return my calls."

"It's not that one woman AUSA that refused to take my name off of Bambie's search warrant is it?"

"No, it's a guy but apparently he is spending all of his time trying to promote himself for US Magistrate. The case was supposed to be transferred to someone else but no one is talking to me. And now we have Goldblatt wanting to cooperate and give up his cartel connections. Screw me!"

"God, man, I can't believe you're leaving. I'm going to miss working with you."

"Yeah, no shit, huh? You generated half of our cases. By the way, Mike, I'll put you in for a reward on this Moreno case. You should probably think about taking a nice prolonged vacation somewhere or relocating when you get these rewards."

Sales had been good but didn't really explode until the weekend before the election. People were in a panic and were buying guns out of fear that the new Obama administration would make efforts to reintroduce the assault weapons ban.

The Small Arms Review in December 2008 was my largest show of the year and was my only three-day show—the first day opening on Friday at noon. By eight in the morning people were lining up outside—eager for the chance to buy an AR-15 rifle. In three days we did almost $200,000 in sales. It didn't look like sales would slow anytime soon, so I placed replacement orders for the inventory sold.

Later in December Lopez called me to tell me that they rounded up Moreno and all of his buddies. "In fact, the only person outstanding is Miguel Sancho. He and Moreno did apparently have some sort of falling out."

"Anybody talking yet?"

"You know, it's funny on these kinds of deals. Usually we put out notice to their lawyers that if they want to have a round table talk we'd be available. The first one to talk usually always gets the best deal. One of the other peripheral kids' lawyers contacted us and said that he'd like to discuss things. So, Moreno won't get the best deal. Based on what we found out though, it looks as though Sancho was the ringleader. He's a big time doper and is most likely hiding in Mexico."

"I wonder what caused the split between Moreno and Sancho."

"I think it had something to do with a girl. Remember how you were asking Moreno if he'd been working out because you said it looked like he'd been lifting weights? Well, when we busted them we found a huge supply of steroids."

"No shit. You think they were for personal use or distribution?"

"I'd say both."

"Did any of them look any bigger?"

"It's funny you mention that because the Montenegro brothers looked huge."

"That's great—you arrested them just in time to have our government pay for their testicular cancer treatments."

Lopez laughed. "Look, Mike, these guys have all made bail but they have GPS ankle bracelets. Let me know if any of them are stupid enough to contact you, and be extra careful."

But I heard nothing. Not anything from Moreno and his crew or Rey Ayala and his family of dyslexic kids, and even Trujillo had been lying low. But Eduardo did resurface.

It was just starting to get dark outside when my doorbell rang. Both dogs ran barking to the door as I got up. I limped to the door unarmed and peeked through the blinds. I saw a short man wearing a baseball cap standing at the door.

My God, it was Eduardo. I turned on the outdoor light and saw him smiling and waving. I looked briefly at his midsection to see if he had a gun. His demeanor seemed non-threatening so I opened the door but kept the outer security door locked.

"Hi Mike, do you remember me?" he asked with a thick accent.

"Hi Eduardo, how are you?" I struggled to pull the dogs away from the door and then realized that this would be a perfect excuse to situate myself before I let him in. "Let me put the dogs outside, OK?"

I grabbed the dogs' collars and pulled them away from the door towards the back door and put them out. As I walked past the door on my way to the bedroom I held up my index finger. "One moment, OK?"

As I walked by the couch, I picked up a little .32 Colt, chambered a round, and stuck it in my waistband and pulled my sweater over it. My digital recorder was sitting on top of my bureau and I turned it on, hit the record button, and placed it in my 5.11 knife pocket.

I walked back to the front door and I could now see two people standing at the door. Oh shit, I thought. Who is he bringing to my house? It turned out to be Charlene with her baby. I unlocked the security door and let them in.

Charlene was holding her little boy. He was over a year old by then and had a full head of hair—he was trying to talk and was already walking. Charlene was wearing a black velour warm-up suit. Her hair looked like she'd just had it teased at a beauty shop, and she was wearing Gucci glasses. She reminded me of the Italian mob princesses from the 1980s. We stood in the foyer and she told me that Eduardo had been in Mexico for a year.

Eduardo pointed to my leg and said something in Spanish. I realized he had seen me limping and laughed, I said, "*Yo soy un hombre viejo.*"—I am an old man.

I invited them into the living room and hit the mute button on the TV remote knowing that the background noise would ruin the recording. I moved my winter jackets on the back of the sofa to make room for them.

They sat down and little Berto smiled and toddled over to see me. He seemed to be a very happy and good-natured baby. He let me pick him up and sat on my knee for a couple minutes while I bounced him up and down. Eduardo spoke and Charlene translated for him. After the pleasantries he asked if he could still buy guns from me for his friends.

Charlene said that they had come to see me at the last gun show but could not find me. I'm sure that he was wondering if I'd been busted or had some legal problems and that may have been his incentive to come check on me.

Not knowing what the ATF would want me to tell him, I explained to Charlene that I had a huge show in December that had wiped out my inventory. "That's why I wasn't at the last gun show. But I'm expecting to get more guns in time for the gun show next weekend."

Eduardo asked if he could come out and see me at the show. He then asked if I had the small AK-47s.

"AK-47s? Do you mean the *pistolas*?"

"*Si, si, las pistolas*," he said.

"I don't have too many—maybe only four or five. Mostly I have the AR-15s."

"*Como este*," he said pointing to the rifle I had leaning up against my entertainment center.

"Yes, just like that."

He said something to Charlene and she translated. "The prices are the same?"

I laughed. I explained what the current situation was with Obama having been elected and the fact that demand had gone way up on those rifles. I told them a gun like that would be about $1,000.

He said that he didn't think his friends would have a problem with that.

I asked him if he had talked with Pedro and he said no. He had just gotten back into town. I told him that Pedro had a problem last year and that he was too afraid to do more business. This was not news to Eduardo—back in October 2007 he had told me he wanted a bunch of .38 Supers but wouldn't give me a deposit because Omar lost his load of guns.

But then I told him that I had spoken with Pedro maybe two months before and that he wasn't in jail and as far as I knew, he wasn't having any problems.

Eduardo asked if he would have to do a 50 percent deposit like before for his orders. I explained that if I already had inventory in hand that he would not have to, but I would need a deposit for items like .38 Supers which I did not keep in inventory in large numbers. He seemed satisfied with my response. Charlene asked if I could give him a business card. I walked out to the office and got a stack of maybe ten cards and gave them to him when I returned to the living room.

"Can he come see you at the show this weekend?" Charlene asked.

That would be great, I thought, because Tucson's ATF office had had a presence at all the Tucson shows for the past four months.

It was a short meeting—only about ten minutes long according to the digital recorder. I would never have imagined having a meeting this cordial with Eduardo, and wondered what influence Charlene had had on that little shithead. He seemed to be a different person with her. She obviously loved him and had some influence over his behavior. This would be very important information to have when the ATF finally questioned her, especially when Lopez played the tape of him having phone sex with Maria.

Then too, maybe he was casing me? Checking out what my security was like? He saw the security iron and the dogs and my rifle leaning against the entertainment center. Only a fool would take those odds.

I walked the three of them to the door. Charlene said Eduardo would call if he couldn't make the gun show that weekend. I nodded and thanked him.

"Do you guys live in Tucson now?" I asked.

"Yes," said Charlene, "we have a house off of Houghton."

"Oh, you kept that house? I thought maybe you had sold it."

"No," she said, "we're in the same place."

I looked out at their car. I really wanted to get the plate but then I figured it would be pushing it. I knew where they lived and there would undoubtedly be surveillances again at their address. I did note, however, that it was a new model red Jeep Grand Cherokee.

I walked back to the living room and turned the recorder off, unloaded the Colt, and staged it again on the back of the couch with an unloaded chamber. I dialed Lopez's cell number. He answered in a tired voice, "Hi Mike—how's it going?"

"Hey man, I have a late Christmas present for you."

"Really? What's that?"

"Eduardo and Charlene just stopped by here."

There was a long pause. In part I'm sure that he was measuring me to see if I was joking. "Get the fuck out."

"Nah, I'm serious."

"No shit, what did he want?"

"He came by to ask if I would still sell him guns for his friends."

"Jesus Christ!"

"Hey," I joked, "you might finally get to shoot that little prick."

We went through the conversation and I told him that Eduardo might come to the gun show that weekend.

"Ah, that's perfect. We could charge him with being a non-immigrant alien in possession."

"Will that fuck up the other investigation?"

Lopez laughed sarcastically. "What other investigation? It doesn't look like they're going to do anything anyway. Besides, these charges can always be tacked on to the other ones."

"I'll make a CD of the conversation for you. But I'll also email it to you— it was only about a ten-minute conversation."

"Get out—you recorded it? Good work!"

"Yep—got the recorder started and was able to slip a pistol in my waistband."

"I didn't have any doubt that you would," chuckled Lopez.

An hour or so later Lopez sent me an email that said he received it and was happy with the information. He had told me on the phone that the whole office was going to be out at the gun show looking for straw purchases again that weekend. It would be the perfect time for them to bust Eduardo.

Maybe Lopez can leave for Albuquerque with a big bust under his belt after all, I thought? He told me to expect a call later in the week.

Just before the weekend, Lopez called me at around eleven in the morning and asked if he could stop by my house with a couple other agents so he could hand me off to the new guys.

Within minutes Lopez, Rob Gaylord, and Matt Cubbie, an agent I had never met before, knocked on the door. They were greeted by Champ and Maya. Lopez explained that they'd been watching Eduardo's house and were trying to get the plate number of his new Jeep.

Gaylord and Cubbie both said that they lived in close proximity to me and if I ever had a problem I should call them and they'd be right over.

I'd met Gaylord the previous summer at a gun show in Tucson and had liked him immediately. I believed he'd be an apt replacement for Lopez. He was from Mississippi and spoke with a thick drawl, and he was personable, athletic, and sharp.

Cubbie had transferred to the Tucson office from Las Vegas. He was soft and sloppy; not what I'd expect of a federal agent. His flaccid physique made me wonder if the ATF had any fitness standards. Even though I was a decade and a half older, I had no doubt I could outrun this agent on my two crippled ankles in a foot race. I found out later that his fellow agents had nicknamed him Chubby Cubbie.

While Lopez took a phone call, Gaylord explained to me that the Assistant US Attorney was going to "throw me under the bus." To get the indictments, they needed to list me as the original source for the Moreno case.

I was dumbfounded. Here I was again about to be screwed over by an Assistant US Attorney. She was fully aware that I'd brought them other cases and had placed myself in some precarious positions to get the ATF the information they needed to make their case. Yet there was no hesitation about exposing me as the CI.

"It's so typical, Mike," said Gaylord. "That's why I hate working with these AUSAs. This cunt cares nothing about you. All she cares about is getting the defendants to plead guilty."

I asked if the kids were still in custody and Gaylord told me that they were all free on pretrial release but not to worry because they had been fitted with GPS anklets.

When Lopez finished his phone call he told me that he'd see me at the gun show that weekend. "If you see Mando or any of the other guys, please don't mention that we were out looking for Eduardo or that we wanted to wrap him up at the gun show."

I agreed to do what he asked, though I didn't understand why that would be important. Maybe if Jack knew that he was looking for Eduardo he would call him off. I still don't know why Lopez asked me to do that.

After they left, I learned that the ATF's public information officer in Phoenix gave my name and contact information to a New York Times reporter who was inspired to write an article after Attorney General Eric Holder's speech of February 26, 2009 in which he detailed that Mexicans were being killed with American guns and that he and President Obama would like to see the Assault Weapons Ban reinstated. If it wasn't bad enough that Department of Justice employees were exposing me as an informant, now an ATF agent was doing the same thing.

Unfortunately, Eduardo never showed up at the gun show and his visit to my house was the last time I would ever see him.

Travis moved to New Mexico in February but we still traded emails occasionally and I had recently sent a Rock River AR-15 rifle to a gun shop in Albuquerque for him. He was applying for the ATF's special response team and wanted to have a weapon of his own to practice with. He was concerned that someone in New Mexico would take advantage of him because of his limited knowledge of the AR-15 and wanted to know if I could give him a good deal. I was driving home from the bank on April 3 when he called me.

"Hey man, I got your email. Am I reading it right when you say you want me to not pay for that rifle?"

"Absolutely, Travis, I've had a good year and I want to do this for you."

"Geez, Mike, I don't know what to say. That's awfully nice of you. Are you sure I can't pay you?"

"I'm happy to do this for you."

"Well, cool Mike, I guess this will just be our secret, huh?"

I told him that Matt Cubbie had called me a couple weeks before and had mentioned that he was going to have a meeting with the female AUSA. I never heard anything back from Cubbie so I asked Lopez if he knew what happened.

"The problem is that the AUSA chick doesn't understand the gun issue. She keeps asking us why we let so many guns go south and our response is 'don't worry about it. It's not your problem. We can justify every gun that went south as necessary to the investigation.'"

"Jesus, is it that simple?"

"Yeah, Mike. We gave them that case on a silver platter and it's a damn shame that they haven't issued the indictments yet. Every time she hesitates I tell her, 'OK, then just sign off on this case and write your reasons for not pursuing it and I'll pass it up the chain of command.' Then she starts back-pedaling because she knows what a problem it will cause if the case gets dropped. She's going to have to indict those people."

It was amazing to me that the case had not yet been indicted and it made me wonder if there were other problems that I didn't know about.

"What else is going on down there, Mike?" Travis asked.

"Not much, it's kind of boring here."

"You miss the adrenaline rushes. You're a junkie like me."

I laughed—he was right and we both knew it.

12

THE UGLY TRUTH

I N OCTOBER 2009 I had an appointment to meet with Special Agent Matt Cubbie and Lori Beavertooth from the US Department of Justice.

I stood in the secure foyer for a few minutes before Joey Pequeno came and let me in. Joey's head was shaved and he was wearing a US Navy lanyard with his ID. I didn't know that he was in the reserves but it didn't surprise me. We chatted for a few minutes.

"I'm going to tell you something that is not public knowledge so if you tell anyone I'll come to your house and slit your throat, OK? Because of its borders with Mexico, Texas has had ongoing problems with gun traffickers. Obama decided to saturate that area with agents doing audits, investigations, and interviews. Now they're talking about doing that here in Arizona."

"How is that different than Project Gunrunner?"

He looked at me funny. "That's exactly what I'm talking about."

"You know it's on ATF's website, right?"

Pequeno giggled.

"Still want to slit my throat?" I asked.

About then Morty Bedouin walked by. He recognized me and made a loop back to say "hi." It looked as though he had lost some weight.

"I just got back from Afghanistan," he said.

"You're in the Army reserves, right?"

"Yeah, I am. In fact I was gathering some info to pass on to Jack. He thinks he'd like to do some government work over there."

"Where is Jack these days? I heard he was in France?"

"I'm not sure where Jack is," he lied.

I thought it was funny how these guys were so well versed in protecting each other. Obviously if he was gathering info on contract work, Bedouin knew where to find Jack. Mando had told me that Jack was in France with his fiancé, an ATF agent who won a sexual harassment case and got her posting of choice.

Just then Rob Gaylord walked by and joined the group.

"Did you get that info I emailed you on that guy?" I asked, trying not to be too specific.

"Yeah I did, but haven't had a chance to look at him yet," said Gaylord.

"Is that why you're down here today?" Morty asked. "Are you bringing us a new case?"

"No, I'm down here on that old Trujillo case. It looks like they're finally going to do something with that."

"No shit! It's about fucking time, huh," said Bedouin.

Pequeno looked up and shook his shaved head. All of those guys knew that case was as well-prepared and packaged as it possibly could be. They had all worked long hours and were invested in the case.

"I'm supposed to meet with Cubbie and an Assistant US Attorney today," I said.

"Oh, so that's who Matt has in Jack's old office," said Pequeno. "What time is your appointment, Mike?"

I looked at my watch. "About five minutes ago."

We chatted for a few minutes more when I heard an office door open and saw Matt. I think the last time I saw him was the first time that I met him with Travis and Rob out at my house the previous December. He seemed puzzled that a group of agents had gathered around me and were shooting the shit. In fact, he seemed reluctant to interrupt us. They each took turns slapping me on the back and wishing me good luck. It was nice to see all of those guys again.

Cubbie led me a short ways down the hall and into an office on the right. It was Jack's old office with the fabulous view west. Inside, behind Jack's desk was a tall, buxom lady wearing a red sundress who had hair tinted an incongruously youthful shade of red. I guessed she was in her late fifties. She stood and offered her hand and smiled, revealing her two very prominent and overlapping front teeth. "Hi Mike, I'm Lori Beavertooth. It's nice to meet you."

Matt offered me a seat anywhere and I chose the love seat against the west wall. Matt sat in a chair across from Lori Beavertooth's desk.

Once we were settled, Lori started. "I'm not sure how much Matt has told you but I'm from Washington and not with the local US attorney's office. I've been here looking at transcripts and reviewing files and I told Matt that it would be nice to actually meet you so I can put a face with all of the information I've been looking at." As she talked, she readied a pad of yellow legal paper and took the cap off of her pen. "Tell me how this case first started? You were approached by Diego Rodriguez at a gun show, right?"

"That's right. Back in February 2006, he came by my tables and bought six AR-15 lowers. I really didn't think he'd pass the background check but he did and he didn't ask for a discount and I liked that even more. He came back the next day and I told him that I would be getting a load of twenty more lowers in the following week. He said that he would take them all. Monday morning I called Special Agent Spencer Edgar to report it."

"And what made you think that he was doing something illegal?" Beavertooth asked.

"Well, anytime someone buys big multiples of the same item I am guessing that they are not just a hobbyist. But when he said that he would take all twenty lowers it became obvious what he was doing with them."

"Why did you report this to Special Agent Edgar?" She looked me intently in the eyes while I took my time answering.

"I reported it because it was the right thing to do. These kids were obviously doing something illegal and my options were to ignore it, be complicit, or to report it."

Beavertooth smiled. Apparently I had given her the answer she was looking for. "What happened next?"

"Well, I sold a bunch of lowers to that Phoenix group before they started taking them to a UPS Store to ship to San Diego. That's when the owner, a former secret service agent, opened one of the boxes thinking it was dope. The SAC in California wouldn't let the shipment go through—something about he didn't want Arizona guns on his California streets, and that stymied the deal. Those kids never bought any more lowers from me. Somewhere along the way Diego stole some money and we all thought he'd been killed."

Beavertooth looked riveted. Some of this information was new to her and it must have sounded like a bad movie script.

"Months later I got a call from him one night. He said that he was now living in Tucson and had some friends that needed guns. So he came over with a bunch of kids and they bought a few guns. With him that night was Pedro Trujillo and he spoke so little that night I didn't even know if he could speak English."

"So that's how you met Trujillo?"

I nodded. "He came out a few more times with Diego but then one night he came out on his own and wanted to know if he could just deal directly with me and cut Rodriguez out of the picture."

Beavertooth chuckled. "Seems like no one liked dealing with Diego."

"I know that I didn't. But then Trujillo started bringing people with him and they started buying too."

Beavertooth looked down at her pad and then asked if this was the first time I had worked with the ATF.

I shook my head and related stories about the Nogales cop and the kidney-failure customer. Both of those cases I'd worked with SA Spencer Edgar but neither were as involved as the cases I had worked the last three years. "I didn't wear a transmitter or recording device for either of those and I was never paid."

"Were there any other cases that you worked on since the Trujillo case?"

"Yes, just recently, I think it was in February that a group of ten was indicted for trafficking." I looked at Cubbie and asked if he was part of the Moreno-Sancho-Rutgers case.

"It wasn't my case but I was in on some of the surveillances. I think they did get busted in February."

"Then there was another case during the Trujillo investigation but this one was handled by the Phoenix office. The ringleader there was Rey Ayala."

She was hurriedly writing down names and I was attempting to spell them for her. "You've been busy!"

"Travis used to call me a shithead magnet."

Beavertooth and Cubbie laughed and nodded. It did seem as though I had a talent for attracting these nefarious sorts.

"When you recorded these individuals, did the office give you a cassette or recorder? What did you use?"

"At first Lopez gave me a cassette recorder with a suction device for recording phone calls. That recorder would have liked to have gotten me killed one night. Not long after that I bought my own digital recorder. That turned out to be much better because then I could burn conversations to a CD or email them."

"What did the recorder look like? Was it small? Was it disguised as something?"

I reached into the knife pocket of my 5.11 khaki pants and removed my Olympus digital recorder and handed it to her.

She turned it over in her hand. "I was imagining something disguised as a ballpoint pen or something. Where did you hide it?"

"I have some hidden pockets on shirts or pants, like these."

"Is it difficult to turn on? Some of the conversations I've listened to sound like they are halfway over when they start."

I thought for a second. Then I realized that she was talking about the phone conversations. "Sometimes I answered the phone when the recorder was in the other room or I couldn't find the ear microphone for it."

She nodded as though it suddenly made sense. "Were there ever any other recording devices used?"

I told her about the Hawk audio and digital video recorder that was usually disguised in a box of Kleenex on my wet bar to record the table where the transactions were conducted. I also told her about the wire or transmitter that I routinely wore during these events.

"There was one evening where the ATF agents placed a clock radio that not only transmitted real time video and audio to a truck that was curbside but also recorded the events. But that was just one evening. Even the Hawk had to be delivered and picked up each session as Hinkley didn't want to take any chances on something happening to it."

Beavertooth made some more notes and looked up at me and smiled. "At any time during this investigation did you make any notes, take any photographs, or otherwise document these events?"

"I started keeping a journal when I realized this would be an ongoing event . . . for a couple reasons. I have a bad memory and there were so many different buys and players that I didn't want the events and people to run together. I also thought that I might write a book one day."

Her eyes brightened. "So you kept notes this whole time?"

"Yep, six hundred pages' worth."

She let her head fall into her hands. I wasn't sure how long Beavertooth had been in town but she obviously had been poring through the transcripts. The last thing she would want to do is read through six hundred pages of my dribble.

"At some point in time we will ask you for a copy of those notes," she said.

"No, I won't give them to you. Besides detailing these buys and criminal interactions, there is too much personal information in them. When I started keeping my journal, no one told me that I might have to turn them over."

"Did Lopez know that you were keeping notes?"

"He did. There were a couple times when he was working on reports that he contacted me asking for dates or names."

"Potentially we would have to let the defense team look at it. We'll just have to see."

"I just told you that I won't give you my notes. This isn't something negotiable. If you turn them over in discovery, it will give the bad guys every detail they need to destroy me."

Beavertooth sat straight in her chair and looked over the top of her glasses. "If we have to, we'll subpoena your journal but it will be much easier for everyone involved if you surrender them. Just so you know, we'll be able to see if you've edited them—made deletions or altered them in any way. I'd like you to bring Matt a CD with your notes on Monday."

I bristled at the rebuke. There I was attempting to help again and she'd pissed me off right out the gate.

"Travis told me at one point that he would have me stop working gun shows and that there would be some support from the government to keep me going during this hiatus," I said.

"Maybe he made that comment with the intent of keeping you safe—out of the public arena?"

"I think that his intent was to throw suspicion off of Mike," said Cubbie.

"I can tell you, just leafing through these transcripts, that it is very obvious to me who the informant was. I'm sure that the defense lawyers won't have any problem either. I'm worried that you'll become a target of the cartel, Mike."

"Obviously, I have spent a lot of time thinking about this. My take is that these people I have dealt with are so low on the organizational tree that they are expendable. I mean, who is more likely to be killed—me or Pedro?"

"Honestly, I would expect that José would target you to protect Pedro. But Pedro obviously has information that could be very damaging to his cartel."

"Which would bring more heat on him—killing me or Pedro?"

"That's something we don't want to gamble on either way. Do you have any questions for me?"

"I do," I said, "how is it that we're just getting started on this right now? Jack Hinkley, the former ASAC, invited me up to this very same office in January 2008. On the floor of his office were stacks of three-ring binders. Probably the same transcripts you're going through right now. He said, 'There's the fruits of your labor, Operation Wide Receiver, and we're going to take them across the street right now and drop them off with the US Attorney's Office.' Why are we just getting some action now when it looked like, for all intents and purposes, the office was going to pass on this case?"

"The Assistant US Attorney became a US Magistrate and the person he handed this case off to said that her caseload was just too heavy to take it on. At least, that was the party line on this case," she said.

"Yeah, but isn't it also true that Tim Bugatti just let this case sit on his floor while he promoted himself for magistrate?" I looked over at Cubbie and he was smiling—obviously enjoying the heat I was applying.

Beavertooth smiled pleasantly. "Well, I wasn't here so it's impossible for me to say what Tim did or didn't do. I can't make explanations for what has happened here in the past but I can say that there is enough here for me to get an indictment from the Grand Jury."

"I wish that I could say that this is the last time that I'll see you down here, Mike," said Cubbie. "But the reality is that we're going to be seeing a lot more of you. I'm going to need help going through files and identifying things. For instance, we were listening to a tape today and it was labeled "unidentified male." On something like that we have you come down and see if you can remember who that person was."

"Sure, whatever I can do to help." As I got up I asked Lori for her business card, and then I walked myself to the door.

When I got home I burned a copy of my journal onto a CD. I was worried. There was so much personal information in those notes that they could turn out to be my Achilles' heel. I was also worried that perhaps Lopez or Hinkley might have asked me to do something that was not 100 percent legal on their behalf and the case would be ruined because I had detailed it so thoroughly in my journal. However, a couple days later I drove down to the federal building and dropped a copy of my notes off with Matt Cubbie.

I was at the University Medical Center waiting for an appointment with an orthopedic surgeon when Lopez called. "Mike, this is Lopez and to say that I am pissed off would be an understatement," he said in a whisper. His voice quivered with anger.

"Travis, what's going on?"

"Your fucking book or screenplay or whatever the fuck it is."

"Oh God," I sighed, "what about it?"

"That rifle! It's going to get me fired. You know I wanted to put in at least twenty years before I leave the agency."

"Oh shit, I'm so sorry. I didn't even think of it when I turned my notes over."

"Cubbie tells me that you recorded some of our conversations. Are you recording me right now?"

"No."

"Are you lying to me?"

"No."

Lopez's anger and resentment was undeniable. He must have been calling from his work office because I could hear other people talking in the background. He spoke in short hisses and I could imagine him talking through clenched teeth with his face contorted with rage.

He asked if I would be willing to change my notes. If I'd be willing to remove the part about his gift rifle and resubmit a new CD to Cubbie.

"Let me call Cubbie, Mike. You have no idea how badly you've screwed me over."

Minutes later Lopez called back. Apparently Cubbie was unwilling to do this favor for his fellow agent.

"It is what it is, Mike. There's nothing I can do about it now. I will have to deal with it."

That was the last conversation I would ever have with Lopez. I felt terrible about what I had unwittingly done to this young agent's career and was unable to get a good night's sleep for months.

In mid-November Matt Cubbie called and told me that Lori Beavertooth and another female AUSA who was handling the Moreno case wanted to meet with me and go over some issues they had with my journal.

Cubbie's tone was terse and abrupt. "Can you meet with us at 10 a.m. on December first?"

"Yes, I can be there."

The phone slammed down on the other end. So this is how it's going to be, I thought. It was going to be a contentious meeting regarding my journal. My only reason for agreeing to meet with them was to see if I could take some of the heat off Lopez for the rifle I had given him.

I arrived at the federal building and went up to the eighth floor and rang the doorbell in the secure foyer. After a few moments Cubbie opened the door a crack.

"We're not quite ready for you, Mike. Wait for us downstairs, okay?"

I went downstairs and stood in the lobby for a little bit and then went outside and sat on the cold stone surrounding the fountains. I was nervous and on edge. Why did I ever try to help these assholes, I wondered?

Twenty or so minutes later Special Agents Cubbie and Gaylord came out and we walked across the street to the federal courts building where my meeting with the two AUSAs would be.

Gaylord tried to lighten my mood by asking me some questions regarding business and the gun shows. Cubbie made no attempt to talk to me. After clearing security, we took an elevator to the third floor where I was ushered into a conference room with a large table and numerous chairs.

Beavertooth made me wait for fifteen minutes before making her grand entrance along with another woman, Mary Jo Kleinbeck. Both took seats opposite me while Gaylord and Cubbie sat several chairs away from me on the same side of the table.

"Well, as you can imagine we have a bunch of questions based on your notes," said Beavertooth.

Cold sweat trickled down my ribs and I felt a heavy pressure in my chest. "Before we get started on my journal," I said, "I'd just like to say that the rifle I gave Lopez was a gift from one friend to another. It had nothing to do with his being an ATF agent and he was no longer my case agent."

"Mr. Detty you are not in trouble for giving a rifle to that agent," said Beavertooth. "You have not had the benefit of attending basic agent training where the rules of ethics are taught. Agent Lopez's solicitation of this rifle has placed an unneeded hurdle in my prosecution of this case. But it is not an insurmountable hurdle and I'd much rather spend today talking about other things."

She flipped through several pages of handwritten notes on her legal pad.

"You have some health problems," she started.

I nodded.

"You're a hemophiliac?"

I nodded again.

"But you look in great shape?"

"I work out for an hour or more every day. I have since I was a teenager."

"How did you manage to get into the Marines?"

"I didn't tell them."

"Why did you choose to enlist?"

"Because I wanted to serve my country and have the right to call myself a good American. Earning the eagle, globe, and anchor will always be my proudest achievement."

"There are quite a few references in your journal to you taking prescription pain medicine."

"Yes."

"How do these pain pills affect you?"

"Usually they make me tired. I take them so I can sleep through the night without waking up in pain."

"Do they affect your ability to think clearly?"

"Sometimes, depending on what I take, I can feel a little foggy. But there's nothing I take that is hallucinogenic. I limit myself to one pill a day and I have never taken more than that. The reason I made journal entries at all regarding this is because it is an issue I am struggling with. It's all about staying productive. It's difficult to be productive when you're in chronic pain. But it's also tough to get work done when the pain pills make you sleepy."

"Would you ever take a pain pill before one of these buys with Pedro or Eduardo?"

"No never."

"Why not?"

"Because in a matter of seconds I might be fighting for my life. I had to be at my best—I couldn't afford to be compromised."

Beavertooth winced and looked through her notes. "There were a number of entries that, I thought, were maybe a bit melodramatic. Specifically, I am alluding to some of your entries where you practiced certain shooting exercises in the desert. I think you also mentioned something about getting out of your car with a rifle and shooting at several targets."

"Considering who I was dealing with, don't you think that type of practice was prudent?"

"Honestly I don't see these people as being that dangerous."

"Really," I said, "then why didn't we sell them guns out of your living room?"

Gaylord and Cubbie broke into laughter. Beavertooth pursed her lips, obviously upset at my rebuke.

I said, "What you're telling me goes against everything the case agent told me. He reminded me before every buy to be careful, to do whatever I needed to do to retain control, and to never let one of these guys get behind me. He also told me that Pedro was not the innocent dolt he pretended to be and to be careful with him. You yourself told me at our last meeting that you were afraid I'd become a target of the cartel."

Beavertooth knew that she pissed me off by intimating that my work for the ATF wasn't dangerous. Her next subject wouldn't fare any better.

"Mike, over the course of three years, our records show that you were paid over $15,000 in informant fees."

"That sounds about right."

"That's going to be another tough hurdle for us to get over at trial."

"Why is that?"

"Well, it looks like you only did this for the money."

"I'm sorry but that's just retarded—$5,000 a year to sell guns to cartel members out of my living room? In a normal year, I write thirty magazine articles. The three years that I worked with the ATF I only had time to write less than ten articles each year. I actually lost money by working with the ATF."

"Well, it will still look bad in front of a jury."

"If you think $5,000 a year made a difference in my lifestyle, you are sadly mistaken. I never solicited funds from the ATF but when they were offered I was glad to accept them. I had no problem bringing this case to the ATF or helping them work it and accepting all of the inherent dangers, but why should my patriotic efforts cost me? You get a paycheck every two weeks, right? These guys sitting next to me get a paycheck every two weeks. I work for myself. My time is my money."

Beavertooth went back to her notes without commenting.

"During the course of the investigation you talked to several people about it. Can you tell me why you spoke to Bryce Chandler about it?"

"Yes, Bryce has been a friend for about ten years and is currently an intelligence asset for one of our most elite military units. I consulted with him when Lopez was attempting to place a tracking device in the buttstock of a rifle. The information that he gave me matched the outcome that Lopez experienced exactly."

"I see," she said, "but why did you feel it was necessary to tell Joe Benedict? I think you made mention that you even copied your journal to a CD and were giving him a copy."

"Joe is my best friend. I've known him since junior high. He's been a police officer since 1981 and I trust him implicitly. If something happened to me, I know that the ATF would issue a release that says something like 'Mike Detty had been a person of interest in an ongoing gun trafficking investigation.' Giving Joe that CD guaranteed a true record of what happened. I can count on Joe to be an advocate for my reputation in the event of my demise."

Beavertooth nodded as if it made sense to her. Then she smiled her snaggletooth smile. "Right now I'm reading about your high school reunion. It sounds as if you had a good time."

A cold chill ran down my spine followed by a nauseous feeling of violation. She was referring to a tryst that I'd had with a classmate at my reunion and had mentioned in my journal. I shot her a look that stopped her dead in her tracks. She went back to her pad of notes.

"So many of these transactions occurred at your home. Weren't you afraid that someone might try to rip you off?"

I looked at her with wide-eyed astonishment. I was incredulous. Hadn't she just told me my criminals were harmless?

"Yes," I said, slapping my hand on the table. "That's why I practiced so often with my rifle and pistol."

Beavertooth threw her pen down so hard on her pad of paper that it bounced off and onto the floor. Cubbie and Gaylord started snickering again.

"Maybe you should take over from here, Mary Jo," she said.

Kleinbeck had been waiting patiently while Beavertooth was questioning me and had made few comments. In front of her she had a dog-eared printout of my journal. She was the AUSA on the Moreno-Rutgers case and while it was not technically part of Operation Wide Receiver, it did share me as the CI and the same gunwalking tactics of the ATF.

"Before we get started, Mr. Detty, I want to address the two agents here regarding what you reported them as saying, that I was going to throw you under the bus," she said looking at Cubbie and Gaylord accusingly.

I wondered if she cared so much about the phrase "throw you under the bus" or Gaylord using the C-word to describe her.

Gaylord leaned across the table and said, "Did you or did you not list Detty as the source for your case?"

"That's not the point. It was not your business to go to a CI's house and tell him that the prosecuting AUSA was going to throw him under the bus."

Gaylord wasn't having any of it and fired back. "It's tough enough for us to work with CIs and protect them without having an AUSA expose them just to make their case easier."

Kleinbeck was fuming. Gaylord didn't back down the way she had hoped and he refused to be intimidated. Her cheeks were red and she was clearly flustered. Taking a moment to regroup she turned her chair towards me again.

"Mr. Detty, as you know I am prosecuting Moreno and his friends. I've read through your journal, at least the parts that pertain to this case, and I have to ask you . . . at any point have you felt the need to exaggerate or embellish these notes?"

I looked at her with a blank expression. By now I was thoroughly pissed off with this inquisition. I stared at her until she diverted her gaze. She flipped through her notes until she found what she was looking for.

"In your notes is a passage about the Moreno brothers. You said, 'They are handsome kids with million-dollar smiles, well built, muscular and athletic and clean-shaven and have no tattoos. They are also articulate and polite and I have to assume the product of good parenting. It's a damn shame they're getting involved in obvious trafficking.'"

I looked at Kleinbeck still saying nothing.

"The reason I asked if you embellished your notes is because I found the Moreno brothers to be the rudest, most arrogant, vulgar criminals I have ever had the displeasure to interview."

Sensing the opportunity to get a dig in I said, "Well you're probably not a people person. It's all in the way you talk to someone."

Gaylord and Cubbie giggled again.

"My experiences with the Moreno brothers were all pleasant," I said. "They spoke to me with respect and were always courteous."

"Well, I think they are lowlife pigs," Kleinbeck snapped.

The anger and forcefulness of her response struck me as humorous. I can only imagine what the Morenos had put that lady through, though I have to admit that at the time I thought it was funny considering how she had unapologetically exposed me as the CI on this case.

"Like I said, you're probably just not a people person."

She smirked and started looking through her post-it notes in the journal. After a few moments she looked up and asked, "Have you given any thought to the consequences of your actions? You have to know that these people are very unhappy with you?"

My God, I thought my head was going to explode. The consequences of my actions? Did she mean reporting these criminals to the ATF so they could build a case and take them off the streets? Did she mean helping the ATF to collect information and intelligence on this gun trafficking case? She made it sound almost as if I had done something illegal rather than helping federal law enforcement.

"Well, the last thing I expected was to be dragged over the coals for my journal. Every word in my notes was the absolute truth. I had no reason to lie or fabricate anything because it was never intended for anyone else's eyes but mine. You should never have demanded it. Now you're pissed because it contains facts that you have to deal with."

"There's a difference between the fallout of your notes and the fallout of the defendants involved in this case. I'm talking about the potential danger you're facing."

"What's your intelligence?"

Kleinbeck smiled. "If I had any intelligence, I wouldn't be in this business," she said smugly—obviously amused by her own wit. Beavertooth and the agents also laughed.

I started to get up from the table. I'd had all I could take from this band of idiots. "I'm fucking glad that my personal safety is a laughing matter for you."

"No, no, no," she said, starting to get out of her chair, "I was just kidding. I'm sorry."

I sat back down, my cheeks burning with anger.

"Mr. Detty, I'm not sure I'm comfortable sharing my intelligence on this case with you," Kleinbeck said when she was sure I wasn't leaving.

"Why?"

"Because once I give it to you, I have no control over what you do with it."

"So, it's up to you to decide what information I get regarding these guys and the potential violence towards me."

She nodded.

"You? The same person who exposed me as the CI? I have to count on you?"

She set her jaw and said nothing.

This time I did get up and leave.

All of my life I had nothing but the greatest respect for federal agents and those who worked in the Department of Justice. Now, for the first time I was seeing them for what they were—lazy, sloppy, self-protecting civil servants who cared more about self-preservation and collecting a paycheck than doing the right thing. The high regard I once had for these people had been replaced with contempt. I'd gone from someone who was extremely proud of my involvement in helping federal law enforcement to someone who was ashamed and embarrassed. I felt betrayed and was disgusted.

Frankly, I didn't care if I never heard from any of these people again. They had gone out of their way to turn a patriot who would have done anything they asked into a disillusioned cynic. The veneer of my naiveté had been sandblasted away leaving nothing but raw nerve exposed.

A few months later I received a phone call from Special Agent Rob Gaylord. The last time I'd seen or talked with him was my December meeting with the two female AUSAs. He wanted to update me on the Moreno case.

"Before Sancho got a lawyer, he talked to me quite a bit and I got some good information. Apparently he was banging this chick in Douglas and she later married a cartel guy. During a trip across the border, she introduced the two and her husband asked if he could get him any guns. He started by selling him an S&W .40 and he used that money as his seed money to start buying guns."

The case snowballed from there with Sancho recruiting his high school football teammates to purchase guns. Even after he and Moreno parted company, the two still kept delivering guns to the same source in Mexico.

Gaylord said, "I wanted you to know that Kenneth Melson, the deputy director of ATF, gave a speech on March 4, 2010 before the House Committee on Appropriations specifically citing this case as an example of the success of Project Gunrunner."

After I got off the phone with Gaylord it took just a few minutes of Internet research to find Melson's speech.

In regards to the Moreno-Sancho case Director Melson said,

I would like to note several examples of our successes in disrupting the flow of firearms to Mexico. In December 2008, ATF agents arrested ten individuals involved in a conspiracy to straw purchase firearms in Arizona for the purpose of supplying weapons to the Sinaloan drug cartel in Sonora, Mexico. We believe they were responsible for trafficking approximately 120 firearms, including .50 caliber rifles. The suspects were indicted in February 2009, and subsequently several cooperated and identified the Sinaloan cartel member who headed the conspiracy, Ruben Javier Elense Ruiz, who goes by the name "Rambo." ATF forwarded Rambo's fingerprints to the FBI who matched them to prints connected to the murder of a Mexican Federal prosecutor in 2004. In March 2009, Rambo and several other cartel members were arrested in Mexico.

What Melson failed to mention was the CI who brought them this case was exposed by the AUSA and he was never paid the promised reward.

The next month I had surgery to replace my right ankle and hip. Looking at a long recuperation, I hired a Colombian nurse to stay with me for six weeks to cook, clean, and take care of the dogs while I was laid up. In August, I had my left ankle replaced which meant a few more months of lying around. My savings were nearly depleted by then.

In November, 2010, I was back at the gun show at the Pima County fairgrounds. For the entire weekend we only sold twelve rifles and two of them were at cost for an NRA raffle. My ankles were still both very sore and I was concentrating on sitting as much as possible to keep the swelling down. As I looked at the customers passing, I saw a smiling face. It was SA Rob Gaylord.

He'd been waiting until no one was around my tables. He extended his hand to shake and asked how I was.

"I'm doing alright Rob, how are you?" I asked, not getting out of my chair.

"Bored to death, Mike. How's business?"

"Shit, I've only sold twelve rifles all weekend."

"Wow, that sucks," said Gaylord as he looked over the ten tables I had with over sixty rifles on display and another forty rifles as back stock under the tables.

"You guys have anything exciting going on?"

"Nothing yet," he said with a smile.

"I got a call from Lori Beavertooth a couple weeks ago," I told him. "She told me that Wide Receiver has legs again and that there should be arrests soon."

"Yeah, how about that?" But the way he said made it seem as though there was something he wanted to tell me but couldn't.

"Why has it taken so long for her to get around to making arrests?"

"There's another case going on in Phoenix. I can't tell you too much about it, other than it makes Wide Receiver look miniscule. I don't understand it and I can't believe the number of guns they're letting walk and it doesn't look like they'll be wrapping up things anytime soon. But they asked us to put off our arrests thinking that somehow it would queer their case. I didn't think so, but its Newell's call." Newell was the Special Agent in Charge of the Phoenix ATF office.

Of course, the case he was referring to was Operation Fast and Furious. I found out later that one of the load cars involved in Fast and Furious stopped at Pedro Trujillo's house on the way to Mexico. That's why they had been afraid to arrest him and his cohorts.

As we talked, he kept scanning the room. He was either looking for other agents or maybe there was someone that he was watching.

"Were you guys working yesterday?"

"Yep, we were here all day."

"That's funny, I didn't see anyone I know."

"There are so many new guys, Mike. Our office is three times bigger than it was a couple years ago. You probably haven't met most of the new guys. Hell, I don't even work downtown anymore."

"I noticed that your last email listed the Research Loop as your address. You like working there better?"

"Oh yeah, it's so much easier getting there than driving into the city. You have anything for me?"

"I'll be sure to let you know if I stumble across anything. You're the one I'll be calling. Cubbie was a real dick to me last year and I won't work with him."

"Mike, you've always been straight up with me and I like you. As far as I'm concerned I'll take whatever I can get but it has to clear Newell's desk and he has a hard-on for you. I'm not even supposed to talk to you."

"He has a hard-on for me? What set him off? Was it my notes?"

Gaylord shrugged. "Hey, I saw Travis a couple weeks ago."

It would make sense that Travis had come over from Albuquerque to meet with Beavertooth and the rest of the team to plan the pending arrests.

"How is he?" I asked.

"He's doing well. I think he's finally done being mad at you."

"Finally, huh? I guess that's good news."

Honestly, I was so sick of worrying about the problems I caused Lopez that I really didn't care anymore. I hadn't heard a word from him since the third week of October 2009, when he called me upset and angry over my notes. It occurred to me that I was never really his friend but someone he used to further his career. When I'd recounted these events to my lawyer at a recent gun show he'd said, "Wait a minute, you gave a guy you considered a friend a $1,500 gun and he had the balls to get pissed off at you? He knows what the rules of ethics are, solicited you for a rifle, and then gets mad because you gave it to him. Makes perfect sense to me."

"Yeah, listen Mike," said Gaylord, "you were way too hard on yourself about that rifle. That's all on Lopez. Don't you think there are gun dealers in Albuquerque who would give a federal agent a good deal? He contacted you because he knew you'd give him the gun. Anyway, I just wanted to say hello and see how you were doing."

On November 10, 2010, I posted some pictures of myself in uniform on my Facebook page in commemoration of the 235th Marine Corps birthday. Dan James, one of my OCS classmates, called me from Fredericksburg, Virginia shortly after I posted the pictures. Mike Vermeil, the Executive Officer of Hotel Company at The Basic School sent me an email wishing me a happy birthday. I responded with a picture of myself and him that was taken Mess Night in 1983.

Just before noon I received this email from Lori Beavertooth.

Sorry, I can't find your phone number or I would have called. Trujillo, Maria Valenzuela, Rodriguez, and Fernando Vasquez were arrested in Tucson yesterday. Valenzuela, Rodriguez and Vasquez were released under supervision of pre-trial services. There is a detention hearing for Trujillo this morning in a few minutes. Izmael was arrested in California yesterday; I don't know how long it will take for him to be brought here. We suspect the remainder may be in Mexico.

I will be sending out discovery next week; this means that the defendants will have copies of the audio tapes as well as transcripts. It probably won't be too hard for the attorneys to figure out that you were working with ATF.

Just wanted to give you an update on things.

Lori Beavertooth
US Dept of Justice Gang Unit

After three years it was kind of anticlimactic. What could I say? All of those promises Jack and Travis had made to keep me safe were bullshit. They knew ahead of time that I'd be exposed. They didn't even bother to give me a heads-up before the arrests.

In December I got a voice mail message from a Washington Post writer saying that she knew I was involved in the investigation in which ten people were arrested and wanted to get a quote from me. I called and left a message on her voice mail telling her that I couldn't talk to her unless someone at the ATF OK'd it. Several minutes later Sari Horwitz called me back and told me that she was publishing a story in the Washington Post the next day and that it would also be on their website. "I just want to get some comments and quotes from you on the arrests of the ten gun traffickers last year," she said.

"Look, I'm afraid that I can't tell you anything unless I get an OK from the ATF office."

"We've already talked to the ATF."

"Who did you talk to?" I asked.

She stammered for a second. "Uh, the SAC in Phoenix, what's his name, Bill Newell. He said that this group bought these guns from you at a gun show and that you were cooperating with the ATF."

"Really," I asked incredulously. "He said that?"

"Yes, listen we just wanted to get some comments on these arrests from the dealers that sold the guns."

"No, I'm not comfortable commenting. Listen, you've put me in a bad position and this is completely off the record—either I am portrayed as a money hungry gun dealer without scruples or as an informant. Neither scenario is good for me."

"Well, let me read you a quote from another dealer who sold weapons to this group. 'We performed a background check on every sale and while we're troubled that some of these guns found their way to Mexico, we did everything required by law to ensure that they were sold legally.'"

In the end, I don't think I gave her anything she could use but still I was shocked by the news that SAC Newell had told her I was cooperating with the ATF.

In truth, I was pissed. It wasn't just that Newell was exposing me to the defendants in the case—that had already been taken care of by AUSA Kleinbeck—but that he was exposing me to the world by giving my name to the Washington Post reporter. A year earlier I had written him a letter asking about the reward Jodi Pederman had promised me and had never received a response from him. Now Gaylord was telling me that Newell had given orders not to accept any new cases from me and was pissed off at me. It was time for me to call Mr. Newell.

Newell's secretary asked for my name and what the call was about and then put me through. Newell answered the phone with a certain amount of apprehension.

I told him that I had been contacted by the Washington Post reporter and she had told me he gave her my name. Newell denied it.

"That's just an old reporter trick," he said. "She was just throwing that out there to get you to talk."

He was adamant he did not give her my name yet she told me he did. If she had gotten my name from another source she could have just as easily named that source. It didn't add up.

"I've been told by an agent here in Tucson that I've managed to get cross-wise with you somehow," I said. "I'm not sure what I did to offend you but I'm certain it was unintentional."

"What? I'd like to know that agent's name. That is a complete misinterpretation of my feelings towards you."

"Agents I've worked with for the last three years now walk past me at gun shows without acknowledging me. Some of them I've even socialized with. It's hard to believe that someone didn't give the order to ignore me."

"That was not an order I ever gave," said Newell. "I'm the top dog here and I can tell you that never happened."

"It seems very strange to me. Last year I sent you a letter asking about a reward that Special Agent Pederman promised me and I never got a response from you."

"Jodi doesn't work out of this office anymore. I forwarded that letter to the Denver office. I'm surprised that you didn't hear anything back."

His response was a lie. If there was going to be a reward it would have had to be approved and issued by his Phoenix office. SA Pederman moving to Colorado meant nothing.

"I was also told that I'd receive a reward for the Moreno-Rutgers case. Yet when I asked my case agent here he said he wouldn't put me in for it because he knew you would deny it."

"I'd sure like to know who this agent is so that I could take corrective action. I believe you absolutely deserve a reward. We could never have made those arrests or got the convictions without your help. We give rewards all the time—it's no big deal."

When I got off the phone with Newell, I sent SA Gaylord an email outlining my conversation with Newell and formally requested that he put me in for a reward on the Moreno-Rutgers case. Minutes later I received this ass-covering response.

Mike

I'm glad that you had the opportunity to talk with Mr. Newell. He is a good man and always has treated me well. I'm not surprised that he treated you the same.

I'll discuss the reward with my supervisor and get back to you.

Let me know if anything else comes up. Take care.

ATF SA Rob Gaylord

December 14, 2010, Border Patrol Agent Brian Terry was shot and killed.

Three days later SA Gaylord called me. "Mike I just wanted you to know that I spoke to Lori Beavertooth and she won't allow the reward for the Moreno case."

I could have guessed. I sent an email to Lori Beavertooth asking her to confirm what he had told me.

Hi Lori,

I just wanted to confirm something. As you know, I have been having a lot of trouble getting ATF to uphold their promise of a reward for the Moreno-Sancho case. Now SA Gaylord says that you told him to cancel my reward? Seriously? This wasn't even your case.

Mike Detty

I went out to my desert shooting spot to chronograph a variety of loads and guns for articles. As I was loading my last target into the back of my Tahoe my cell phone rang and I could see that it was from the Washington DC area code. I knew it must be Lori Beavertooth.

She started in a stern voice, "Every email that you send asking about your reward only makes it look like you are money hungry. All of those emails have to be turned over in discovery. Can you imagine how bad that will make you look if you have to testify?"

I gave an apathetic, "Uh-huh."

She continued the same way a school teacher would scold a wayward student.

"Now you and I both know that the money is not your prime concern. But these types of emails will do nothing but support a defense attorney's argument that you're only interested in money."

I was already in a bad mood as I had shot my old chronograph (an electrical instrument used to measure a bullet's velocity) square through its circuit boards. Right now I could give a fuck about her or her case. "Let me tell you something, Lori," I said. "The reason I sent an email is so I could have a record that it was sent. What am I supposed to do when I don't get an answer? It's been six months now since the Moreno–Sancho case wrapped up and three years since the Rey Ayala case in Phoenix was finished. I have no advocate saying, 'You know, we should really get Mike Detty the reward we promised him.' I spoke to Rob Gaylord last week and he said that he wanted to hold off on the reward because Bill Newell was pissed at me. I called Newell on Monday and he was hot. He wanted to know who was mischaracterizing his opinion of me and said he was appreciative of everything I had done for the agency. He also said that he thought that I was deserving of a reward. Now I have to ask myself why Gaylord thought it would be a good idea to have me think that Newell hated me."

My retort took Beavertail by surprise and stymied her aggressive tone.

"I can't answer those questions, Mike," she said.

There I was, three years removed from this case and still dealing with the fallout from it. I was tired of being treated like a criminal. I had done everything these people had asked of me and now I was feeling like a piece of used Kleenex.

March 2, 2011, I drove down to the Federal Courthouse for a 10 a.m. meeting with Lori Beavertooth. I had no idea what she wanted to see me about and feared that it might be some sort of cover-up for what was going on with ATF leadership over the guns walking into Mexico as part of investigations.

I put my wallet, cell phone, and digital recorder into the basket before passing through the metal detector which set off an alarm immediately. The elderly security agent said that I must have forgotten something. "No, it's these new ankles and hip." He waved his wand around me, smiled, and reached over to get the basket with my articles.

He picked up my digital recorder and said I couldn't take it upstairs. I told him the US Attorney was counting on me bringing it. "OK, I'll have to call a US Marshall to have it escorted upstairs with you."

I stood idle, watching the court schedules flicker across the large flat screen TVs in the lobby. After several minutes, I realized that it was not going to be a speedy process so I texted Beavertooth and told her that I was stalled at security downstairs. Minutes later, I saw SA Tom Goodman walk into the lobby. He saw me and walked over to shake my hand. I had the feeling that even though he knew my name and face he had not quite put them together yet. I asked if he was there today on my case and he nodded in affirmation as he held up a three-ring binder and manila envelope. I told him that they had snagged my digital recorder and that I was waiting for a Marshall to escort me upstairs.

Just then Lori Beavertooth walked into the lobby from the elevators. I explained that they were holding my recorder.

"Oh no—you are not recording anything! Do I make myself clear?" she said loudly.

"I'm recording you right now," I said as I aimed one of the buttons from my 5.11 shirt at her as though it was a miniature camera.

She broke into a toothy smile. "Are you so paranoid that you feel like you have to record our conversation?"

I gave her the stink eye. "Are you new? Have you forgotten how I've been treated by the ATF the last year?"

Her smile quickly disappeared and she gave me a conciliatory look. "Yeah, well, regardless, the recorder cannot go upstairs."

Goodman offered to lock it in his pistol cube in the lobby of the courthouse so we walked over, picked up the recorder, and secured it.

The three of us went up to the fourth floor where Goodman signed me in as a guest of the courthouse and I was issued an "Unescorted Guest" adhesive badge, and then we went back to the elevators and down to the third floor where the Assistant US Attorneys offices were located.

"I'm so important that they gave me this huge office," said Beavertooth as she pointed out her cubicle-size office.

"At least you have a window," I said, noting the view of the federal building and Pima County courthouse.

We walked past her office into a conference room. She took a chair on one side of the table and Goodman took one on the other, leaving me the seat at the head of the table.

My chest was tight. I had no idea what to expect and I had already made up my mind that I wasn't going to take any more crap from her or the ATF. My only purpose was to gather as much information as I could.

"I wanted to talk to you today in preparation of the trial of Fernando Vasquez," said Beavertooth.

My mind started racing. I remembered when she told me he'd been arrested as part of the Operation Wide Receiver round up and I didn't recognize his name then. The other name I didn't recognize was LaFourcade.

"To tell you the truth, Lori, that is a name I don't recognize."

"According to your notes, Fernando Vasquez came out with Omar and Pedro Trujillo on the evening of March 20, 2007. Vasquez did the paperwork for a .38 Super and Trujillo handed you money for the gun. Once the paperwork was completed, Vasquez walked over and handed the gun to Omar."

"Who then held that pistol to his girlfriend's head at the Mexican restaurant?"

"Well, that is what she said in her TPD complaint."

"Yep—got it. It's all coming back to me now."

"That's OK—after all, it's been four years."

"According to Pedro he was arrested, taken to Florence prison, and eventually deported," I said.

Beavertooth nodded. "Yes, he was deported. It looks like everyone is going to plead—at least that's what we're hoping for, with the exception of

Fernando Vasquez and his lawyer wants to take it to trial. I mean, we have him dead to rights. It is the classic definition of a straw deal. He did the paperwork and then handed the gun to Omar."

"Who then sat on my couch and snapped the hammer a couple hundred times before he left," I said.

Goodman nodded giggling—he had obviously read my notes.

"Your notes are very detailed and it clearly outlines that he did the paperwork and then handed the gun off to the person you call Skunkhead in your notes."

"Yes, that much I remember clearly. I do, however recall that Pedro told me that when the police came to the restaurant that Fernando was trying to tell them that it was his gun—presumably so they wouldn't charge Omar, who was an illegal alien in possession of a firearm."

"Yes," said Beavertooth, "His lawyer is so ridiculous. 'In twenty-five years of practicing law, I finally have an innocent client.' He's very theatrical and flamboyant—kind of like a Kevin Klein figure."

I wondered why this case would be so important to Beavertooth in the grand scheme of things. Clearly it was important in terms of the DOJ scoreboard and headlines, but it was just one gun compared to the hundreds that Trujillo and Eduardo had bought.

"I think the judge on the case wanted to give up something since we had won so many of the battles and in this case he said that he would slice off the Vasquez case for a separate trial. But, I think that now he has to put it in writing that he's having an issue with it."

"You mean that Rodriguez, Trujillo, and Valenzuela will all be tried at the same time?"

Beavertooth looked surprised, "Yeaaaaahh! That's the idea. But Vasquez wants his own trial and I'll need to start preparing for that. Have you ever testified?"

"No."

"I want you to know that I've gone through your notes and redacted some things I didn't think were relative. You know, like things about your dogs or your sexual escapades and even some back and forth chatter between you and Lopez. One thing that will cause some issues is the emails that you sent where you identified yourself as the "star witness" in Operation Wide Receiver." She use her fingers to accentuate imaginary quotation marks.

At first I was unaware of what she was talking about and then I realized that it was the email I sent before my Warning Conference. I turned to

Goodman and asked him if he knew what she was talking about. He shook his head in the negative.

I explained that ATF's Industry Ops had sent out two hapless investigators, Dan Davidson and Destani Hula, who spent three weeks performing a perfectly screwed up audit. During their inspection they managed to lose eighty serial numbers that were there. I explained that all of those numbers were in my master cases of stripped Rock River Arms AR-15 lower receivers.

"I'm not saying that it was Dan, but it was Dan that opened these cases of twenty-four each and counted three or twelve or twenty of twenty-four pieces and then closed the box and stopped counting. That's where all the missing numbers were. If I hadn't gone back and physically recounted everything they did I would have never found those missing numbers and would have lost my license. He told me I was going to lose my license and face probable criminal action. But the point here is that they decided that I needed to be formally reprimanded. It was decided that my deficiencies were so bad that they actually had to have a conference to warn me that my records were substandard. I couldn't have cared less—it was a slap on the wrist but my question was; do you really want to formally scold a dealer when he may have to testify in a major trafficking case? That's why I sent you, Lori Beavertooth, an email, as well as Bill Newell, Rob Gaylord, Matt Cubbie, and the new Tucson ASAC. I was worried that one hand of the ATF didn't know what the other hand was doing. Do you know how many responses I got from that email?"

Beavertooth shrugged her shoulders.

"Not one! So, you can complain all you want about that email and make a big deal out of calling myself the star witness but the truth is that in this instance I was the only one with the foresight and who cared enough to raise it as an issue."

Goodman's face was red and he was shaking his head back and forth as if it was hard for him to believe.

"I'll tell you Lori, if you had just picked up the phone or emailed me back, then this wouldn't have become an issue."

She smiled, looked down and shook her head softly side to side.

Frankly, I could care less if she agreed with me or not. My concerns were about Wide Receiver not about the Warning Conference. It pissed me off no end that they would try to make me out to be the bad guy when I was the only conscientious person in the whole gaggle.

"Mike, I've known you for a while," said Goodman finally, "and I apologize for all those times that I stopped and talked to you at gun shows without really knowing who you were or what you've done for this office. And, I apologize because clearly you weren't treated right. But I do want to let you know that I'm handling the case now and if you have any problems or concerns, all you have to do is let me know. I'll be as responsive as I possibly can."

"Look, Tom, I appreciate that, but really you don't need to apologize for anyone else. What pisses me off is people lying to me and ignoring me. If someone tells me that they're going to give me a reward, then give me a reward. Don't jerk me off. I'm not some drug addict trying to stay out of prison. I'm just a guy who wanted to be a good American and I brought you some pretty damn good cases and put myself in some significant danger to help your office. I didn't deserve the bullshit treatment that I've received for the past year and a half. And don't make me out to be some malcontent when I'm trying to help and nobody has the decency to get back to me," I said, turning to Beavertooth.

"OK—duly noted," said Beavertooth, clearly wanting to get off this topic as quickly as possible.

"Whatever happened to Ira Goldblatt?" I asked, changing gears.

"I can't tell you," said Beavertooth.

I looked out the third-floor window towards the federal building. "I'm guessing that he's cooperating with you and had probably moved and even taken on a new identity?"

"I can't tell you—at least not right now. At some point in time I may be able to unseal his folder and fill you in."

I nodded, satisfied that she had told me all that she could.

"But I do have to tell you that I think he's a very nice young man," she added.

Her words took me by surprise. "My impression of him was that he was caught up in living the gangster lifestyle and enjoying it."

"That may very well be but he's had the opportunity to turn over a new leaf and seems to be an incredible young man."

Now it became clear that he had cooperated with the ATF and that he had a chance to start over. I nodded and looked outside. "What about Eduardo?"

"He's going to trial with Rodriguez."

"I didn't know that you'd arrested him."

"Oh, I'm sorry. I thought you meant Izmael. No, Eduardo is dead," she said matter-of-factly.

"Dead? What happened?" Even though I didn't really believe it, I had to admit I felt a little gleeful about the news of his demise.

"He was sitting in his pickup in Hermosillo," said Goodman, " and someone walked up and shot him in the head."

After I got home I looked through my notes to find the spelling of Eduardo's last name and then Googled it. Apparently, he was sitting in his truck in the southern part of the city and someone walked up to him and shot him twice in the arm and once in the head with a 10 mm pistol.

"Hey Mike," said Goodman, "what was his wife or girlfriend's name?"

"Let me think for a second." I rubbed my forehead trying to remember when I introduced myself to her at the gun show. "It's Charlene Saucedo."

"That's right," said Goodman. "Matt Cubbie is part of a multi-agency anti-terrorism team and he called me a couple days ago with a question about her."

"I remember Travis telling me that he thought her father was involved in a cartel somehow."

"I'm not sure if we were ever able to confirm that but it might make sense as to how Eduardo hooked up with her."

"What a little prick that guy was. I remember Travis and I used to joke over who was going to get to shoot him. I guess we both lost."

"Well. I never had the displeasure of meeting him," said Beavertooth, "but I could tell by your writing that you had nothing but contempt for him. That came through loud and clear."

"Absolutely! He was such an obnoxious punk and seemed to have no trouble screwing anyone over."

"May God bless his soul," said Beavertooth as she smiled her bunny smile.

I laughed. I was feeling more at ease and not as ready for a fight as when I'd walked into the meeting. But I wanted to make the most of it and gather as much information as possible.

I looked at Lori, cocked my head and smiled. "So, what do you think about what ATF's leadership is saying about guns crossing the border?"

Goodman dropped his head into his hands with a dull thud. "Oh God," he moaned as if he'd been punched in the stomach.

She looked at me and said with a straight face, "What are you talking about? I haven't been keeping up."

I looked over at Goodman, who was now acting like he was in the midst of an appendicitis attack, and laughed. "Have you been under a rock?" I asked in disbelief.

"What's going on?"

Goodman straightened up in his chair. "This all has to do with the Border Patrolman that was shot last December. The gun that he was shot with was one of the guns that was part of Operation Fast and Furious. Newell and Melson have both publicly said that no guns crossed the border as part of any investigation."

"That's interesting," said Beavertooth.

It was more than just "interesting." The Inspector General's report had documented emails between Beavertooth and high-ranking officials at DOJ in which Beavertooth reported that guns had been allowed to walk across the border and how to portray this in the best light to the press. In an effort to keep the gunwalking aspect out of the case, Beavertooth narrowed the scope of the case to straw sales. Each of her defendants was charged with lying on their form #4473, the background check form filled out when a gun is purchased, in that they were not the actual buyer of the firearm.

"I got a call yesterday from an agent in Phoenix who wanted to know about Wide Receiver because Senator Grassley's office had called and asked for specific information regarding this case," said Goodman.

I felt a warm rush and fought hard to contain my smile. Someone had listened! I had been in touch with both Congressman Issa and Senator Grassley's offices.

In March, 2011, I was at a gun show at the Pima County Fairgrounds when I saw Dan Kochs and a friend walk by. Dan was an AUSA in Tucson and was dating an old friend of mine, Barbie, who had introduced us at an earlier gun show. With him was Tim Bugatti, who at one time had been the AUSA on Wide Receiver. I answered some gun-related questions for the two. After a while our discussion turned to the ATF. Tim seemed uninhibited in his criticism of the ATF and the Fast and Furious investigation. He made mention of the third gun found at Border Patrol Agent Terry's murder site and the ensuing cover up. "This could be Obama's Watergate," he offered.

"You know, Mike," said Tim, "I have to apologize because I have seen you at many gun shows. But it took me a while to figure out that you at the gun shows was the same Mad Dawg that I read about in all the reports."

We both laughed and I remembered to myself how much I used to resent Tim. Field agents, specifically Lopez, had told me that the reason Wide Receiver was not prosecuted was because Bugatti ignored it while he promoted himself for US Magistrate.

"Tim, I have to ask you a question. Why is it that you never prosecuted Wide Receiver? I should tell you that the agents I worked with blamed it on you."

"They're right," Bugatti said sharply. "I never prosecuted that case because the ATF lied to me."

I sensed that I was about to receive some monumental information.

"Look, I'm not blaming Travis because I don't think he did anything other than repeat what someone above told him. I don't want to believe that he's complicit because he's a nice kid. But I was told at first that they had arranged for Mexican authorities on the other side of the border to interdict or at least follow your guns."

"Yeah, they told me that too," I said.

"I was lead to believe that there was ongoing cooperation with the Mexicans on this case. When I found out that they were lying to me, I wasn't going to devote any more time or work to that case. The last thing I was going to do was take a case to court that was based on lies. Why should I ruin my personal integrity and professional credibility because they screwed up so badly?"

So, there it was. It took me three years to learn the truth and it was nothing close to what Lopez had told me. The ATF had screwed up badly and had based an entire investigation on lies to the AUSA. Their arrogance and assumption that Bugatti would go along with their deception caused them to lose years of manhours, resources, money and, most importantly, credibility. The person responsible for this mess had to be the supervising Special Agent in Charge, Bill Newell.

"When I left to become magistrate, I handed the case file over to Sarah and she refused to touch it too. Now they brought this new AUSA in from DC to prosecute it? Really? Nothing has changed—it's still the same screwed-up case. I was working the dope angle with ICE and they just couldn't wrap themselves around a very simple concept. Eduardo was more important and dangerous than anyone at ATF could have guessed."

"Who was calling the shots there? Was it Newell?

"I dunno if it was Newell or someone above him but it's a damn shame that they are so screwed up. I still can't believe that they had you selling to those guys out of your house. They should never have exposed you to that danger."

The following Sunday evening I checked my email and found a note from Dan Kochs's girlfriend, my old friend, Barbie.

Dan told me last night that after he and Tim left the show and were driving home, Tim started telling Dan that he thought you were under the impression the people you were dealing with were not big players and not that dangerous. Tim said based on his knowledge of the case, those guys you were dealing with were big time and they were/are very dangerous, and given what has gone down (and I don't know the details but am under the impression that you do) you really do need to take precautions and watch your back.

Dan was telling me this, and I asked if you were in any danger, and he said very possibly. When I asked if you had been told that he said he didn't think so. I asked why not. He didn't know until on the way home or he would have taken you aside and told you. I said that was easy to fix right then and there, because it wasn't fair for you not to know. He agreed we should email you.

So that is all I know, which is really only bits and pieces. I don't want anything to happen to you because (1) I don't, and (2) I certainly don't want to see you get hurt because you were willing to step up to the plate and do what was right.

So seriously, take care. Barbie

So, the original AUSA on Operation Wide Receiver thought I was in danger even though Lori Beavertooth continued to tell me these criminals were harmless—even after telling me that Eduardo had been assassinated. She only cared about getting her convictions. She certainly couldn't care less about me or my welfare.

On April 1, 2011, SA Tom Goodman called me as I was setting up my tables at the state fairgrounds in Phoenix in preparation for the weekend's gun show. He told me that Beavertooth wanted to meet with me to arrange for pretrial case preparations. I thought about it for a second. Given the way that she had treated me I saw no reason to help her any further. I told Goodman to tell her that I would not be taking part in pretrial preparations but if I was subpoenaed, I would arrive on time and testify truthfully to the best of my recollections.

The following month Lori Beavertooth and two ATF agents came out to my house. She had requested that I come down to the federal building to meet with her and I told her no. I was recovering from the ankle surgery I'd had the previous week to fine-tune the new ankle I received the previous August and remove two large bolts. My left foot was in a large walking cast and I was using a walker.

I had a crew in the backyard working on my pool so both of my dogs were inside and they swarmed my company. Maya's white hair covered Beavertooth's business suit in a matter of minutes. Champ crawled up onto the couch between me and Beavertooth and put his head in her lap.

One of the ATF agents sat on the other end of the L-shaped sectional. He had Samoan tribal tattoos, thick shoulders, and a high-speed, "rich kid" watch worn with its face on the inside of his wrist.

"Navy?" I asked.

He nodded, confirming my suspicion that he'd been a Navy operator of some sort. The other agent sat behind me in the kitchen. I turned just in time to see him push Maya's head away from him. She was a friendly dog giving him a smiling greeting and he pushed her face away.

"Don't like dogs?" I asked.

He didn't say anything.

"You're here at my invitation," I said. "If you don't like my dogs you can go sit out in the driveway."

He smirked at me and that pissed me off. I started to get out of my chair and turned completely. "Maybe you didn't understand me. I am telling you to leave my house."

Beavertooth turned around and told him to wait in the car. He reluctantly got up and left.

Beavertooth's purpose was to drop off some transcripts that she wanted me to go through. They were of different buys that had happened at my house and the transcripts were made from my recordings. I looked through several stacks of them and saw that they had each voice identified but there was now a thick black line drawn through the name.

"I'd like you to listen to your recordings and identify each voice," said Beavertooth.

"Someone has already done that."

"Lopez did it originally. But we need you to do it as well so we can be 100 percent certain in court of who said what."

I looked at the thick stack of transcripts and it made my stomach turn. There were days and days worth of work there.

"Don't you feel bad doing this to me?"

"No I really don't," said Beavertooth. "You can work on these while you recover."

Her arrogance struck a chord with me.

"I can write an article and make money. It will cost me money to do this for you."

"Nonetheless, I need you to do it—the sooner the better."

After she left, I dropped an email to my attorney and asked if she could force me to do it.

"Yes and no," he replied. "If she forces you to do that transcript work she has to divulge that in discovery and it won't look good for her."

I started working on the transcripts, listening carefully to the recordings on my hard drive and trying to attribute the correct name next to each statement. It was harder than I expected and required me to constantly rewind and listen again. After two hours, I had only completed four pages of the first transcript.

When my girlfriend came home from work she asked what I was doing. I explained it all to her and showed her the stack of transcripts. She was livid.

"How long do you have to do those?"

"She wants them as soon as possible."

"Are they paying you to do this?"

I shook my head from side to side.

"How many article assignments do you have right now from your publisher?"

"Eight."

"So you're putting off roughly $5,000 of work to do this?"

I nodded. I felt my face flush. I was embarrassed.

"Isn't this the same woman who has lied to you, taken your reward away, and dragged you over the coals about your journal?"

She wasn't telling me anything I didn't already know but to hear it from someone else put things into perspective for me. I turned off my computer and threw the transcripts on the floor.

"Seriously, Mike, haven't you done enough for these people? Haven't you fulfilled your patriotic obligation already? They don't care if you get shot. Screw them!"

I thought about a lot of things that night—like my willingness to help my government without question, the risks I took on their behalf, and my tremendous naiveté in believing that not only would I be instrumental in taking down a cartel but also in believing that people I worked with, for whom I once had such great respect, would protect me.

I had been a fool!

The next morning I wrote and sent the following email. Besides sending it to Beavertooth, I copied every ATF agent I had ever worked with including Bill Newell. I was sick of being used and would not allow it to happen again.

Definition of FORESIGHT

1: an act or the power of foreseeing : prescience

2: provident care : prudence <had the foresight to invest his money wisely>

3: an act of looking forward; also : a view forward

— fore·sight·ed \- sī-təd\ adjective

— fore·sight·ed·ly adverb

— fore·sight·ed·ness noun

— fore·sight·ful \- sīt-fəl\ adjective

Examples of FORESIGHT

1. They had the foresight to invest the money wisely.

2. His career choice shows a lack of foresight.

3. ATF showed a complete lack of foresight by fucking Mike Detty around without realizing that they would need his help in the future.

Lori—I will not be doing the transcripts. I find it amazing that you keep coming back to me asking me to do these favors for you. While you might be able to legally force me to do this work, you would also need to turn that over as discovery.

I first brought these cases to the attention of the ATF as a concerned patriot. I allowed myself to be placed in conditions of danger time after time without flinching. But what I did not bargain for was agents lying to me and treating me like I was a drug addict trying to keep myself out of prison.

The fact that I blindly put my faith in ATF and followed their orders exactly is now a huge embarrassment. The morons that designed Project Gunrunner and administrated Wide Receiver are the ones that should be on trial. A bigger group of liars I have never been associated with! What started as a noble effort on my part is now a matter of great shame to me.

You make a big deal about the CI money that I took during the 3 years that I worked for ATF. Take a look at the volume of work that I did and the risks that I took on their behalf. I'd be happy to give that money back if you would just leave me alone. Would you take $15,000 to have cartel assholes in your living room? In every case that I have worked I have been exposed as the CI-twice by AUSA's.

While on the topic of money-it was YOU that gave an order to Gaylord to NOT put me in for a reward for a case that you were not even involved in. This was after I already had been stiffed on another Phoenix investigation and finally had a conversation with SAC Newell where he acknowledged that I should get a reward for the Moreno-Sancho-Rutgers case.

So, again, do not ask me to do any more work for you. As I said before, I will show up at the time noted on the subpoena and will testify honestly. Beyond that-do not count on a single thing from me.

Best regards,
Mike Detty

In September, 2011, I drove up to Phoenix to do an interview with CBS investigative reporter Sharyl Attkisson. I had been talking and corresponding with Sharyl since February, 2011 when she was trolling www.cleanupatf.org looking for information on Fast and Furious. I supplied her with details regarding Wide Receiver for her report which aired October 5, 2011. Of all the mainstream news outlets, Attkisson's reports were the most accurate and ground-breaking. Attkisson, by far, was the most skilled of all the media people I'd dealt with in terms of putting me at ease and conducting an effective interview. While ATF and DOJ were still saying that they never allowed guns to walk across the border, SA John Dodson from the Phoenix ATF office had the balls to come forward and blow the whistle on SAC Newell and his gang in an interview with Attkisson.

I started making an outline of notes for what would eventually become this book. Reading through my journal, I decided to listen to my first meeting with Eduardo. In particular, I wanted to hear the exchange when his bodyguard was standing behind me in an intimidating manner.

When I clicked on the audio file I got an error message that read "File deleted or damaged." I clicked on another file in the folder and then another until I realized that every file in my Wide Receiver folder had been corrupted. There were hundreds of recorded conversations in this folder—every buy, every phone call with Trujillo and friends. I thought for a minute and decided to check my emails to Lopez where I had attached many of the phone call conversations.

Lopez had three email accounts that I used. ATF, DOJ, and a private Yahoo account. Lopez often had me send phone recordings to his Yahoo account because the government had some sort of filter on their email accounts that limited file size. I searched for all emails sent to that account—there were none. I then searched for emails to his other work accounts and none showed up there either.

Other folders were untouched—my phone conversations with Lori Beavertooth, my call to Bill Newell, all of the Moreno-Rutgers conversations were still there. Just a couple months earlier I'd used some of the files to work on Beavertooth's transcripts. Before giving in to paranoia, I called my friend Bryce Chandler, who works in the intelligence field and had previously given me some advice in regards to installing tracking devices in weapons to see what he thought. He asked me a series of questions regarding the types of files and my wireless system and said that he'd talk to his IT guys.

Chandler called me back a couple hours later.

"Most likely someone sat outside your house and used your wireless internet system to break into your files. My guys think they could figure out who it was if you want to fly out here with your laptop."

"They'd be willing to do that for me?"

"Sure. But here's the rub. Let's say we find out exactly who did this. Then what? Who do we take that information to—the same people that have been screwing you over? My guys wouldn't be able to testify on your behalf. But based on what you've told me, all fingers point in one direction."

"Yeah, Lopez," I said. "He's the only one who would have benefited from this. He even went to the trouble of deleting our emails back and forth."

"Mike," said Bryce in a pleading manner, "tell me that you back up your computer to an external hard drive."

"Yes, of course. I guess that was something whoever did this wasn't counting on."

"Well, whoever it was, was worried enough to make that gamble. After you restore your files, go to one of the office supply stores and buy a bunch of thumb drives. Copy all of the files pertaining to these ATF cases and send them to trusted friends around the country. That way, if they destroy your computer and get hold of your external hard drive, you'll still be covered. Who knows what they'll try next? Breaking into your house? Don't underestimate these guys, Mike."

I had left a voice mail message for Lori Beavertooth to let her know about my computer being hacked and see what her response would be. I mentioned that if she needed my files I would have happily given them to her.

Mike,

Not sure when you left the message about your computer being hacked as there was no date/time, but I just got it today (I am not at this number frequently). Neither I nor Tom Goodman requested any government agency to surreptitiously retrieve the recordings that you indicate were stolen, nor do I have reason to believe that any govt agency did so. If you wish to report this incident, you should probably start with Tucson Police Department or whatever law enforcement agency serves your location (I'm not sure if you are within the City of Tucson, or how that works in your location).

Lori Beavertooth

I was worried. What if this invasion wasn't just a matter of Lopez trying to cover his ass? All of DOJ and ATF now had my notes. Who was it I pissed off and what were they so afraid of? What would their next move be?

In October, Fox News investigative reporter William LaJeunesse flew in to do an interview with me. He and his crew spent some time with me at my home and then we went out to a place in the desert where they could video me shooting the types of weapons I had sold to the Narcos. He used his piece to illustrate that Fast and Furious was not the only case where the ATF had let guns walk across the border.

Paul Barrett, a writer for *Businessweek* magazine, flew into Tucson to interview me for a piece he titled, *The Guns That Got Away*. We spent several hours talking in the lobby of his hotel and the next day he came out to my house to actually see where the transactions with the cartel associates took place. I had a gun show at Cardinal's Stadium in Glendale, Arizona, that weekend and Barrett came up to see the event firsthand. A couple weeks later *Businessweek* published his four-page report. I was impressed that his report did not contain more anti-gun vitriol, as *Businessweek* is owned by gun-control proponent and New York City mayor, Michael Bloomberg.

When Bill Newell testified in front of Congressman Issa's Oversight Committee in July, I sent him an email calling him a lying bastard and may have made some crude remarks inferring that his sex life would improve once he goes to prison. I had no idea that his email was being monitored. I received this response an hour or so later.

Mr. Detty,

Your recent complaint about Bill Newell was referred to our office by ATF Internal Affairs. Our office is currently conducting an investigation of the ATF Phoenix investigation commonly referred to as Operation Fast and Furious, to include any other ATF investigations that utilized similar tactics/techniques. In your e-mail to Mr. Newell, you mentioning that he had lied under oath during his recent congressional testimony. We would like to speak with you about your allegation and any other relevant information that you may have that would assist our investigation.

You can respond via e-mail or contact me at one of the below listed telephone numbers.

Sincerely,
Jeff McCatskill
Senior Special Agent
Office of Inspector General

In November, 2011, I met with two investigators from the Office of Inspector General. They had asked me to meet them at the federal building but I declined. I had several reasons but the most important one was that I wanted to record the meeting and would not be able to get my digital recorder through security at the federal building. Of course, I didn't tell them I wanted to record our conversation so I told them I would feel intimidated meeting at the federal building where I would surely run into some of these agents I had worked with. So we arranged to meet at the La Paloma resort where the two agents were staying.

The male agent started a digital recorder, which sat on the table between us, while the female Investigative Counsel swore me in. I had already started my own recorder before entering the conference room. I was pleasantly surprised at how well the two were prepared. Obviously both of them had read through my notes and had sharp, pointed questions that were absolutely designed to get to the bottom of who most likely orchestrated this investigation and let guns walk to Mexico. There were many questions as to whether or not Jack Hinkley might have done this on his own and my answer was absolutely not. Jack was so close to retirement that he would not have wanted to do anything that may screw it up. In my opinion, everything he did was approved through the Phoenix office—meaning SAC Newell.

I arrived at 10 a.m. and I think we adjourned around 1 p.m. It seemed to be a pleasant meeting and not in the least confrontational. I had the opportunity to vent about Lori Beavertooth, the haggard prosecutor who had somehow made Wide Receiver a prosecutable case even after two AUSAs had declined it. I also had to vent about the ATF and their lies.

I had brought my laptop computer with me and filled a thumb drive with my files for them. The Office of Inspector General was my last hope for the truth to be told and for those who had been lying and obsfuscating to be punished.

The two told me that they would publish their public record probably in mid-2012. From there it would be up to congress or DOJ to make changes based on the OIG's recommendations.

Later I received this distressing email from the Investigative Counsel.

Dear Mr. Detty:

We have since reviewed the materials on the thumb drive you gave us and determined that we need to give the recordings and manuscripts to Lori Beavertooth – this does not mean that everything will be handed over to the defense, but simply that Beavertooth will have to evaluate them to see what information, if any, has to be disclosed.

I understand the sensitivity of this issue and that you are likely to have concerns. If you would like to discuss this, please do not hesitate to give me a call at 202-305-xxxx. I will do my best to answer any questions.

Best regards,
Judy McConnelly
Investigative Counsel
U.S. Department of Justice

The files she gave Beavertooth included surreptitious recordings I'd made of conversations with her, Newell, and other agents whom I did not trust. Plus another two hundred or so pages of notes I had made since Beavertooth got my last journal. Why in the world would an investigator for the Inspector General turn files over to the very people they were investigating? It didn't make sense to me and did nothing but erode what little trust I had in the government and those who worked for it.

After Christmas of 2011 Dan Kochs, my friend who worked as an AUSA here in Tucson came over to have me replace the gas block on his rifle with one that has an integral folding front sight. While I worked on his rifle we talked.

"There were some long faces walking around the federal building last month," said Kochs.

"How long were the IG investigators there?"

"All week. They even came and talked to me. Tim had to talk to them too."

"I asked them when they thought they'd be done with the report and they told me it would probably be summer before it was published."

"Yeah, nothing moves fast when it involves our government."

"Dan, what do you really think was going on with Wide Receiver? I mean nothing makes sense to me."

"Anytime you have an operation like this you have to ask yourself; what is the end gain? Was it to take out a cartel?"

"That's what they told me," I said.

"How? By what mechanism? How do you shut down a cartel when all of their assets are in another country?"

"I wondered about that."

"Was it to find out what cartels these guns were going to? Thanks to you they had that information within the first couple buys. Was it to track the guns to see where the cartels are operating? That's ridiculous—we already have that intelligence."

I looked up from my work. He made it all sound so simple.

Kochs said, "I can only think of one reason that Newell would allow American guns to continue to cross the border and show up at Mexican crime scenes." He cocked an eyebrow for emphasis.

At last I understood the ugly truth. All of the risks I took, all of the work I performed, all of the man hours and resources poured into this case by the ATF were not to take down a cartel. In my opinion, the reason that guns were allowed to cross the border in Wide Receiver as well as Fast and Furious was to have American guns show up at Mexican crime scenes.

With American guns being used in ruthless savagery across the border, a push could be made for a new assault weapons ban here in the United States. There is no other explanation why guns would be continually allowed to cross the border after the purchasers, their cartels, and ports of entry had already been identified.

I believe there was never a plan to take down a cartel. The end result of Wide Receiver was ten people being charged with lying on their form #4473 by indicating the gun purchase was for themself. I think the maximum sentence was thirty-six months. Remember, Beavertooth had to narrow the scope of the charges to get the defendants to plead without addressing the whole gunwalking controversy. Fernando Vasquez, who had a sharp lawyer and pushed for his own trial, had all charges dropped when it came time to go to trial. That's a far cry from taking down a cartel or toppling a drug kingpin!

The one common denominator between Wide Receiver and Fast and Furious was Bill Newell, the Special Agent in Charge of the Phoenix ATF office. Newell took over the Phoenix office just a few months after Wide Receiver started and was there from start to finish for Fast and Furious.

Both cases were politicized with Republicans blaming the Obama administration for Fast and Furious and Democrats saying Bush did it too with Wide Receiver. I've seen it reported in mainstream media that in Wide Receiver guns had tracking devices attached so they could be collected on the other side of the border. It's also been reported that Wide Receiver had the full cooperation of Mexican authorities. Both assertions are completely false.

People have asked where the policy of gunwalking originated. The answer is simple. It originated with Operation Wide Receiver and was initiated at the field level. Newell OK'd it and looked no further for approval from his superiors.

While the Inspector General's report does mention that in Operation Wide Receiver there were several instances of contact with Mexican authorities, there was never any coordination regarding the following of guns once they crossed the border yet guns continued to flow across the border. In Fast and Furious, according to the report, there was zero communication with Mexican authorities. If the goal were to take down a cartel you would think there would have to be a certain level of cooperation between the United States and the very country the cartels operated out of. At very least, professional courtesy would have dictated that someone alert Mexican authorities that several thousand weapons would be flowing across the border and into cartel hands.

Even though there has been documentation between Department of Justice officials regarding their concern over Newell's policy of letting guns walk across the border in Wide Receiver there was no official admonishment for his actions. Under the anti-gun Obama administration why wouldn't he continue his plan on a grander scale? Newell had Dennis Burke as his US Attorney in Phoenix. Burke had been one of the authors of the 1994 Assault Weapons ban.

I believe Bill Newell realized long before I did that my journal would become problematic. My notes detailed each and every purchase made by these cartel associates as well as where the guns were going and who they were going to. In each case, we learned these specifics early on, yet purchases were encouraged to continue by ATF leadership. Because I had bought my own digital recorder and used my personal laptop to download the files, I possessed information that would prove damning to Newell and the ATF. Whoever it was who corrupted my audio files understood this. I believe the detailed journal I kept that caused such heartburn with everyone is also what kept me safe from government reprisals.

Leverage is a wonderful thing when you have it. You can make someone do something that they normally wouldn't do. In this case, ATF and DOJ had no leverage on me. I was an informant for all of the right reasons. I hadn't been forced to become a CI to reduce a prison term or stay out of jail. I was a good American trying my best to fulfill a perceived patriotic obligation. As unhappy as those at ATF and DOJ were with me there was little they could do to shut me up.

I have to say one of my greatest disappointments was that when ATF and DOJ leadership maintained that they never let guns walk across the border, none of the agents I worked with came forward to dispute this. Agents I had trusted my life to and once held in such high regard sat silently while their bosses continued to perpetrate this lie. Men of honor, men of integrity would never have allowed this to happen.

But being a good American doesn't always involve doing what government authorities tell you to do. In this case, it required speaking out against the government when they were clearly wrong in their actions. Unfortunately, it took the death of an American hero for this ugly scheme to come to light.

INDEX